Executable UML

The Addison-Wesley Object Technology Series

Grady Booch, Ivar Jacobson, and James Rumbaugh, Series Editors

For more information, check out the series Web site [http://www.awl.com/cseng/otseries/].

Ahmed/Umrysh, *Developing Enterprise Java Applications with J2EE™ and UML*

Arlow/Neustadt, *UML and the Unified Process: Practical Object-Oriented Analysis and Design*

Armour/Miller, *Advanced Use Case Modeling: Software Systems*

Binder, *Testing Object-Oriented Systems: Models, Patterns, and Tools*

Blakley, *CORBA Security: An Introduction to Safe Computing with Objects*

Booch, *Object Solutions: Managing the Object-Oriented Project*

Booch, *Object-Oriented Analysis and Design with Applications, Second Edition*

Booch/Rumbaugh/Jacobson, *The Unified Modeling Language User Guide*

Box/Brown/Ewald/Sells, *Effective COM: 50 Ways to Improve Your COM and MTS-based Applications*

Carlson, *Modeling XML Applications with UML: Practical e-Business Applications*

Cockburn, *Surviving Object-Oriented Projects: A Manager's Guide*

Collins, *Designing Object-Oriented User Interfaces*

Conallen, *Building Web Applications with UML*

D'Souza/Wills, *Objects, Components, and Frameworks with UML: The Catalysis Approach*

Douglass, *Doing Hard Time: Developing Real-Time Systems with UML, Objects, Frameworks, and Patterns*

Douglass, *Real-Time UML, Second Edition: Developing Efficient Objects for Embedded Systems*

Fowler, *Analysis Patterns: Reusable Object Models*

Fowler/Beck/Brant/Opdyke/Roberts, *Refactoring: Improving the Design of Existing Code*

Fowler/Scott, *UML Distilled, Second Edition: A Brief Guide to the Standard Object Modeling Language*

Gomaa, *Designing Concurrent, Distributed, and Real-Time Applications with UML*

Gorton, *Enterprise Transaction Processing Systems: Putting the CORBA OTS, Encina++ and Orbix OTM to Work*

Graham, *Object-Oriented Methods, Third Edition: Principles and Practice*

Heinckiens, *Building Scalable Database Applications: Object-Oriented Design, Architectures, and Implementations*

Hofmeister/Nord/Dilip, *Applied Software Architecture*

Jacobson/Booch/Rumbaugh, *The Unified Software Development Process*

Jacobson/Christerson/Jonsson/Overgaard, *Object-Oriented Software Engineering: A Use Case Driven Approach*

Jacobson/Ericsson/Jacobson, *The Object Advantage: Business Process Reengineering with Object Technology*

Jacobson/Griss/Jonsson, *Software Reuse: Architecture, Process and Organization for Business Success*

Jordan, *C++ Object Databases: Programming with the ODMG Standard*

Kruchten, *The Rational Unified Process, An Introduction, Second Edition*

Lau, *The Art of Objects: Object-Oriented Design and Architecture*

Leffingwell/Widrig, *Managing Software Requirements: A Unified Approach*

Marshall, *Enterprise Modeling with UML: Designing Successful Software through Business Analysis*

McGregor/Sykes, *A Practical Guide to Testing Object-Oriented Software*

Mellor/Balcer, *Executable UML: A Foundation for Model-Driven Architecture*

Mowbray/Ruh, *Inside CORBA: Distributed Object Standards and Applications*

Naiburg/Maksimchuk, *UML for Database Design*

Oestereich, *Developing Software with UML: Object-Oriented Analysis and Design in Practice*

Page-Jones, *Fundamentals of Object-Oriented Design in UML*

Pohl, *Object-Oriented Programming Using C++, Second Edition*

Quatrani, *Visual Modeling with Rational Rose 2000 and UML*

Rector/Sells, *ATL Internals*

Reed, *Developing Applications with Visual Basic and UML*

Rosenberg/Scott, *Applying Use Case Driven Object Modeling with UML: An Annotated e-Commerce Example*

Rosenberg/Scott, *Use Case Driven Object Modeling with UML: A Practical Approach*

Royce, *Software Project Management: A Unified Framework*

Ruh/Herron/Klinker, *IIOP Complete: Understanding CORBA and Middleware Interoperability*

Rumbaugh/Jacobson/Booch, *The Unified Modeling Language Reference Manual*

Schneider/Winters, *Applying Use Cases, Second Edition: A Practical Guide*

Shan/Earle, *Enterprise Computing with Objects: From Client/Server Environments to the Internet*

Smith/Williams, *Performance Solutions: A Practical Guide to Creating Responsive, Scalable Software*

Stevens/Pooley, *Using UML: Software Engineering with Objects and Components*

Warmer/Kleppe, *The Object Constraint Language: Precise Modeling with UML*

White, *Software Configuration Management Strategies and Rational ClearCase®: A Practical Introduction*

The Component Software Series

Clemens Szyperski, Series Editor

For more information, check out the series Web site [http://www.awl.com/cseng/csseries/].

Allen, *Realizing eBusiness with Components*

Cheesman/Daniels, *UML Components: A Simple Process for Specifying Component-Based Software*

Szyperski, *Component Software, Second Edition: Beyond Object-Oriented Programming*

Executable UML

A Foundation for Model-Driven Architecture

Stephen J. Mellor

Marc J. Balcer

✦▾Addison-Wesley

Boston · San Francisco · New York · Toronto · Montreal
London · Munich · Paris · Madrid
Capetown · Sydney · Tokyo · Singapore · Mexico City

Many of the designations used by manufacturers and sellers to distinguish their products are claimed as trademarks. Where those designations appear in this book, and Addison-Wesley was aware of a trademark claim, the designations have been printed with initial capital letters or in all capitals.

The authors and publisher have taken care in the preparation of this book, but make no expressed or implied warranty of any kind and assume no responsibility for errors or omissions. No liability is assumed for incidental or consequential damages in connection with or arising out of the use of the information or programs contained herein.

The publisher offers discounts on this book when ordered in quantity for special sales. For more information, please contact:

Pearson Education Corporate Sales Division
201 W. 103rd Street
Indianapolis, IN 46290
(800) 428-5331
corpsales@pearsoned.com

Visit Addison-Wesley on the Web: www.aw.com/cseng/

Library of Congress Cataloging-in-Publication Data

Mellor, Stephen J.
  Executable UML : a foundation for model-driven architecture /
Stephen J. Mellor, Marc J. Balcer.
      p.   cm.
Includes bibliographical references and index.
  ISBN 0-201-74804-5
  1. Object-oriented programming (Computer science) 2. Computer
software--Development. 3. UML (Computer science) I. Balcer, Marc
J. II. Title.
  QA76.64 .M45 2002
  005.1'17--dc21   2002002815

ISBN 0-201-74804-5
Text printed on recycled paper
1 2 3 4 5 6 7 8 9 10—MA—0605040302
First printing, May 2002

To Sally

in memoriam

Contents

List of Figures

Chapter 11 Synchronizing Objects

Chapter 12 Using Lifecycles

Chapter 13 Relationship Dynamics

Chapter 14   Domain Dynamics

Chapter 15   Domain Verification

Chapter 16   Model Management

Foreword

Creating a modeling language that is also an executable language has long been a goal of the software community. Many years ago, in 1968 to be exact, while working with software components to successfully develop a telecommunications system, we created a modeling language that was the forerunner to UML. To model components we used sequence diagrams, collaboration diagrams, and state transition diagrams (a combination of state charts and activity diagrams). Our modeling language then seamlessly translated the component models into code. Each code component was in its turn compiled into an executable component that was deployed in our computer system. The computer system was a component management system—thus we had "components all the way down."

Thanks to the seamless relation between the modeling language and the programming language, almost 90% of the code could be generated. Changes in the code could translate into models. However, this had to be done manually, because at that time we didn't have the tools to do the job. It was almost a clerical event. We called it a job for monkeys. Of course, I asked myself the question, if we only need the programming environment to create 10% of the code, do we really need two languages? Couldn't we integrate the modeling language and the programming language and make one language with a visual as well as a textual syntax and with common semantics. Having such a powerful language would dramatically eliminate work and it would make life more enjoyable to the developers. In 1980, I suggested this move in writing as a next step in the development of our products.

Several years latter, the International Telecommunication Union (ITU), headquartered in Geneva, created a standard for object modeling, known as the Specification and Description Language (or SDL). SDL was very much inspired by the modeling language we were using in developing our telecommunication system. We referred to it as "The Ericsson Language". In the early 1980s we added to SDL constructs to formally define algorithms and data structures. It was very simple, but at last we had a language that would allow us to execute our design models long before these models had been translated into a programming environment.

Steve Mellor and Marc Balcer now move the concept of "executableness" a step further. Steve in particular, advances the idea of making an abstract, platform independent, executable model of a software system which then, with specially designed tools (bridges), generates or transforms the model into executable software to run on target computer systems. The specially designed tools transform platform independent models to platform dependent code.

Steve has long been an advocate of this idea. I remember that Steve was on a panel discussing this several years ago. He was met by a lot of skepticism by other panelists. After the panel I told him, "There is in my mind no doubt that you will be proven right—in particular for a small stereotypical class of systems, but it may take 25 years to get there for the majority of software development." After five more years and all the work done by Steve and others, I think we can get there even sooner.

Steve has now moved his work from Shlaer-Mellor notation to UML as the base modeling language. He has been the driving force behind the work on action semantics in UML, which was the missing piece to make UML an executable language. This is now part of the OMG standard for UML. He has gone even further. His work on transforming from a platform independent executable model to executable code via bridges is one of the cornerstones on which rests the OMG's new initiative: Model Driven Architecture (MDA).

However, to quote Winston Churchill, "This is not the end. It is not even the beginning of the end. But it is, perhaps, the end of the beginning." Having an executable UML for modeling platform independent software is a great step forward. We can work on abstract models, validate (debug if you want) them early before we introduce the platform dependencies and make sure that the system behaves functionally as expected. However, I believe we need to take one step further to eliminate a very expensive impedance in software development. We should move forward and design the missing link to make UML the language to also execute platform dependent software, to make UML a third generation language that eventually will replace existing programming languages. This is not a technical problem. This could be done today if the big platform vendors wanted to do it. We would eliminate the two-language problem (having both a modeling language, UML, and a programming language like C# or Java). We would get a language that would be both. A language that would be used for use cases, for platform-independent design, for platform dependent designs whether this would be done by transformers as Steve advocates or by doing the job by interconnecting components—some of which being new, some of them already being harvested.

Getting an executable UML—to be used both for platform independent models as Steve and Marc describe in this book and for platform dependent ordinary source code—will be an important step in the future of software development.

Ivar Jacobson

Preface

At one time, the title for this book was *Executable UML For Model-Driven Architectures (MDA) Using Aspect-Oriented (AO) Techniques with Extreme Programming (XP), Agile Modeling (AM), and Other Agile Alliance (AA) Processes as an Instance of the Rational Unified Process (RUP).*

Eventually, we settled instead on *Executable UML: A Foundation for Model-Driven Architecture.* This title is snappier, but it's not as fully buzzword-compliant as the original.

So what is this Executable UML? It is a profile of UML that allows you, the developer, to define the behavior of a single subject matter in sufficient detail that it can be executed. In this sense, the model is like code, but there's no point in writing "code" in UML just to rewrite it in Java or C++, so it's rather more revealing to examine what executable UML *doesn't* say that code might.

An executable UML model doesn't make coding decisions. It makes no statement about tasking structures; it makes no statement about distribution; it makes no statement about classes or encapsulation. An executable UML model describes only the data and behavior, organized into classes to be sure, about the subject matter at hand. In other words, an executable

UML developer describes subject matters at a *higher level of abstraction* than she would in a programming language.

To build a system, we build an executable UML of each subject matter. Typically, the system includes subject matters such as the application, a user interface, and some general services. The executable UML models for each of these subject matters are then woven together by an executable UML *model compiler.*

The model compiler targets a specific implementation embodying decisions about "coding:" tasking structures, distribution, data structures (which may be quite different from that suggested by the class structure), as well as the language. Model compilers can be extremely sophisticated, taking care of cross-cutting concerns such as transaction safety and rollback, or they can be sophisticated in a different way, targeting small footprint embedded systems with no tasking or other system support.

In general, a model compiler compiles several executable UML models, each of which captures a single cross-cutting concern to yield the running system. In this sense, executable UML makes use of the concepts in *aspect-oriented* programming.

Executable UML models support a new Object Management Group initiative, *Model-Driven Architecture* (MDA). This initiative is in its early stages, but its goal is to allow developers to compose complete systems out of models and other components. This goal requires at least an interface as contract and, behind the interface, the ability to express a solution without making coding decisions. That would be executable UML, or some variation.

This book does not describe model-driven architecture or its implications. Rather, this book focuses on one aspect of MDA that we believe to be critical: the ability to model whole subject matters completely and turn these models into systems. This ability, we believe, relies on being able to execute models. Hence executable UML.

Because the developer builds models as executable as a program for each subject matter, all the principles of *extreme* programming and *agile* processes can be applied. Indeed, many of the principles of these processes having nothing to do with coding *per se.*

You can use executable UML in a deliberate process or, because the models are executable, an agile one. Our preference is agile and incremental because it keeps the focus on delivering working software.

And what about RUP? As one of our reviewers, Martin Fowler, so memorably said: "My biggest concern with RUP is that it's so loose that any process seems to qualify as an instance of RUP. As a result, saying you're using RUP is a semantics-free statement." So we can reasonably assert that the process described by this book is an instance of RUP. (And if you want, we do.)

Frequently Asked Questions

Is this the only possible Executable UML? No. This rendition views each object as potentially having a state machine that can execute asynchronously and concurrently. We view this approach as necessary for today's distributed computing environments. However, one could define an executable UML that relies on synchronous method calls between objects to produce a completely synchronous model of the subject matter. Similarly, our particular use of the statechart diagram is not the only possible one.

Is Executable UML a standard? Yes and No. The notational elements you see in this book conform to UML, and so qualify as a *profile* of that standard. In addition, the execution semantics defined here conform to UML, though we do both subset UML and impose certain rules to link the elements together. What is not yet a standard is the exact content of what can and should be interchanged so that we can guarantee that any and all model compilers, irrespective of vendor, can compile any arbitrary executable UML model.

Throughout this book, we use standards as much as they are established. In some areas, the book is intended to provide a basis for discussion of what should ultimately become a standard.

Will there be a standard one day, and how might it differ? Yes, we hope so. Work has begun informally to define a standard and we will encourage and support it. We expect the standard to define an underlying semantics quite similar to that outlined here, and to layer increasingly rich syntax on top.

Does that mean I should wait? Not at all. This technology is taking off, and the basic elements are already established. Get ahead of the learning curve.

I know hardly anything about UML. Is this book too advanced for me? We assume you have an intuitive understanding of the goals behind UML, but nothing more. We will show you all the elements you need to build an executable UML model.

I'm a long-time UML user. Do I need this book? If you want to garner the benefits of Executable UML, then you'll have to learn the elements that make it up. Focus on the definitions we use and the chapters that show how to build and execute models. Skip the notational stuff. Be prepared to unlearn some UML and habits of mind required to model software structure, but not required to specify an executable model.

What happened to adornments such as aggregation or composition? We don't need them for Executable UML. UML enables you to model software structure, but that's not our purpose here, so those adornments, and many others, are not in our profile.

Some of this seems familiar. Is this just Shlaer-Mellor in UML clothing? Shlaer-Mellor focused on execution and specification of an abstract solution, not on specifying software structure. UML can be used for both the expression of software structure and the abstract model. Executable UML brings Shlaer-Mellor and UML together by using UML notation and incorporating concepts of execution. We hope this will make execution accessible to a broader community.

I've used Shlaer-Mellor before. Is this any different? A lot can happen in this industry in ten weeks, let alone the ten years since the publication of *Object Lifecycles*. First of all, of course, we all now use UML notation and vocabulary. (Resistance was futile.) Executable UML takes a more object-oriented perspective, no longer requiring identifiers or referential attributes, or other traces of Shlaer-Mellor's relational roots.

The addition of an action semantics to the UML is a major step forward. We hope the action semantics, and the very concept of an executable and translatable UML may one day be seen as a significant contribution of the Shlaer-Mellor community.

Progress in tools has also made certain conventions, such as event numbering, less critical to model understanding, though they are still helpful in keeping our minds clear.

Why do you say "Action Semantics?" Because UML defines only the semantics of actions, it does not define a language.

But how can you execute without an action language? We use an action semantics–conforming language that is executable today. We show several other action languages to illustrate that syntax is unimportant.

You use an Online Bookstore case study. Can I use this if I'm a real-time developer? Yes. We chose a more IT-oriented case study to increase the reach of the approach. You can find a completely worked out real-time case study in Leon Starr's book *Executable UML: The Elevator Case Study.*

How can I get an Executable UML tool? All of the examples in this book were developed using Project Technology's tool, BridgePoint. A copy of BridgePoint can be downloaded from the book's website, *www.executableUMLbook.com.*

How is this different from the old "draw the pictures, get some code" CASE tools? There are two main differences. First, compiling models produces the whole system, not just interfaces or frameworks. Second, there are many different model compilers available to buy, and even more that can be built, to meet exacting software architecture needs.

Where has Executable UML been used? Executable UML has been used to generate systems as large as two million lines of C++, and as small as handheld drug delivery devices. Executable UML has also been used in lease-origination, web-enabled executive reporting, and intermodal transportation logistics systems.

Why did you write this book? Because we had nothing better to do? No: There are lots of books out there that tell you about UML notation, but few of them focus on the subset you need for executability. Many books use UML to describe software structure. We explicitly spurn this usage.

Why should I buy this book? Because it describes completely everything you need to know about executable UML: It's the Executable UML handbook.

Stephen J. Mellor
San Francisco, California

Marc J. Balcer
San Francisco, California

March 2002

Acknowledgments

First and foremost, we must acknowledge our debt to the late Sally Shlaer. She started this ball rolling in the mid-1970s with a project that generated FORTRAN from a set of primitive data and program files, with daily builds and—perhaps astonishingly—many of the trappings of today's agile processes. The system, a radiation treatment facility, had only five bugs in its first full system test. None lasted over forty-eight hours. And a good job too, given the subject matter. We deeply miss her warmth, her unparalleled concern for people, and especially her steel-trap mind.

In our work together in the late eighties, we focused on objects as an organizing principle for describing data and behavior, culminating in the two Shlaer-Mellor books. Execution was then, and is now, the goal. Since then, of course, the UML has become the *lingua franca* of object modeling, but the UML, until the recent past, has not been executable. This book is intended to link together the executable ideas of Shlaer-Mellor with the universality of UML.

Someone, someday, should write a paper about the four stages of review and how they correspond to the four stage of grief. First there's disbelief, then denial, then bargaining, and finally acceptance. The paper should discuss the correspondence between "denial" and the abuse heaped upon the reviewers as it becomes all too clear that the work needs to be revised. Fortunately, we didn't send too many of the hate mails we composed.

The table below lists our unfortunate reviewers. Those reviewers marked with a * were a part of the formal review team. We thank them all for their sterling efforts and apologize profusely to their burning ears.

* Conrad Bock	Mark Blackburn	Alistair Blair
* Dirk Epperson	Scott Finnie	* Martin Fowler
* Takao Futagami	Kazuto Horimatsu	Yukitoshi Okamura
* Edwin Seidewitz	* Leon Starr	* William G. Tanner

We would especially like to thank Conrad Bock, Director of Standards at Kabira Technologies, one of the few people worldwide who has the whole UML in his head, who provided a most detailed—and so, if he'll forgive us, an especially annoying—review.

We would like to thank the many talented analysts and developers at ThoughtWorks (http://www.thoughtworks.com), including Chief Scientist Martin Fowler, for keeping our focus on executability and its impact on agile development.

Our thanks, too, to William G. Tanner, Software Development Manager at Project Technology, Inc., who is apparently able to review executable models with a model compiler in his head.

This book would not be possible without the professionalism of the staff at Addison Wesley. Susan Winer, our copy editor, moved better than 50% of our commas and performed countless acts of linguistic hygiene. Kate Saliba, who leads the marketing team, has kept the project on track as it moved into production. John Fuller has been tolerant as we have attempted to do his job as production editor. Finally, our thanks to Paul "Eyebrows" Becker, alternately patient and a pain, who has cajoled us into finishing this project. Authors are not (always) easy to get along with!

Finally, we'd like to thank members of the community who have long understood the benefits of execution and modeling at a high level of abstraction. You know who you are, and we wouldn't still be here if it weren't for you. Thanks.

1

Introduction

Organizations want systems. They don't want processes, meetings, models, documents, or even code.[1] They want systems that work—as quickly as possible, as cheaply as possible, and as easy to change as possible. Organizations don't want long software development lead-times and high costs; they just want to reduce systems development hassles to the absolute minimum.

But systems development is a complicated business. It demands distillation of overlapping and contradictory requirements; invention of good abstractions from those requirements; fabrication of an efficient, cost-effective implementation; and clever solutions to isolated coding and abstraction problems. And we need to manage all this work to a successful conclusion, all at the lowest possible cost in time and money.

None of this is new. Over thirty years ago, the U.S. Department of Defense warned of a "software crisis" and predicted that to meet the burgeoning need for software by the end of the century, everyone in the country would have to become a programmer. In many ways this prediction has come true, as anyone who has checked on the progress of a flight or made a stock trade using the Internet can tell you. Nowadays, we all write our own

---

[1] Robert Block began his book *The Politics of Projects*[1] in a similar manner.

programs by filling in forms—at the level of abstraction of the application, not the software.

1.1   Raising the Level of Abstraction

The history of software development is a history of raising the level of abstraction. Our industry used to build systems by soldering wires together to form hard-wired programs. Machine code allowed us to store programs by manipulating switches to enter each instruction. Data was stored on drums whose rotation time had to be taken into account so that the head would be able to read the next instruction at exactly the right time. Later, assemblers took on the tedious task of generating sequences of ones and zeroes from a set of mnemonics designed for each hardware platform.

Later, programming languages, such as FORTRAN, were born and "formula translation" became a reality. Standards for COBOL and C enabled portability between hardware platforms, and the profession developed techniques for structuring programs so that they were easier to write, understand, and maintain. We now have languages such as Smalltalk, C++, Eiffel, and Java, each with the notion of object-orientation, an approach for structuring data and behavior together into classes and objects.

As we moved from one language to another, generally we increased the level of abstraction at which the developer operates, requiring the developer to learn a new higher-level language that may then be mapped into lower-level ones, from C++ to C to assembly code to machine code and the hardware. At first, each higher layer of abstraction was introduced only as a concept. The first assembly languages were no doubt invented without the benefit of an (automated) assembler to turn the mnemonics into bits, and developers were grouping functions together with the data they encapsulated long before there was any automatic enforcement of the concept. Similarly, the concepts of structured programming were taught before there were structured programming languages in widespread industrial use (*pace*, Pascal).

Layers of Abstraction and the Market

The manner in which each higher layer of abstraction reached the market follows a pattern. The typical response to the introduction of the next layer of abstraction goes something like this: "Formula translation is a neat trick, but even if you can demonstrate it with an example, it couldn't possibly work on a problem as complex and intricate as mine."

As the tools became more useful and their value became more obvious, a whole new set of hurdles presented themselves as technical folk tried to acquire the wherewithal to purchase the tools. Now managers wanted to know what would happen if they came to rely on these new tools. How many vendors are there? Are other people doing this? Why should we take the risk in being first? What happens if the compiler builder runs out of business? Are we becoming too dependent on a single vendor? Are there standards? Is there interchange?

Initially, it must be said, compilers generated inefficient code. The development environment, as one would expect, comprised a few, barely production-level tools. These were generally difficult to use, in part because the producers of the tools focused first on bringing the technology to market to hook early adopters, and later on prettier user interfaces to broaden that market. The tools did not necessarily integrate with one another. When programs went wrong, no supporting tools were available: No symbolic debuggers, no performance profiling tools, no help, really, other than looking at the generated code, which surely defeated the whole purpose.

Executable UML and the tooling necessary to compile and debug an executable UML model are only now passing from this stage, so expect some resistance today and much better tools tomorrow.

But over time the new layers of abstraction became formalized, and tools such as assemblers, preprocessors, and compilers were constructed to support the concepts. This has the effect of hiding the details of the lower layers so that only a few experts (compiler writers, for example) need concern themselves with the details of how that layer works. In turn, this raises concerns about the loss of control induced by, for example, eliminating the GOTO statement or writing in a high-level language at a distance from the "real machine." Indeed, sometimes the next level of abstraction has been too big a reach for the profession as a whole, of interest to academics and purists, and the concepts did not take a large enough mindshare to survive. (ALGOL-68 springs to mind. So does Eiffel, but it has too many living supporters to be a safe choice of example.)

Object Method History

Object methods have a complex history because they derive from two very different sources.

One source is the programming world, whence object-oriented programming came. Generalizing shamelessly, object-oriented programmers with an interest in methods were frustrated with the extremely process-oriented perspective of "structured methods" of the time. These methods, Structured Analysis and Structured Design, took functions as their primary view of the system, and viewed data as a subsidiary, slightly annoying, poor relation. Even the "real-time" methods at most just added state machines to the mix to control processing, and didn't encapsulate at all. There was a separate "Information Modeling" movement that was less prominent and which viewed data as all, and processing as a nuisance to be tolerated in the form of CRUD++. Either way, both of these camps completely missed the object-oriented boat. To add insult to injury, one motivation for objects—the notion that an object modeled the real world, and then seamlessly became the software object—was prominently violated by the emphasis in transforming from one (analysis) notation, data flow diagrams, to another (design) notation, the structure chart.

Be that as it may, the search was on for a higher level of abstraction than the programming language, even though some claimed that common third-generation programming languages such as Smalltalk had already raised the level of abstraction far enough.

The other source was more centered in analysis. These approaches focused on modeling the concepts in the problem, but in an object-oriented way. Classes could be viewed as combinations of data, state, and behavior at a conceptual level only. In addition to the model, reorganization of "analysis" classes into "design" classes, and re-allocation of functionality were expected. There was no need to model the specific features used from a programming language because the programmer was to fill in these details. Perhaps the purest proponents of this point of view were Shlaer and Mellor. They asserted classes with attributes clearly visible on the class icon seemingly violating encapsulation, with the full expectation that object-oriented programming schemes would select an appropriate private data structure with the necessary operations.

These two sources met in the middle to yield a plethora of methods, each with its own notation (at least 30 published), each trying to some extent to meet the needs of both camps. Thus began the Method Wars, though Notation Wars might be more accurate.

UML is the product of the Method Wars. It uses notations and ideas from many of the methods extant in the early nineties, sometimes at different levels of abstraction and detail.

As the profession has raised the level of abstraction at which developers work, we have developed tools to map from one layer to the next automatically. Developers now write in a high-level language that can be mapped to a lower-level language automatically, instead of writing in the lower-level language that can be mapped to assembly language, just as our predecessors wrote in assembly language and translated that automatically into machine language.

Clearly, this forms a pattern: We formalize our knowledge of an application in as high a level language as we can. Over time, we learn how to use this language and apply a set of conventions for its use. These conventions become formalized and a higher-level language is born that is mapped automatically into the lower-level language. In turn, this next-higher-level language is perceived as low level, and we develop a set of conventions for its use. These newer conventions are then formalized and mapped into the next level down, and so on.

1.2   Executable UML

Executable UML is at the next higher layer of abstraction, abstracting away both specific programming languages and decisions about the organization of the software so that a specification built in Executable UML can be deployed in various software environments without change.

Physically, an Executable UML specification comprises a set of models represented as diagrams that describe and define the conceptualization and behavior of the real or hypothetical world under study. The set of models, taken together, comprise a single specification that we can examine from several points of view. There are three fundamental projections on the specification, though we may choose to build any number of UML diagrams to examine the specification in particular ways.

The first model identifies, classifies, and abstracts the real or hypothetical world under study, and it organizes the information into a formal structure. Similar "things," or *objects*, in the subject matter under study are identified and abstracted as *classes*; characteristics of these objects are abstracted as *attributes*; and reliable associations between the objects are abstracted as *relationships*.

Concept	Called	Modeled As	Expressed As
the world is full of things	data	classes attributes associations constraints	UML class diagram
things have lifecycles	control	states events transitions procedures	UML statechart diagram
things do things at each stage	algorithm	actions	action language

Figure 1.1   *Concepts in an Executable UML Model*

Operations do not appear explicitly as entries in Figure 1.1 because Executable UML derives operations from actions on state machines.

Invoked actions may be shown as operations on classes, but their existence is normally dependent on the invocation that occurs in a state machine.

We express this first model using a *UML class diagram*. The abstraction process requires that each object be subject to and conform to the well-defined and explicitly stated rules or policies of the subject matter under study, that attributes be abstractions of characteristics of things in the subject matter under study, and that relationships similarly model associations in the subject matter.

Next, the objects (the instances of the classes) may have *lifecycles* (behaviors over time) that are abstracted as state machines. These state machines are defined for classes, and expressed using a *UML statechart diagram*. The abstraction process requires that each object be subject to and conform to the well-defined and explicitly stated rules or policies of the world under study, so each object is known to exhibit the same pattern of behavior.

The behavior of the system is driven by objects moving from one stage in their lifecycles to another in response to events. When an object changes

Executable UML is a single language in the UML family, designed for a single purpose: to define the semantics of subject matters precisely. Executable UML is a particular usage, or *profile*, the formal manner in which we specify a set of rules for how particular elements in UML fit together for a particular purpose.

This book, then, describes a profile of UML for execution.

state, something must happen to make this new state be so. Each state machine has a set of *procedures,* one of which is executed when the object changes state, thus establishing the new state.

Each procedure comprises a set of *actions.* Actions carry out the fundamental computation in the system, and each action is a primitive unit of computation, such as a data access, a selection, or a loop. The UML only recently defined a semantics for actions, and it currently has no standard notation or syntax, though several (near-)conforming languages are available.

These three models—the class model, the state machines for the classes, and the states' procedures—form a complete definition of the subject matter under study. Figure 1.1 describes the concepts in an Executable UML model.

In this book we will informally make use of other UML diagrams, such as use case and collaboration diagrams, that support the construction of executable UML models or can be derived from them. We encourage using any modeling technique, UML-based or otherwise, that helps build the system.

1.3   Making UML Executable

Earlier versions of UML were not executable; they provided for an extremely limited set of actions (sending a signal, creating an object, destroying an object, as well as our personal favorite, "uninterpreted string"). In late 2001, the UML was extended by a semantics for actions. The action semantics provides a complete set of actions at a high level of abstraction. For example, actions are defined for manipulating collections

Executable UML isn't just a good idea, it's real. There are several Executable UML vendors, and the models in this book have been executed to ensure they are correct. The case study models and the toolset are downloadable.

For the latest information on executable UML, go to
http://www.executableumlbook.com.

of objects directly, thus avoiding the need for explicit programming of loops and iterators. Executable UML relies on these new actions to be complete.

For UML to be executable, we must have rules that define the dynamic semantics of the specification. Dynamically, each object is thought of as executing concurrently, asynchronously with respect to all others. Each object may be executing a procedure or waiting for something to happen to cause it to execute. Sequence is defined for each object separately; there is no global time and any required synchronization between objects must be modeled explicitly.

The existence of a defined dynamic semantics makes the three models computationally complete. A specification can therefore be executed, verified, and translated into implementation.

Executable UML is designed to produce a comprehensive and comprehensible model of a solution without making decisions about the organization of the software implementation. It is a highly abstract thinking tool to aid in the formalization of knowledge, a way of thinking about and describing the concepts that make up an abstract solution to a client problem.

Executable UML helps us work out how we want to think about a solution: the terms we need to define, the assumptions we make in selecting those terms, and the consistency of our definitions and assumptions. In addition, executable UML models are separate from any implementation, yet can readily be executed to test for completeness and correctness.

Most important of all, together with a model compiler, they are executable.

1.4   Model Compilers

At some level, it is fair to say that any language that can be executed is necessarily a programming language; it's just a matter of the level of abstraction. So, is executable UML yet another (graphical) programming language?

An executable UML model completely specifies the semantics of a single subject matter, and in that sense, it is indeed a "program" for that subject matter. There is no magic. Yet an executable UML model does not specify many of the elements we normally associate with programming today. For example, an executable UML model does not specify distribution; it does not specify the number and allocation of separate threads; it does not specify the organization of data; it does not even require implementation as classes and objects. All of these matters are considered decisions that relate to hardware and software organization, and they have no place in a model concerned with, say, the purchase of books online.

Decisions about the organization of the hardware and software are abstracted away in an executable UML model, just as decisions about register allocation and stack/heap organization are abstracted away in the typical compiler. And, just as a typical language compiler makes decisions about register allocation and the like for a specific machine environment, so does an executable UML model compiler make decisions about a particular hardware and software environment, deciding, for example, to use a distributed Internet model with separate threads for each user window, HTML for the user interface displays, and so on.

An executable UML *model compiler* turns an executable UML model into an implementation using a set of decisions about the target hardware and software environment.

There are many possible executable UML model compilers for different system architectures. Each architecture makes its own decisions about the organization of hardware and software, including even the programming language. Each model compiler can compile any executable UML model into an implementation.

The notion of so many different model compilers for such different software architecture designs is a far cry from the one-size-fits-all visual modeling tools of the past.

Here are some examples of possible model compilers:

1. Multi-tasking C++ optimized for embedded systems, targeting Windows, Solaris, and various real-time operating systems. [3]
2. Multi-processing C++ with transaction safety and rollback. [2]
3. Fault-tolerant, multi-processing C++ with persistence supporting three processor types and two operating systems.
4. C straight on to an embedded system, with no operating system. [3]
5. C++, widely distributed discrete-event simulation, Windows, and UNIX.
6. Java byte code for single-tasking Java with EJB session beans and XML interfaces.
7. Handel-C and C++ for system-level hardware/software development.
8. A directly executing executable UML virtual machine.

A single model compiler may employ several languages or approaches to problems such as persistence and multi-tasking. Then, however, the several approaches must be shown to fit together into a single, coherent whole.

Of these, some are commercially available, as indicated by the references provided above, and some are proprietary, built specifically to optimize a property found in related systems produced by a company, such as the fault-tolerant multi-processing model compiler. Some are still just proto-types or twinkles in our eyes, such as the last three.

As a developer, you will build an executable UML model that captures your solution for the subject matter under study, purchase a model compiler that meets the performance properties and system characteristics you require, and give directives to the compiler for the particular application. Hence, a system that must control a small robot would select the small footprint C model compiler or one like it, and a system executing financial transactions would prefer one with transaction safety and roll-back.

The performance of the model compiler may depend on the allocations of application model elements, and a model compiler may not know enough to be able to allocate a particular class to that task or processor for the best performance. Similarly, a model compiler that provides persistence may not know enough about your subject matter to determine what to make persistent. Consequently, you will also need to provide model compiler–specific configuration information. Each feature provided by the model-compiler that does not have a direct analog in executable UML will require directives to determine which feature to use.

These choices will affect performance of the model compiler. One particularly performance-sensitive feature is static allocation to tasks and processors. Allocating two classes that communicate heavily with different processors could cause significant degradation of network performance and of your system. If this is so, of course, it's a simple matter to re-allocate the elements of the model and recompile. This is why executable UML is so powerful—by separating the model of the subject matter from its software structure, the two aspects can be changed independently, making it easier to modify one without adversely affecting the other. This extends the Java notion of the "write once, run anywhere" concept; as we raise the level of abstraction, we also make our programs more portable. It also enables a number of interesting possibilities for hardware-software co-design.

1.5   Model-Driven Architecture

Executable UML is one pillar supporting the Model-Driven Architecture (MDA) initiative announced by the Object Management Group (OMG) in early 2001, the purpose of which is to enable specification of systems using models.

Model-driven architecture depends on the notion of a Platform-Independent Model (PIM), a model of a solution to a problem that does not rely on any implementation technologies. A PIM is independent of its platform(s).

A model of a online bookstore, for example, is independent of the user interface and messaging services it employs.

A PIM can be built using an executable UML.

Some proponents of MDA hold that a specification of the interface in a language such as the OMG's Interface Description Language (IDL), plus some constraints, is sufficient to specify without overspecifying. The views of these two camps are not contradictory, but complementary. There is no technical reason why a PIM specified using an executable UML cannot be bridged to one specified in terms of interfaces and constraints. One is just a more complete version of the other.

It is because an executable model is required as a way to specify PIMs completely that we view an executable UML as a foundation of model-driven architectures.

MDA also defines the concept of a Platform-Specific Model (PSM): a model that contains within it the details of the implementation, enough that code can be generated from it. A PSM is produced by weaving together the application model and the platforms on which it relies. The PSM contains information about software structure, enough information, possibly, to be able to generate code. Executable UML views the PSM as an intermediate graphical form of the code that is dispensable in the case of complete code generation.

At the time of writing, MDA is still being defined. However, some variation of the concepts of executable UML will, in our opinion, be required to support MDA. We offer our view on executable UML concepts here. Describing and defining MDA is another project and another book.

1.6   References

[1] Block, Robert: *The Politics of Projects.* Yourdon Press, New York, NY, 1983.

[2] Kabira Technologies URL: *www.kabira.com*

[3] Project Technology, Inc. URL: *www.projtech.com*

2

Using Executable UML

Processes may be characterized along a spectrum from agile to deliberate. Agile processes, the exemplar of which is Extreme Programming (XP) [1], focus primarily on adaptation and feedback. They view running software as the primary measure of progress on a project. Consequently, agile processes generally disdain model building because a model does not provide feedback in the same way as code.

Deliberate processes, more commonly associated with model building, are more predictive in nature, viewing a model as a blueprint for construction. A common analogy for deliberate processes has been manufacturing, and software development has been viewed as a manufacturing process for which the models are the blueprint. The construction part of software has always been the automated part: compiling, linking, building, and so forth. A model compiler extends this automation to include repetitive coding decisions and so does away with the idea of model as blueprint.

You can use executable UML models at any point along this process spectrum. At the agile end, you can build a model and immediately verify its behavior, without the need to make coding decisions. You can use a model verifier to run tests automatically, and a model compiler for frequent builds. At the other, more deliberate end, you can know that the construction of an executable UML model helps us understand the system so you can select an appropriate organization for the software expressed as a model compiler.

This chapter describes how to use executable UML. Of necessity, the description of activities is linear, but that is not meant to imply that executable UML must be used in a strict, sequential order. To show how executable UML can be used in a modern iterative process, we describe the key iteration checkpoints at the end of each section.

2.1   The System Model

We build an executable UML model for each subject matter, or *domain*, in the system. To establish the domains, we gather requirements expressed as use cases and sort them, based on their vocabularies, into the various subject matters in the system.

Requirement-gathering and domain identification go together. Sometimes we know what the domains are and build use cases against them, and sometimes we have use cases but have to work out what the domains are. Typically, of course, it's a mixture of the two, so we iterate between the two activities.

2.1.1   Domain Identification

Each domain is an autonomous world inhabited by conceptual entities. The conceptual entities in one domain require the existence of other conceptual entities in the same domain, but they do not require the existence of identified conceptual entities in other domains.

Each domain, except for the application, provides services to other domains, and each domain can make use of other domains. We show the domains and the relationships between them on a *domain chart* (Figure 2.1). Ancillary notes define the meaning of each element on the chart.

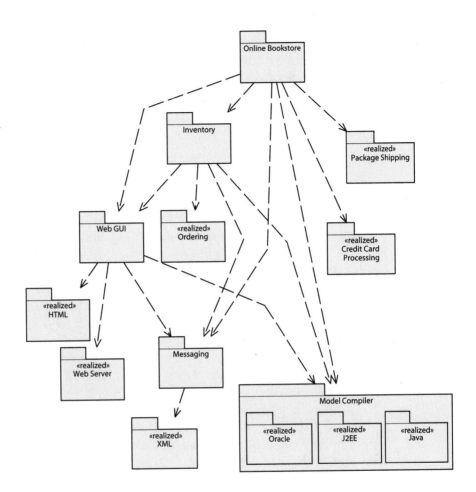

Figure 2.1   *Domain Chart*

Each package symbol on the domain chart represents a domain, and the dotted lines are domain dependencies. The example domain chart shows an online bookstore relying on the existence of a web GUI. However, the online bookstore has no knowledge of the concepts housed by the web GUI; in fact, the web GUI could be replaced by any other user interface, even the Vulcan mind-meld. Domain dependency is a different beast from compilation dependency between packages, so we give it a different name, a *bridge*.

A domain may be too big for a single team, in which case we may divide it into parts called *subsystems,* which we also represent as packages. Subsystems may explicitly make use of concepts from other subsystems in the same domain because boundaries between subsystems are essentially arbitrary, selected for convenience and the manageable size of the resulting subsystems.

2.1.2   Use Cases

The functional, or behavioral, requirements on the system can be expressed textually or more formally in terms of *use cases.*

Systems respond to requests from actors, and each collection of responses, an interaction, is a use case. Each use case is a set of behavioral requirements placed on the system by the role played by the actor.

Initial use cases may span several domains. In our bookstore example, a use case to place an order will affect the application, a user interface, a database to capture the order, and so on. To build an executable UML model for a domain, each use case should be expressed solely in terms of the vocabulary of that domain. Hence, we would frown on the use case "Select a book to purchase from a pull-down menu," because it mixes up what is being done ("Select a book to purchase") with the mechanism used to make it happen ("Select an arbitrary item from pull-down menu"). Rather, these should be represented as separate use cases for the book store and for the user interface.

The vocabulary used in the expression of the use case should match the vocabulary of the associated domain. Hence, the use case "Select a book to purchase from a pull-down menu" would be acceptable if "book" and "pull-down menu" were both concepts in the same domain. Consequently, as you work the use cases, it can change your view of the domains, and vice versa.

Use cases help establish the domains for which we build executable UML models. Use cases also provide us with the vocabulary we need to be able to build appropriate abstractions in each domain.

2.1.3   **Iterating the System Model**

The domain chart provides the highest-level view of the system. Consider a very simple system with a small application and a limited number of services, such as a user interface, and with no layering of the content of the application. Creating the initial domain chart might take one hour, and it would be updated once or twice throughout the project's lifetime.

At the other end of the spectrum, consider an application with a great deal of layering and a good number of services, such as messaging or decision support. Creating an initial picture of the system may take a day or two and require monthly updates as the interfaces between the layers become better understood.

By design, domains are semantically autonomous of one another, so we can build domain models for each one independently, but when we have limited resources, we need to select which domain(s) to model first. Select the domain(s) based both on available expertise and on the relative risk of being surprised by a unexpected requirement.

Unexpected requirements can come about when one domain provides services to another. An incomplete understanding of the domain requesting the service can lead to incomplete requirements for the domain providing the service. When in doubt, model the domain requesting the service in preference to the one providing it.

Sometimes when building the class models it becomes clear that the whole domain is at the wrong level. This should trigger revisiting the domain chart.

2.2   **Modeling a Single Domain**

After gathering and understanding requirements for a domain, we select or invent the appropriate abstractions and make detailed decisions about how the domain works. (This abstraction step is often overlooked, but it is critical to success.) The result is an executable UML model that defines the behavioral requirements for a domain in excruciating detail.

Models are both abstract and detailed at the same time. The abstraction Order, for example, abstracts away all sorts of detail, but the total cost of the order and the delivery address can't be vague, wishy-washy, or incompletely specified.

We abstract away irrelevant detail to see the fundamental details of the abstraction more clearly.

To find domain abstractions and describe each domain precisely, the developer must understand the domain's mission and have sufficient detailed information to make decisions about the exact behavior of the domain.

The executable UML model for each domain (or subsystem in a domain) comprises a set of tightly connected class, state, and action models.

2.2.1   Classes

On the first iteration, we have a domain chart that outlines each domain and a set of use cases for each domain. Next, we are ready to begin modeling each of the domains.

A domain is full of real and hypothetical things. We abstract like things and call them classes. In forming such abstractions, we choose to ignore most of the things. Those remaining are grouped according to perceptions about what it means to be "like." Our ideas of what constitute appropriate criteria for establishing likeness depend on the purpose we have in mind—in other words, on the purpose or mission of the domain.

We choose attributes that support the ideas of likeness we have in mind when we abstract the class. Relationships exist between the things in the domain, and we abstract them as associations between classes.

The result of the abstraction process is a *class diagram* (Figure 2.2) comprising classes, attributes and associations, and descriptions for each element.

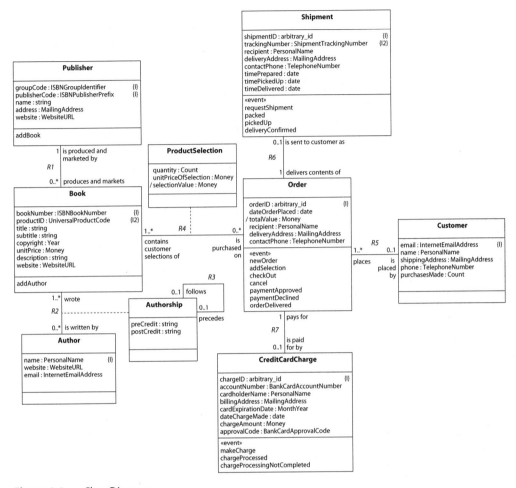

Figure 2.2   *Class Diagram*

2.2.2   **State Machines**

Many things go through various stages in their lifetimes. The collection of stages is called a *lifecycle*. A state machine formalizes a lifecycle in terms of states, events, transitions, and procedures with their actions. At any given time an abstraction representing some aspect of a thing is in exactly one stage of its lifecycle. Hence, a Person abstraction may be At Work while the same person, acting as an Employee abstraction, is In Meeting.

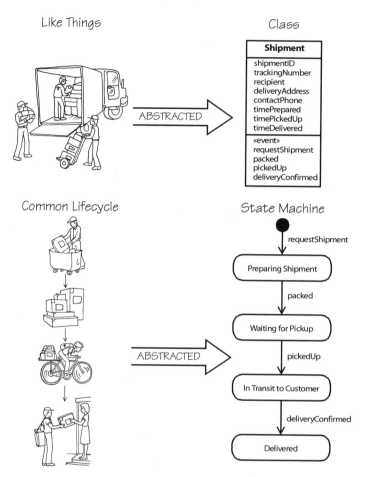

Figure 2.3   *One State Machine for Each Class*

Like things have a common lifecycle, so when a group of like things is abstracted as a class, the common lifecycle is abstracted as the object's state machine. This correspondence is illustrated in Figure 2.3.

The state machine is represented using a subset of the statechart diagram, as shown in Figure 2.4. This subset is chosen to be rich enough to model the lifecycles of the abstractions, in contrast to the more complex statechart diagrams required for modeling software structure. The subset is also chosen to be sparse enough to ease model compilation: A complex language requires more complex model compilers.

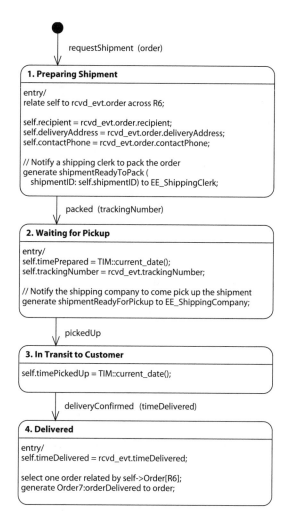

Figure 2.4   *Statechart Diagram for Shipment Class Showing Executable Actions*

To ensure completeness, a state machine can also be rendered as a state transition table that has one cell for each state and event. Checking whether there is a transition for each cell is often beneficial, revealing missing transitions and behaviors.

Objects communicate by sending signals back and forth. A collaboration diagram, such as the one in Figure 2.5, shows the communicating signals between objects.

> **Models vs. Diagrams**
>
> A statechart diagram and a state transition table are both representations of the same underlying model, and they must be consistent with respect to one another.
>
> Executable UML is careful to distinguish the concept of a *model*, the underlying data, behavior or computation, from its *representation*. The representation is typically a diagram or a table, though it could be any representation you can imagine.
>
> Executable UML model-building tools can either prevent the construction of inconsistent models, provide auditing tools to find inconsistencies, or treat some diagrams as primary and generate the rest (for example, generate a collaboration diagram from the several statechart diagrams).
>
> UML defines the semantics (more properly, the "abstract syntax") of each of the diagrams. Executable UML addresses the problem of defining the semantics of an underlying model.

2.2.3   Procedures

Each state on the statechart diagram has an associated *procedure* that takes as input the data items associated with the event that triggered entry into the state. Each procedure comprises a set of *actions*, and each action carries out some functional computation, data access, signal generation and the like. Actions are like code, except at a higher level of abstraction, making no assumptions about software structure or implementation.

UML has a definition of the semantics of actions, but it does not yet have a notation for action models. In Figure 2.6 and throughout the book, we use an existing, action semantics–compliant language [2] for actions.

2.2.4   Iterating the Domain Models

Typically, the very first time one builds a domain model, building the class model is an easy, short-lived task, but that simple class model makes the state-modeling activity almost impossible: The state machines are too large and very complicated. The problem is incomplete factoring of the classes. Often a first-time class diagram has only classes that model tangi-

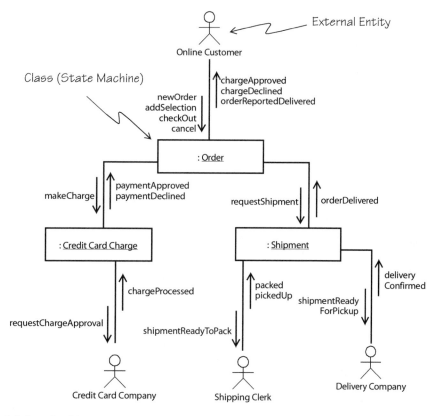

Figure 2.5   *Collaboration Diagram*

```
        // Make this the shipment for the order
        relate self to rcvd_evt.order across R1.'contains product selected as';

        // Copy the delivery information for this shipment from the Order
        self.deliverTo = order.deliverToCustomer;
        self.deliveryDestination = order.deliveryDestination;
        self.deliveryContactPhone = order.deliveryContactPhone;

        // Notify the shipping clerk that a shipment is ready to pack.
        generate shipmentReadyToPack to ShippingClerk;
```

Figure 2.6   *Procedure for State Creating Shipment Consisting of a Series of Actions* ble things, but no classes for desired behavior. Instead, the behavior is allocated to the tangible things, which, of course, makes them extremely complex.

The solution is to refactor the classes so that each class is simpler, abstracting just one role as a class, instead of the many roles taken on by a single thing. Then the state machines for the classes become significantly easier to build. The class diagram and the statechart diagrams are tightly connected, but with practice, the work can be carried out without too much iteration between the two kinds of model.

We often find that the action-modeling step is key to finding missing attributes—sometimes entire missing classes and associations. It also helps locate navigational and hidden constraints that have been incorrectly or incompletely specified.

2.2.5   Iterating between System and Domain Modeling

Abstracting classes in the domain requires some distance from the previous steps in the process because use cases can easily lead to poor abstractions. For example, use cases that outline a set of reports to be produced can easily yield classes that produce each report instead of a report generator based on a set of configurable fields. Similarly, requirements for producing time sheet reports for a small consulting firm could lead to a lot of special-purpose code, when a spreadsheet would be faster, more economical, and far easier to maintain.

These examples, and many like them, share several common properties. First, the abstraction required is one layer of abstraction removed from the original requirements. Instead of the model capturing the details of each specific report, the model captures field, type, and heading in the first example. Similarly, for the second example, the correct abstractions are cell, formula, and cell format, not consultant, client, project, or hours.

Second, the details of the specific application are expressed in data, while the logic for the abstractions remains constant. In the time sheet example, the model has classes cell, formula, and cell format, while the instances of cells can contain the name of the project, the name of the consultant, the number of hours worked, and the formula that produces the bills.

Third, because the application is expressed in data as instances of the more abstracted classes (project name as an instance of cell, for example) the model is highly reusable in other contexts. We simply replace the instances with data describing the new application.

For these reasons, you must be willing to go back and refine, even completely reconstruct, the domain chart as you build the domain models.

2.3   Verification and Execution

As we build the executable UML model, we need to verify its behavior. This work takes place continuously; we test the models as we go along. Similarly, we can compile the model into an implementation as we proceed, checking that the performance of the generated code is adequate for the system.

2.3.1   Model Verification

Having worked our way through all of these steps, we now have the executable UML work products. The very intent of executable UML is to provide a way to prototype the domain without having to construct a complete product. We can verify the finished system without making any decisions about software structure. We can be certain that we have designed the proper behaviors without being concerned with the performance of our network and database. We can also use this approach to test the performance of specific underlying services without needing to have the entire application in place.

There are two kinds of verification. Static verification is like a syntax check that a compiler does. In the early eighties, a lot of work was done on "structured editors" for programming languages. The goal was to provide a way to enter the code without syntax errors to make the programmer more efficient. By using a modeling tool that truly understands the formalism of executable UML, the amount of human intervention in static checking will be less than if you use a general-purpose drawing tool or "flexible notation" modeling tool.

Dynamic verification requires real objects and a scenario to execute with real values. Each scenario should correspond to an instance of a use case or a portion thereof, though the scenarios are built more from the models than the original use cases from which the test cases were derived. When the scenario is executed, the resulting instances and their values can be checked for correctness with the user and even changed contemporaneously.

2.3.2   Model Compilation

A *model compiler* turns an executable UML model into a implementation using a set of decisions about the target hardware and software environment.

The model compiler is therefore an implementation of a subject matter that has the conceptual entities required to execute an arbitrary UML model.

Select a model compiler appropriate to the performance requirements of your solution. Direct the model compiler so it treats each part of the application in the manner you desire (allocation of components, persistence, state execution strategies, static populations that can be optimized in storage, in short, any feature of the model compiler that can be applied differentially to the application).

Then each time you compile your models, you have a running system on which you can verify the behavior of the application and other domains and verify that the performance is adequate. If performance is not adequate, re-allocation of the application components, or even a new model compiler, could help.

The worst case is that no known model compiler meets the performance properties required. In this case, you can hand-code performance-critical portions of a problem and "wrap" them to link up with the generated code. In all cases, 100% of the model is generated, even if the generated code represents less than 100% of the system. Do not modify generated code.

You could also purchase a model compiler that is closest in performance and modify it to generate higher-performance code uniformly. This book does not address this topic.

2.3.3 Iterating Verification and Execution

The last two steps, verification and applying the model compiler, both concern system execution. The former allows for model interpretation so that you and your users can check that the system behaves as desired. Any errors found here will lead to reconstruction of the domain models.

Model verification should take place as each increment of a subsystem is modeled. Executing the model increases our confidence that the model does the right thing. Such verification should be carried out continually as the models are constructed. Indeed, you may build the test cases before you build the models.

The second step, applying the model compiler, is akin to program compilation. Because there are several model compilers available, you may choose to change the model compiler if the performance is not adequate.

Of course, the model being compiled has to be "efficient." A better model compiler won't fix performance problems caused by building a statement for every transaction, instead of grouping transactions monthly. On rare occasions, you may need to modify the application domains to meet performance constraints caused by the model compiler.

2.4 The Big Picture

This chapter has provided an overview of the entire process. The remainder of the book covers the details of what exactly needs to be done to build and compile Executable UML models.

Chapter 3 and Chapter 4 address the topics of working out what needs to be modeled in the first place, addressed in this chapter as Section 2.1: The System Model.

Chapter 5 and Chapter 6 cover the class diagram, addressed here as Section 2.2.1: Classes.

Chapter 7 covers action semantics and action language (Section 2.2.3: Procedures) and Chapter 8 covers constraints on the class diagram.

Chapter 9 covers the basics of statechart diagrams (Section 2.2.2: State Machines). Chapter 10 through Chapter 14 cover ways to build sets of communicating statechart diagrams.

Chapter 15 covers model verification (Section 2.3.1: Model Verification).

Chapter 16 covers model management.

Chapter 17 and Chapter 18 cover weaving the models together so they will execute (Section 2.3.2: Model Compilation).

2.5   References

[1] Beck, Kent: *Extreme Programming Explained: Embrace Change.* Addison-Wesley, Boston, 2000.

[2] BridgePoint Object Action Language *www.projtech.com/pdfs/bp/oal.pdf*

3

Domains and Bridges

Building a system involves understanding many different subject matters and gluing them together to make a coherent whole. In an online bookstore, for example, we need to understand the application itself, the look and feel of a user interface, the details of user-interface screen layout using, say, HTML, messaging between computers, networking, and so on. In addition to these subject matters, we must also state how they relate to one another, so we can put them together into a complete system.

Each subject matter is a *domain*, capable of being understood and modeled using executable UML. We build one or more executable UML models for each domain.

Domains are semantically autonomous. For example, we can understand an online bookstore application without having to understand networking, and vice versa. But domains also depend on one another: The online bookstore makes assumptions about the existence of a networking domain and so places requirements on it. This assumption–requirement pair is a *bridge*.

At implementation time, the models of each domain are woven together by specifying a set of *join points* between the models. The joining together of two domains is an implementation of a bridge. We take up this topic in Chapter 18: Model Compilers.

This chapter describes the concepts of domains and bridges, introduces a domain chart to visualize the relationships between them, and discusses how requirements relate to both systems and domains.

3.1 Domains

Domains represent the different subject matters that we need to understand to build a system.

Definition: A *domain* is an autonomous, real, hypothetical, or abstract world inhabited by a set of conceptual entities that behave according to characteristic rules and policies.

For a given system, we first identify the several domains that make up the system as a whole. Generally, systems comprise domains such as an application, a bookstore for example; some implementation technologies, such as Java, HTML, a relational database, and XML; and some intermediate abstractions, such as a Web GUI, messaging, and workflow.

We then understand and model the application and intermediate abstractions using executable UML and apply various implementation technologies to realize the abstractions in the application and intermediate domains.

3.1.1 Domain Missions

Each domain should have a clear mission that drives the modeling work for that domain. Each domain therefore has a *mission statement*—a sentence or two that's the systems development version of a domain's "elevator pitch." Figure 3.1 shows some domains for the online bookstore project, along with their mission statements.

Each domain has a set of conceptual entities that support the mission. An online bookstore has customers, orders, and the business rules governing their use, while a user interface domain involves windows and forms

Domain	Mission Statement
online bookstore	provides a way for customers to place orders for books and other goods
Web GUI	provides a way for online users to interact with a system
messaging	provides a way to communicate information between the application and other independent software systems
HTML	provides a way to render user interface displays as pages that can be displayed in a web browser, and for user input to be captured in web forms and transmitted back to the application

Figure 3.1   *Sample Mission Statements*

together with their entirely different set of operating policies about how those entities behave.

3.1.2   Domain Autonomy

Each domain forms a cohesive whole, semantically autonomous of other domains. This has a number of implications.

First, a conceptual entity is defined in exactly one domain. Orders and customers are part of the bookstore, while pages and icons are part of the user interface.

It is possible to have two entities with the same name in different domains, but they must mean different things. For example, a Table in HTML means "rows and columns," while a Table in a Furniture Manufacturing domain means "top and four legs."

Second, the conceptual entities in a domain require the existence of other conceptual entities in the same domain. An order makes little sense without a customer, and an icon requires a page on which to appear.

Third, the conceptual entities in one domain do not require the existence of conceptual entities in other domains. Customers and orders can exist without windows or icons, and windows and icons can exist without customers.

This is a most crucial idea: When we build a model of an online bookstore, that model will be complete and detailed—about bookstore things. Done properly, the model will contain nothing that makes any assumption about a particular user interface, programming language, database, or other implementation technology.

3.1.3   Domain Replacement

Domain autonomy implies that one domain can be replaced with another. For example, a model of networking could be replaced by another one using different conceptual entities.

When you identify the different domains in a system, verify that each domain is truly cohesive and autonomous by mentally replacing a domain with another that has the same mission but a different set of conceptual entities.

It is good practice to plan a system so we can realize the application with different implementation technologies without needing to rethink, and remodel, the whole application. Though we usually intend to use one specific user interface, for example, we should think about the system as if it were likely that others could be used. Developers often face the problem of applying new technologies to existing applications: "Can this system be WAP[1]-enabled in three months?"

Similarly, we want to be able to reuse UI standards or messaging schemes, and to do so they need to be separate from the applications. The user interface design we use for the online bookstore, for example, could be applied in another context, in an accounting system or a mortgage system.

Complete autonomy of the domains is critical for rapid redeployment. Designing systems in terms of domains that can be replaced with others with the same mission but different conceptual entities improves the reusability of all domains. Domains are the largest units of reuse.

We can also identify other domains as generic, reusable services. The bookstore might need to track assignment of tasks to people in an organization. The assignment of tasks to people would be modeled as a

---

[1] WAP = Wireless Application Protocol: a sort of HTML for mobile phones

Workflow domain without any knowledge of its use in the bookstore, and the Bookstore domain would make no reference to the conceptual entities in the Workflow domain. The same Workflow could then be used to track credit approval in a Mortgage system. Any necessary links between the two domain models are maintained separately from both domains.

Domain partitioning gives us the tools to represent the application subject matter separately from the implementation. It goes further, encouraging the construction of systems as layered abstractions.

3.2　**Domains and Requirements**

Dividing a system into its subject matters helps us control an undifferentiated mass of requirements by assigning each requirement to the appropriate domain. Domain requirements then drive the modeling for each domain.

When we model a domain, we use the vocabulary of that domain and no other. The bookstore domain will include concepts such as "add item to order" and "provide credit card number," but there is no statement of how these behaviors might be achieved. The domain modeler assumes that somewhere, somehow, a collection of mechanisms exists that can satisfy these statements.

For our purposes in organizing modeling, we want to work with requirements that affect a single domain. The vocabulary of a domain-level requirement is completely within the subject matter at hand, and each domain-level requirement employs a vocabulary consistent with the domain. But consider the following typical requirements:

> ***Add item to order:*** The customer selects a book from the catalog page by specifying a quantity *in a text box and pressing the Add Item button next to* the catalog entry.

> ***Check out order:*** A returning customer simply enters his account number and password. *The password appears as a row of asterisks.* The order is then processed using the credit card and shipping address already on file for the customer.

These requirements commingle application and user interface vocabulary. (The latter is shown in italics.)

With knowledge of the potential domains in the system, we can partition these system-level requirements, allocating each to an identified domain. The first requirement above becomes two separate requirements, each for a single domain:

> ***Online Bookstore:*** Customer adds an item to an order by specifying a book and quantity.

> ***User Interface:*** The catalog menu allows selection of items and quantities via a page containing a table with a check box, a text box, and a button on each row.

Each individual domain-level requirement applies to a single domain, so that modeling for each domain may proceed. Working by domains—not just by individual requirements or functional areas—helps avoid fragmented systems that fail to exploit opportunities for commonality and reuse.

If you have no prior knowledge of the domains in the system, you can still partition requirements based on their distinct vocabularies. For example, the partitioned requirement for the preceding user interface example still contains two vocabularies, one associated with a GUI toolkit with pages, tables, check boxes and the like; and another separate domain, an application user interface that identifies the specific kinds of menus, such as the catalog menu. Separate these into two domains:

> ***(Application) User Interface:*** A catalog menu allows selection of items and the selection of quantities.

> ***(HTML) GUI:*** A page contains a table with a check box, a text box, and a button on each row.

3.3   **Bridges**

Domains are autonomous, but they rely on the existence of other domains. For example, an online bookstore domain can be modeled without reference to any mechanism that selects the item the customer wants or the desired quantity. The user interface mechanism could be HTML, voice recognition software, or some other yet-to-be-invented technology.

We implicitly assume that there is some way to determine the specific items and quantities of them to add to the order. This implicit assumption in turn embodies requirements that somehow the customer can communicate with the bookstore application. A *bridge* exists between the bookstore domain and some other domain that can satisfy the requirement implied by the assumption.

Definition: A *bridge* is a layering dependency between domains. One domain makes assumptions, and other domains take those assumptions as requirements.

These assumption–requirement pairs form an asymmetric dependency: The bookstore needs a user interface to do its job, but the user interface domain does not rely on the online bookstore application for its existence. We maintain domain autonomy using the bridge as intermediary.

A domain makes assumptions about a bridge, and the bridge then places requirements on another domain. For example, the bookstore has a requirement to find out the requested item and quantity. Only when we decide to communicate with users specifically using menus does the bridge place the requirement on a specific user interface domain that supplies the menus. Hence, we think of a bridge as having two parts. The first part contains a set of assumptions that one domain makes, and the second part contains a set of requirements placed on a domain.

Multiple domains may place requirements on their respective bridges, all of which could be satisfied by a single domain. For example, the application may assume the existence of a scheme to communicate with the credit card company, while the web browser assumes the ability to communicate with a host. Both requirements can be accomplished with a single messaging domain. Hence, a bridge can have many domains that

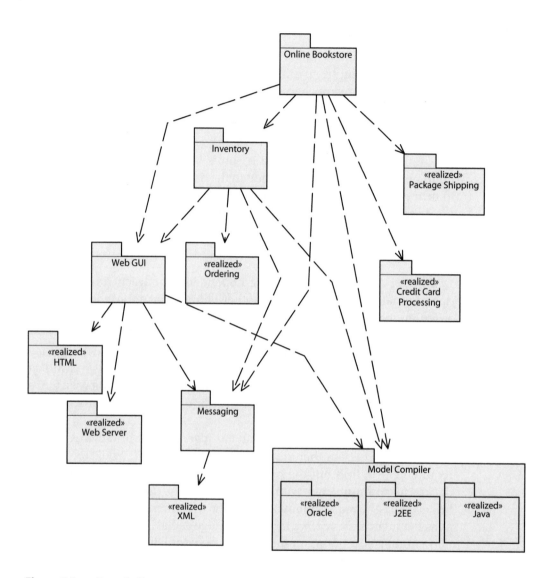

Figure 3.2   *Domain Chart*

make assumptions about it and a single domain that satisfies those requirements.

Each domain is represented as a UML package, and each bridge is shown as a dotted dependency line between them.

Domain: Web GUI

> *Mission statement:* Provides a way for online users to interact with a system.
>
> *Unallocated Assumptions:* Selection menus can accept a quantity, such as "15 copies of this book."
>
> *Bridge to Web Server:* All display communication will be over secure communication.
>
> *Model Compiler:* All class instances persist in a redundant store. All event communication is by sending XML messages.

Figure 3.3   *Domain Mission Statement, Including Bridge Descriptions*

Some domains are groupings of other subject matters into a single whole with a single united interface. We show this situation by placing folders inside a larger folder. In Figure 3.2, the model compiler has a single interface used by messaging, the Web GUI, and the bookstore. In turn, the model compiler uses Java, Solaris, Oracle, and Xerces.

Some domains are not modeled, but are instead already realized as code. These domains are stereotyped «realized». (The «» indicate a stereotype [i.e., a special form or use of some UML element]. These symbols are called *guillemets* ["ghee-yu-may," with a hard G].)

The domain chart is very high level, providing only a name for each domain. To flesh out the definition of the domain, build a mission statement for the domain that will drive the modeling of that domain, as shown in Section 3.1.1: Domain Missions. Note how the domain mission statements are very short—only a phrase or a few sentences. The objective is to communicate information succinctly, not to be textual representations of the models.

As soon as an assumption is identified, add it to the end of the domain's mission statement. If you can identify the bridge that can satisfy the assumption, allocate the assumption to the appropriate bridge, as in Figure 3.3.

Bridges represent flows of assumptions and requirements, not flows of control.

Many systems carry out their functions only in response to some user request, and as a consequence, control flows from the user interface domain to the application. A web-based online bookstore application, for example, might begin by asking the user for the account number and password, and then move on to a screen for buying and selling. Nothing is done until the user makes a request, except possibly a time-out if there is no activity.

The customer log-in screen, however, exists only because the application needs it. There is an assumption–requirement dependency between the application, which needs customers to log in, and the appearance of specific menus and buttons that allow the customer to do so.

As the project proceeds, especially once modeling has begun, it is critical to reconcile the various clients' assumptions to ensure they form a complete set of requirements on specific domains. See also the discussion in Section 2.1.3: Iterating the System Model.

To the extent that domain-level requirements have been identified, these requirements are more specific forms of the general requirements identified on a bridge. Domain-level requirements for the domain therefore "belong" with the bridge *to* the domain in question.

3.4   Aspects and Join Points

The principle of domain autonomy allows us to build models of domains that are quite separate from one another. From the point of view of the user interface domain, the meaning of what is selected from a menu is both irrelevant and unknown, and from the point of view of the application the fact that a catalog item was selected from a menu list is irrelevant.

At construction time, when we have already built complete executable UML models of each domain, we will need to build a correspondence between different elements of each of the participating domains. The correspondence is between a specific type of thing in the application (catalog item) and an instance, expressed as data, in the user interface (the list of allowable items in the menu).

The two domains, the application and the user interface, need to be woven together, and the combination then translated to form the implementation. More generally, the several domains must be woven together and translated by the model compiler into the implementation.

This is the same problem taken on by various aspect-oriented programming environments. Analogously, each domain is an *aspect*[2] and each bridge is a set of *join points*. The join points are simply correspondences between elements in two aspects that are then compiled into code. (For a useful introduction to aspect orientation, see [1].)

We take up several ways of doing this in Chapter 18: Model Compilers. For the purposes of specification in executable UML, the key issue is to link specific elements in one domain with the specific elements in another that implement it as part of the construction process.

3.5   **Domains and Aspects**

Domain partitioning is a way to factor out a single cross-cutting concern as a single subject matter. Each domain constitutes a single aspect of the system. As such, domains are the largest unit of reuse, because domains form cohesive wholes, autonomous of one another.

We represent domains and the bridges between them as UML packages and dependencies, respectively, though this is a stretch because UML does not directly support the concepts. Nonetheless, domains are important because each domain becomes a set of executable UML models with defined behaviors.

To build the executable UML models, however, we need to gather and understand the requirements. One approach to this problem is use cases, the topic we pick up in the next chapter.

---

[2] While aspects can contain anything a programmer chooses, a well-chosen aspect corresponds to a single domain.

3.6   References

[1] *Communications of the ACM*, Volume 44, Issue 10.
(The entire issue is devoted to aspect-oriented development.)

4

Use Cases

A recurring problem in systems development is getting started with the requirements and organizing them into some comprehensible framework. In this chapter we will see how to gather the requirements for the system and organize them into separate domains.

Use cases view a system from the outside—they take an external view of the system in terms of what *happens*. Executable UML models, on the other hand, take an internal view of a domain in terms what the conceptual entities *are* and how they behave.

Use cases, then, are a useful tool for gathering requirements, but they do not immediately yield classes. Figuring out the classes requires abstraction based upon the requirements.

Once we have built the executable UML models, we can assign specific values to the current state of the system and the data that activates the use case. These scenarios become the test cases for the system. We take up this topic later, in Chapter 15: Domain Verification.

There are many fine books on organizing requirements and writing use cases. This chapter is not intended to replace these for those purposes. Rather, it is intended to describe how to apply the appropriate level for use cases to organize information for modeling, to expose the different subject matters in a system, and to form the basis for test cases.

4.1   Basics of Use Cases

Systems respond to external signals by carrying out some desired activity, often with varying outcomes depending upon the system's state. Each desired activity is a functional requirement, such as:

- A customer can order a book by selecting a book number and quantity.
- A customer checks out an open order by entering the credit card number and shipping information.
- The credit card company approves or declines a charge.
- If the customer's credit card charge is approved, the requested items are packed and shipped to the customer.

Use cases are a tool for organizing system requirements by understanding the interactions between the *actors* that make a request and the responses, or *activities*, made by the system. (These terms were first defined in [1].)

4.1.1   Actors

Definition: An *actor* is a role played by an external entity that requires something from the system in one or more interactions with the system.

Roles played by people are the most obvious actors. In an online bookstore we have obvious roles such as:

Online Customer   Delivery Person   Warehouse Clerk

Organizations can also be actors:

Credit Card Company   Delivery Company   Product Supplier

The use case diagram's value is like a table of contents—it provides a graphical overview of the actors and use cases. To quote Alistair Cockburn, "If you spend much time studying and worrying about the graphics and the relations, you are expending energy in the wrong place."[2]

Similarly, because "time" is not a person or organization, it is possible to argue that time is not an actor, or that it's ridiculous to model time as a stick figure. Practically speaking, this is about as useful as arguing about how many angels can dance on the head of a pin. It really makes no difference. Invent a clock symbol; use a stick figure; don't show the timer.

Sometimes there may be situations where different actors may all request the same activity. For example, a delivery person delivers the order to the customer, but the dispatcher notifies the system. Who is the actor? The delivery person? The dispatcher? In this case, an effective strategy is to abstract away the mechanism and focus on the eventual source of the request, in terms of the role, in this case the customer.

People and organizations are not the only actors. Use cases may be initiated by the expiration of a delay, or the arrival of an external signal that signals some absolute time. For example, the store requires that an order more than five days old that hasn't been checked out be automatically canceled and deleted from the system. In this example, no active user of the system is initiating the use case. Instead, a timer is set when the order is first made and canceled when the order is checked out. The timer is the actor and the expiration of the timer initiates the use case.

4.1.2   Use Cases

Definition: A *use case* specifies an interaction between the system and one or more actors together with the activities performed by the system.

For example, in the online bookstore, customers start orders, add and remove items, change the quantity of items, and cancel orders. We may represent this graphically, using a stick figure for an actor and an oval for a use case, as shown in Figure 4.1.

We name an activity so it does not include the name of the actor. Hence, we prefer Order Merchandise over Customer Orders New Merchandise.

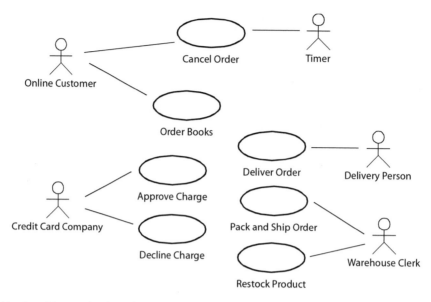

Figure 4.1   *Use Case Diagram for the Online Bookstore*

This naming scheme has the advantages of reducing redundancy (why state the actor twice?) and flexibility (other actors can start a new order).

Consequently, any time a single use case is referred to by more than one actor, the activity's behavior is the same regardless of the actor. If that is not the case, we have distinct activities that must also be named differently. So one oval pointed to by two actors is different from two ovals, as in Figure 4.2.

We have also found it useful to represent the use case diagram as a table, as shown in Figure 4.3.

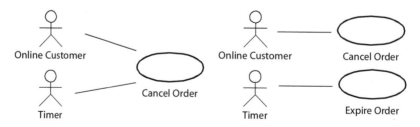

Figure 4.2   *Different Use Cases for Different Actors*

Actor	Activity
Customer	Order Books Cancel Order
Timer	Expire Order
Warehouse Clerk	Pack and Ship Order Restock Product
Credit Card Company	Approve Charge Decline Charge
Delivery Company	Deliver Order to Customer

Figure 4.3   *Use Cases Listed as a Table*

4.1.3   External Signals

A line to a use case shows the initiating actor. The actor does something or requests something from the system and so is seen as a source of an external signal that initiates the activity. The system itself receives the external signal to inform it of the request to carry out the activity.

External signals often carry data, say, the book number and quantity to restock the product. These data values act as parameters, as shown in Figure 4.4.

External Signal	Parameters
Order Books	book number quantity credit card number customer name delivery address
Approve Charge	charge amount customer name credit card number
Restock Product	book number quantity

Figure 4.4   *External Signals with Their Parameters*

Real-Time Systems

In many embedded and real-time systems, we don't have "users" in the same way that business systems do. In an elevator control system for example, a passenger may well know that he wants to go a particular floor, but when it comes to organizing requirements into use cases, an ordinary elevator passenger is not likely to be much help. Instead, we will find our users in the various experts in the problem space: mechanical engineers, hardware engineers, and so on.

Similarly, we will find that use cases are not always initiated by people but also by devices. An actor is anything that interfaces ot interacts with the system. People, machines, external systems, and sensors are all candidate actors.

For example, the use cases for an elevator might include:

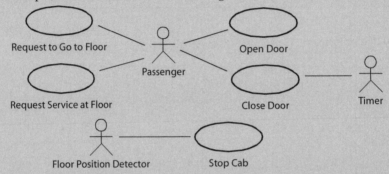

Note that the Passenger actor is acting as a surrogate for external devices (e.g., buttons and sensors) that actually initiate the use case. This is similar to the technique for managing the user interface in IT systems.

In real-time systems, the external signal may be a signal (a control value), the arrival of data values, a data item reaching a value (position of the elevator reaching a floor), or the expiration of a timer (either absolute or relative).

There may be computation involved in recognizing the external signal. For example, the external signal may be the result of a comparison of values, such as the position and speed of the elevator. This comparison is carried out by an *event recognizer*. For system engineering purposes, however, it is worthwhile to note the requirement for an event recognizer and any additional communication required with actors.

Similarly, if the only way to know whether a condition is true is to examine the actor, then the system may need to track the state of an actor, or even interrogate the actor periodically. Again, these interfacing solutions are properly system-engineering issues, not requirements. They should be noted, and not allowed to obscure the essentials of the use case.

The way in which the system becomes aware of the external signal is not relevant to the essential requirements of the application, so it should not appear as part of the use case. This formulation effectively separates the interfacing technology, the user interface, from the problem at hand.

Whatever you do, do not model every field on some screen as a separate use case. Exactly how those data values were accumulated is not relevant. Likewise, if a particular UI design requires stepping through multiple windows and menus, do not treat each of these elements as its own use case.

Instead, at some point, a group of related data items are ready and confirmed by the actor. Treat the entire unit as a single external signal that starts the activity.

It is helpful to note any proposed interfacing solutions as part of a description of the external signal, but these possible solutions should not be allowed to obscure the essentials of the use case.

4.2   Working with Use Cases

Often candidate use cases include items that require an actor's intervention to complete the activity. This intervention is itself a separate activity that could become its own use case. Consider, for example, a use case Order Books. When the customer completes an order, the system sends a message to the credit card company to approve the charge. It is unclear whether the response from the credit card company is a separate use case or not. In addition, this informal description introduces vocabulary ("message") that does not belong in the Bookstore domain.

This section provides guidance on working with use cases that span several domains and when a use case should be decomposed into other, smaller use cases.

4.2.1   Single-Domain Use Cases

As noted in Section 3.2: Domains and Requirements, for our purposes in organizing modeling, we want to work with a vocabulary consistent with the domain. It is therefore critical that the description of each use case

1. The customer starts a new order by selecting a book *from the catalog page* and specifying a quantity.
2. The customer can continue to add more books to the order. He can also cancel the order entirely.
3. Once the customer is satisfied with his selections, he checks out the order by entering a credit card number, name, billing address, and shipping address. *The system sends a message* to the credit card company to process the charge.
4. If the credit card company approves the charge, Shipping *receives a Shipping Order and a label on their printer*. The delivery company *receives a message* that an order will be ready for pickup.
5. The shipping clerk packs the order and *scans the barcode* to indicate the shipment is packed.
6. The delivery company *sends back a message* to confirm when the order will be picked up.
7. A shipping clerk records each shipment picked up by the delivery company.
8. The delivery company notifies the bookstore when the order has been delivered to the customer. The bookstore then *e-mails* the customer to inform him that the order has been (or shortly will be) delivered.

Figure 4.5   *Typical Flow Description for an Order Books Use Case*

employ the vocabulary of the domain under study. The flow description shown in Figure 4.5 describes requirements on domains other than the Bookstore domain. These "extra-curricular" requirements are shown in italics.

The flow description should be rewritten to use only the single vocabulary of the domain under study. Figure 4.6 shows a revised the flow description using only the vocabulary of the Bookstore domain.

4.2.2   Levels of Use Cases

So, what is the right level of detail for use cases? Cockburn [2] identifies several different levels of use cases. Those at the "sky" level involve a broad system goal, such as Order Books. These use cases are useful for getting a grip on the problem as a whole, without being overwhelmed by too much detail.

The next level of use cases, those at the "kite" level, are the more detailed steps a user takes to achieve a goal. For the bookstore customer, these would include Start New Order, Add Item to Order, and Check Out Order. Constantine and Lockwood [3] conceive of use cases primarily at this

1. The customer starts a new order by selecting a book and specifying a quantity.
2. The customer can continue to add more books to the order. He can also cancel the order entirely.
3. Once the customer is satisfied with his selections, he checks out the order, specifying a credit card number, name, billing address, and shipping address. The credit card company must approve (or decline) the proposed charge.
4. If the credit card company approves the charge, a shipping clerk packs the order and indicates the shipment is packed.
5. Once packed, the delivery company is informed that an order is ready for pickup.
6. The delivery company confirms when the order will be picked up.
7. A shipping clerk records each shipment picked up by the delivery company.
8. The delivery company notifies the bookstore when the order has been delivered to the customer. The bookstore then notifies the customer to inform him that the order has been (or shortly will be) delivered.

Figure 4.6   *Revised Flow Description for an Order Books Use Case*

level, at the level of user goals. These use cases tend to be written in the language of the user, so they naturally apply to a single domain.

"Sea level" use cases are single system interactions: The actor requests a service, and the system is capable of making a complete response, with no additional interaction with *any* actor. For example, the kite-level use case Check Out Order needs other actors to carry out the checkout process: The credit card company approves the charge, a shipping clerk packs the order, and a delivery company picks up and delivers the order. Each of these actors initiates system interactions that involve no other intermediate intervention while contributing to the overall kite-level goal of checking out an order. Figure 4.7 shows a use case diagram with a set of single-interaction use cases.

"Mud-level" use cases are even lower than single system interactions and generally describe the mechanics of how the system will implement functionality. These often mix in the vocabulary of the mechanics of a particular user interface, middleware, or messaging technology.

Note that some "kite-level" use cases such as Start New Order also appear as single-interaction "sea-level" use cases, because they are both at the level of a user goal, and they happen not to involve other actors. Because use cases can be expressed at a number of different levels, it is quite tempting to decompose use cases and to form a neat hierarchy all the way

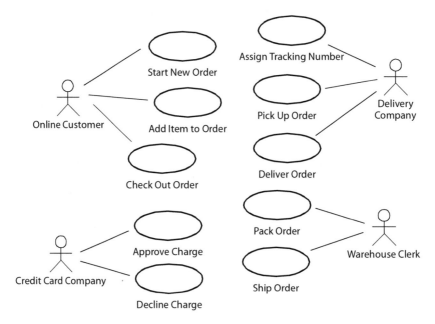

Figure 4.7   *Order Books Identified as Single-Interaction Use Cases*

down into the mud. However, our objective is not to analyze the system with use cases (the dreaded "abuse by decomposition" [4]), but rather to understand enough about the domain to build executable models.

4.2.3   Applying Use Cases

We recommend using use cases in two ways: to provide a foundation for modeling and as fodder for test cases.

Use cases and modeling. Use cases are helpful in learning the vocabulary of the domain from a user perspective. As the problem becomes better understood, it is your job as developer to abstract the requirements expressed in the use cases into a set of classes and their behaviors, as described in subsequent chapters. This abstraction frequently increases the semantic gap between the models and use cases, and that's a good thing.

Generally, sky-level use cases are useful to get you started, but are too high-level to provide enough detail (by themselves) for modeling. Sea-level use cases, in particular those developed before any modeling is started, can easily overwhelm you with too much detail, though it is occasionally useful to drill down some especially difficult use cases to that level. Mud-level use cases that incorporate other domains, particularly the user interface, are worse than useless.

Kite-level use cases provide the level of use cases needed for modeling.

Use cases and test cases. The second application of use cases is as fodder for test cases. A good use case, with a definition for the required behavior, describes the behavior that needs to be tested well. For this, sea-level use cases are best, assembled into larger kite use cases as required. Chapter 15: Domain Verification covers in detail the process of testing models.

4.3   Activity Diagrams

When we have a lot of use cases, especially sea-level use cases, it can be difficult to understand how the individual use cases interact. The use case diagram shown in Figure 4.7 is a table of contents of the use cases in Order Merchandise. While it shows actors and activities, it does not show any context to those activities. How can we show these user activities and how the individual use cases are sequenced to carry out those activities?

Figure 4.8 shows an activity diagram that presents the use case Order Merchandise as a sequence of single-interaction use cases.

Each oval is an activity, corresponding to a use case. The arrows between the activities show sequence: Start a New Order, then Add Item to Order. Arrows that loop back indicate an iteration, so the example allows for several items to be added. To help visualize activities that encompass use cases initiated by several distinct actors, divide the activity diagram into *swimlanes*. These divide the activities into individual columns by actor.

An activity diagram can also show alternatives and decision logic. For example, the Customer may add more items or check out; the credit card company can either approve or decline the charge.

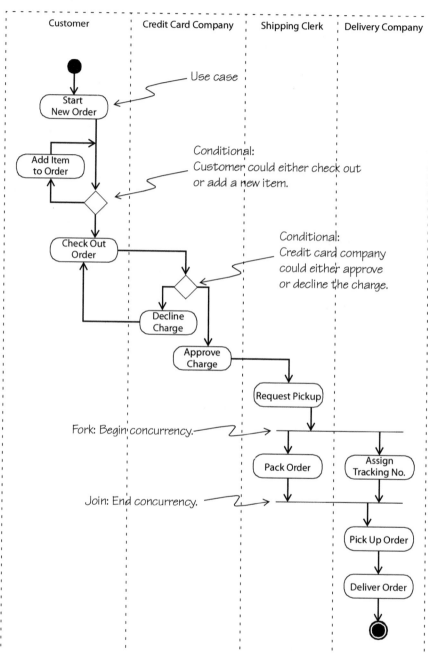

Figure 4.8   *Activity Diagram for the Use Case Order Books*

Concurrency and synchronization can also be shown to place use cases in context. If several use cases can all be executed concurrently, use a *fork* to show where the concurrency begins and a *join* to show where the concurrent paths are re-synchronized.

4.4 Formalizing Use Cases

The initial description of a use case is text. We can formalize the definition of a use case in terms of *preconditions* and *postconditions*. Preconditions state what must be true for the use case to execute. Postconditions state what must be true when the use case has completed.

The formulation of a use case in terms of pre- and postconditions is both precise and concise, in no way presupposes a particular design, and avoids the pitfall of specifying the use case in an overly procedural form.

4.4.1 Preconditions

Each use case may have zero or more preconditions.

Definition: A *use case precondition* denotes a relevant, verifiable property of the system that is required to be true before the use case is performed.

To help identify preconditions, examine the use case's parameters. For example, Add Item to Order has the parameters Order Number, Book Number, and Quantity. This raises questions about each of these items. What must be so? In the case of Add Item to Order, then, we expect the following to be true:

- There is an unexpired Order not yet checked out.
- The item selected is a book carried by the store.
- The quantity selected is a number greater than zero and less than stock on hand.

4.4.2 Postconditions

Each use case has at least one postcondition.

Definition: A *use case postcondition* represents what must be true when the use case has completed.

After Add Item to Order completes successfully, we expect the following to be true:

- The order is no longer empty.
- The order is not checked out.
- The book is included in the order with the given quantity.
- The total value of the order is increased by the unit price of the book times the quantity selected.

We can write a use case in terms of preconditions and postconditions, as seen in Figure 4.9.

4.4.3   Linked Use Cases

One use case's postcondition is often another's precondition. This is especially true when we have sequences of use cases characterized as activities, as you can see in Figure 4.10.

4.5   Scenarios and Testing

The actual execution of a use case, with real data values, is called a *scenario*. (A scenario is also sometimes defined as an instance of a use case.) We formally define a scenario in Chapter 15: Domain Verification:

> A scenario is the planned execution of a use case with ranges of values for signal parameters, initial states for state machine instances, and ranges of values for attributes of objects, so that there is only path through the model.

A scenario is therefore an excellent way to define a test case, but running the test depends on having values for attributes, states, and parameters. At this stage in a system's development, we can supply values for only one of the three: the parameters.

Add Item to Order (Order Number, Book Number, Quantity)

Add Item to Order adds a quantity of a given book to an existing order. The quantity requested must be capable of being satisfied from the stock on hand.

Preconditions:

- The Order identified by Order Number exists, has not expired, and is not yet checked out.
- The book identified by Book Number is stocked by the store.
- The Quantity is a number greater than zero and less than the stock on hand of the book.

Postconditions:

- The Order identified by Order Number is no longer empty, is not checked out, and has not expired.
- The quantity on hand of the book identified by Book Number is reduced by the Quantity selected.
- The book is included in the order with the given quantity.
- The total value of the order is increased by the unit price of the book times the quantity selected.

Figure 4.9   *Preconditions and Postconditions for Add Item to Order*

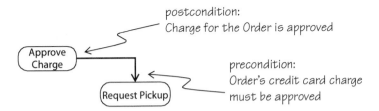

Figure 4.10   *Connecting Preconditions and Postconditions*

To define the test cases completely so that they can be executed, we must first build the models. Once we have executable UML models, we can supply values for the attributes and states of the system and use the scenarios as test cases. We take up this topic in Chapter 15: Domain Verification.

4.6 System Modeling

Domains and use cases go together. The subject matter represented as a domain has a set of requirements captured by the use cases, and the use cases employ a vocabulary consistent with the subject matter.

With the domain mission and the use cases in hand, it is now time to begin the abstraction process required to go from the external view of the subject matter (supplied by the use cases) to the internal view employed by the executable UML models. We begin this process by abstracting classes.

4.7 References

[1] Jacobson, Ivar, et al.: *Object-Oriented Software Engineering: A Use Case Driven Approach.* Addison-Wesley, Reading, Mass., 1992.

[2] Cockburn, Alistair: *Writing Effective Use Cases.* Addison-Wesley, Boston, 2001.

[3] Constantine, Larry, and Lucy Lockwood: *Software for Use: A Practical Guide to the Models and Methods of Usage-Centered Design.* Addison-Wesley, Reading Mass., 1999.

[4] Fowler, Martin: "Use and Abuse Cases." In *Distributed Computing,* April 1998.

5

Classes and Attributes

The requirements and use cases we gather for a domain provide an external view of its required behavior. Once we have a handle on a good number of use cases, we can begin abstraction of those requirements into a model that formalizes knowledge about the domain. The resulting model is an internal view: It expresses our *solution* to meeting the requirements.

Many possible executable formalisms could be used to model the domain. Executable UML is an abstract, object-oriented formalism; hence, it employs classes, attributes, and other object-oriented constructs as a way to organize abstractions.

5.1   Classes

We base the abstractions on the conceptual entities in a domain. An online bookstore, for example, will process many shipments to send orders to customers.

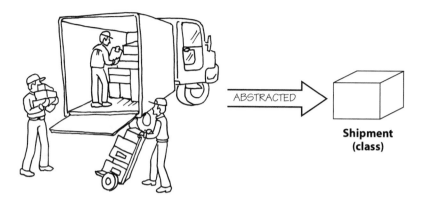

Figure 5.1   *Instances and Classes*

We abstract these shipments into the *class* Shipment, as shown in Figure 5.1.

Definition: A *class* is an abstraction from a set of conceptual entities in a domain so that all the conceptual entities in the set have the same characteristics, and they all are subject to and behave according to the same rules and policies.

Put another way, a class abstracts common characteristics and common behavior.

5.1.1   Finding Classes

Start out by asking yourself, "What are the *conceptual entities*[1] in this domain?" Most of the concepts are likely to fall into the following five categories: tangible things, roles, incidents, interactions, and specifications. These categories aren't offered as a classification system but as a set of starter ideas for finding classes in a new domain.[2]

---

[1] More colloquially, we might say "thing" instead of "conceptual entity." However, as we shall see, conceptual entities need not be tangible: Indeed, the BookProduct abstraction captures not a physical book, but a kind of book, as in "Do you have a copy of *Executable UML*?"

[2] This classification scheme, and much of the text describing it, was first proposed in [1].

Tangible things. These are the easiest to find. Given the appropriate domain, it's hard to miss:

Airplane	Pipe Support	Magnet	Book
Nuclear Reactor	Racehorse	National Landmark	Dog
Circuit Breaker	Power Supply	Vehicle	Car

Underlining the nouns in a requirements document or in the use cases sometimes helps find the simple tangible things, but this technique has a tendency to stifle the abstraction process; also, it does not help identify the more interesting and valuable kinds of classes described below.

Roles played by people or organizations. This category is described by examples:

Doctor	Shipping Clerk	Client	Department
Patient	Tenant	Employee	Taxpayer
Customer	Account Holder	Supervisor	Trustee

Frequently, if you have one role, you will have others also. This comes about when distinguishing between different roles played by the same or different people; hence, one would expect to find Customer, Shipping Clerk, and Salesperson in a model of a bookstore. By creating separate classes, we allow for a Shipping Clerk also to be a Customer, with the characteristics and behavior of a Customer classified separately from that of a Shipping Clerk. Strong models make heavy use of role classes.

The alternative is to model the tangible thing Person, and then to constrain its behavior in a variety of difficult-to-check ways so as to distinguish among the cases. (Can a Shipping Clerk ship a book to a Customer? What if they are the same person? This is not just an academic question: Many systems prohibit a Payroll Clerk from approving his own paycheck.)

Combining multiple roles into a single class does not "save classes." It just makes a lot of extra work during state modeling.

Incidents. Incidents represent an occurrence or event: something that happens at a specific time. Some reasonable incidents are:

Flight	Accident
Performance (of a play, for example)	Event (in a physics experiment)
System Crash	Service Call (appliance repair)

Abstract an incident to capture data about it, such as the departure time of a flight. Classes abstracted from incidents often have behavior: The flight is scheduled to occur at some time; at some time, a plane is available; the flight departs at some time and eventually lands. We will model this lifecycle behavior with a statechart diagram.

Interactions. Interactions generally have a "transaction" or "contract" quality, and relate to two or more other classes in the model. Examples are:

Purchase (relating buyer, seller, and thing purchased)

Credit Card Charge (relating an account and a purchase)

Arc (relating two nodes in a graph)

Interaction classes may also come up when modeling geometrical or topological systems: an electrical network, the piping in a refinery, or the trackwork of a railroad.

Specifications. Specification classes are used when a set of things all share certain characteristics.

For example, you and your colleague may have a copy of "the same book." The title of the two physical books are the same—that's what it means to be "the same"—but the books are themselves different ("This one's mine, that one's yours."). Examples are:

Insurance Policy Product, which specifies policy types you can buy

Book Product, which specifies the book you can buy

Credit Card Type, which specifies the brand of credit card used on a charge

Specification Class	Actual Class
Insurance Product	Insurance Policy
Book Product	Selected Book
Credit Card Type	Credit Card Account

Figure 5.2   *Specification Classes and Actual Classes*

When you have a specification class, you generally also have another related class that represents instances of things that meet the specifications. For example, your insurance policy has attributes that capture premiums paid, amount paid out, and so on, while the insurance product captures the deductible that applies to all insurance policies, yours included, that conform to this insurance product.

These "actual classes" need not represent something tangible: They could represent roles or incidents. See Figure 5.2 for examples.

To avoid confusion between the name of the specification class and the related class, write class descriptions (see Section 5.4.2: Class Descriptions) to define each of the names properly.

5.1.2   Naming Classes

A good choice of names for the classes will contribute significantly to the clarity of the model. Strive for names that are clear, direct, and honest. As in real life, this is not always easy.

We prefer to name a class in the model with the common name used for a typical thing in the domain. Unfortunately, this often turns out to be difficult. Unless the organization involved has been through a terminology formalization process in the recent past, one is likely to find that a single common name refers to two or more different things, and two or more common names refer to the same thing.

Although this can be confusing for the unfortunate developer, it leads to less confusion in the organization than one might expect, as most terminology references take place in ordinary conversation, which supplies context for each reference. Terminology references are exchanged among application experts—people who have large amounts of special knowledge in and context for the subject at hand.

People are extremely adept at using context information to establish meaning. When it becomes necessary to transfer the special application knowledge to experts in a different area (to us developers, for example), imprecise context-dependent terminology frequently causes confusion and misunderstanding. It is critical, therefore, to formalize that knowledge, selecting clear and unambiguous names and representing that knowledge in our model.

A class diagram, acting in Executable UML as a semantic information model, can be dramatically helpful in exposing and resolving these problems. For this reason, it is useful to regard the class diagram as a dictionary in which each name has only one meaning. Against this background, we offer the following suggestions in naming classes.

Common names. Use common names where these are, or can be made to be, well-defined. For example, Signaling Unit is OK, but Traffic Light is better. On the other hand, if a traffic light is just one of several ways of signaling, all of which have the same behavior, Signaling Unit could be acceptable. As another example, Part Transporter is OK, but Conveyor Belt is better.

When there is confusion in common names for the layperson, use industry-standard names.

Should both these strategies fail, use a made-up name. Sometimes your work will identify an abstraction for which no common name exists.

Strong names. Use strong, everyday words with extended meanings in preference to vague, unnecessarily technical, or esoteric terms. For example, the concept described as "a room, closet, or defined warehouse area used to store..." could be named as a Storage Environment, but Room would be better. Similarly, the concept "a cupboard, refrigerator, set of open shelves, or freezer used to store..." could be named a Storage Location, but Cabinet would be better because the term is both strong and common.

Precise names. Append adjectives to common short names to make names more precise. The name Storeroom describes "a room, closet, or defined warehouse area used to store..." more precisely than Room.

Same dimension names. Use names that contrast in the same dimension. The pair of names High Voltage Power Supply and Continuous Power Supply can be confusing because it raises the question, "Is a High Voltage Power Supply pulsed and high voltage? Or is the Continuous Power Supply necessarily low voltage?" If the fundamental difference between the two is that one power supply is pulsed and the other is continuous, then it is better to use names that make that distinction: pulsed vs. continuous.

Names based on essential nature. Use made-up names, even if they are lengthy, if they capture the essential character of the abstraction better than more customary, but less precise terms. For example, this concept:

> A piece of territory, not necessarily contiguous that is defined by the intersection of all election districts. As a consequence of the mechanism by which a territory is defined, all voters residing in the territory receive identical ballots for any particular election.

is commonly known as a Precinct or Precinct-Split, but the essence of the concept is better captured in the name Smallest Territorial Unit. (It is the smallest because the intersection of all districts is necessarily indivisible.)

Content-based names. Name the class by its information content, not by the form or document commonly used to carry information. Hence, a person legally entitled to operate a motor vehicle shouldn't be named Driver's License. The content is better captured by the name Licensed Driver. Note that the class name "Driver's License" might be appropriate if the concept we're naming were "a little piece of paper, about 2.25 by 3.25 inches, bearing an identifying number...".

Avoid abused words. And finally, avoid "abused words" in naming your classes—words that have many meanings or great context dependence. Everyone knows what they mean, but no one seems to agree in any given situation. Exactly what constitutes an abused word depends a great deal on the audience for your model, but the following are classic examples: person, user, account, order, task, form, operation, schedule, part, and assembly.

5.2   Attributes

Definition: An *attribute* is the abstraction of a *single* characteristic possessed by all the entities that were, themselves, abstracted as a class.

The goal is to obtain a set of attributes for a class that is:

- Complete—They capture all information about the class.
- Fully factored—Each attribute captures a separate aspect of the class abstraction.
- Mutually independent—The attributes take on values independently of one another.

5.2.1   Finding Attributes

For each class, start out by asking yourself, "What characteristics do all the things in the domain possess (that we care about)?" Another approach is to go back to the abstraction and ask, "What information is inherent to this abstraction that makes the abstraction what it is?"

Attributes fall into three informal categories: descriptive, naming, and referential. These categories are offered only as a way to ease finding attributes for classes.

A *descriptive attribute* is an attribute that describes an intrinsic characteristic of the thing, such as the amount of the order, or the customer's address. These attributes can be found by considering what describes each thing.

A *naming attribute* is an arbitrary name or label used to refer to a thing. You can change the names or labels of each thing without changing what it is: That is, if we re-number an airplane, it is still the same airplane. Naming attributes help identify things from outside the domain. (Inside the domain, we have object references.)

A *referential attribute* provides facts about links. For example, an Order may have a customer attribute that refers to the Customer who made the order. Referential attributes formalize associations (e.g., "the Order's Customer"), a topic we address in Chapter 6: Relationships and Associations.

5.3 Attribute Data Types

The set of values an attribute can take on constitutes its *data type*. Each attribute must have a data type.

Tools today capture this information through dialog screens and in some cases by data type definition as a part of the action language. Since there is no compact standard way to capture all this information, we shall use an informal textual notation.

Data types in Executable UML are based on a two-level scheme:

- Domain-specific data types, which define the type in terms of the domain. Hence, the online bookstore domain has attributes of type Currency and MailingAddress.
- Core data types, which are universal types defined by Executable UML.

Each data type has a domain-specific name, used on the class diagram, and a definition: the formal, detailed part.

5.3.1 Core Data Types

Definition: A *core data type* is a fundamental datatype from which other domain-specific datatypes can be defined.

Core data types include boolean, string, integer, real, date, and timestamp. We summarize these in Figure 5.3 overleaf.

5.3.2 Domain-Specific Data Types

While attributes may be defined in terms of core data types, by defining attributes in terms of individual domain-specific data types, the developer can specify precisely the values that are legal for an attribute and can identify those attributes that can take on the same kinds of values.

Definition: A *domain-specific data type* is a definition of the set of legal values that can be assigned to attributes in a domain model.

Core Type	Meaning
boolean	binary value true or false
string	a sequence of characters
integer	whole number
real	decimal number
date	calendar date and clock time
timestamp	clock time
arbitrary_id	an arbitrarily assigned identifier value

Figure 5.3   *Core Data Types*

Domain-specific data types can represent subsets of values of the core data type (for example, a range of positive integers). In addition, domain-specific data types can be defined to represent symbolic enumerations and composite values.

In all cases, the assignment of domain-specific data types to actual implementation data types is handled by the model compiler, based on the specific performance properties supported by that model compiler.

Numeric types. Domain-specific numeric types provide for values that have units, range, and precision.

The data type Currency may be defined, in keeping with the example above:

> **type** *Currency* **is** *real* **range** *[0..100000]* **precision** *0.01*

which specifies that Currency is of type numeric, with a range from 0 to 100000, with a precision of 0.01.

String types. String types provide for values that contain textual data. These can be specified in terms of a size and a pattern.

> **type** *NorthAmericanTelephoneNumber* **is** *symbolic* **pattern** *"nnn-nnn-nnnn"*
> **type** *postalCode* **is** *symbolic* **length** *6*

A proper specification for a domain-specific type avoids stating how the value is to be stored because a type may be transformed into different implementations. For example, the Currency values between $0.00 and $1000.00 could be expressed as an integer between 0 and 100,000—it does not have to be stored as a real. Similarly, a SupplyVoltage that can vary between 0.7 and 25 volts can be represented as an integer 0..253 (and stored in a byte!).

Enumerated types. Enumerated types are described by a list of values.

type *CompassPoints* **is** *(North, East, South, West)*

Composite values. A type may be composite, but the corresponding attribute must always be treated by the domain as a single unit. For example, MailingAddress and TelephoneNumber are valid types, but no operations in the domain can access the city as a part of the mailing address, nor an area code as a part of the telephone number. (Another domain, on the other hand, may choose to treat these attributes as objects, and their components as separate attributes.)

5.3.3 Using Types

Each attribute has a type. These are shown in the class definition (and the class diagram as in Figure 5.4) as the attribute name, type, and an optional initial value.

Hence, for a class Customer

purchasesMade : Count = 0

specifies that the attribute Customer.purchasesMade has a type, Count, and asserts an initial (default) value of zero.

Syntax vs. semantics. Define attribute types in terms of the meaning of the data (the semantics), not merely in the form of the data. Good models should use domain-specific types as much as possible and refrain from using the core data types if more meaning is available. Hence, defining an attribute merely as real is not as good as using a domain-specific type, such as Currency or SupplyVoltage.

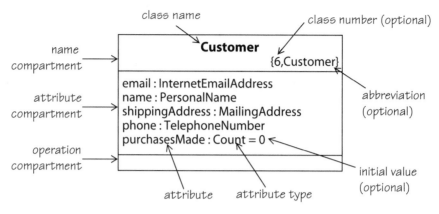

Figure 5.4   *Class Box with All Components*

5.4   Documenting Classes and Attributes

5.4.1   Diagramming Classes and Attributes

Figure 5.4 shows how classes are shown on a class diagram as boxes divided into three compartments.

Class name. The top compartment identifies the class: It contains the class's name along with an optional number and abbreviation ("key letters"). UML, as opposed to Executable UML, allows only for the class name.

Class number. A class may have a sequential number that provides the ordering for the descriptions. This is optional and some tools may provide an option to suppress its display.

Class abbreviation (key letters). A class may have a small abbreviation used as a shorthand to refer to the class, especially in class actions. By using the abbreviation, we can maintain a readable name in the diagram while keeping actions succinct. Like the number, it is optional. If the abbreviation is not shown, it is assumed to be the same as the class name.

```
        ┌─────────────────────┐
        │      Customer       │
        ├─────────────────────┤
        │  email              │
        │  name               │
        │  shippingAddress    │
        │  phone              │
        │  purchasesMade      │
        ├─────────────────────┤
        │                     │
        └─────────────────────┘
```

Figure 5.5   *Class Box with Types and Tags Suppressed*

Attribute compartment. The middle compartment contains the attributes and their types. In addition, attributes may have an initial (default) value.

Operation compartment. The operations compartment contains operations performed by the class. We describe operations later when we discuss actions and procedures.

Suppressed display of diagram components. UML allows parts of a class box (e.g., the attribute types, class numbers, attributes, and operations) to be suppressed in the display of a diagram. We will suppress some information on some diagrams in this book, such as the class box in Figure 5.5, to make the diagrams more readable. But we will suppress the information only when it is not essential to the example at hand.

5.4.2   Class Descriptions

A model without descriptions is like a dictionary without definitions for the words. Even the best class names can be confusing without context.

A *class description* is a short, informative statement that allows one to tell, with certainty, whether or not a particular thing is an instance of the class as conceptualized on the class diagram. Class descriptions include descriptions of each of the class's attributes.

Write a description for each class in the model. Start drafting descriptions early in the modeling process—this will frequently tell you if you are getting off track. Here are some informal technical writing hints that we have found helpful in producing good descriptions.

Domain statements vs. model statements. In writing a description, make statements about the reality being formalized in the model as well as statements about the model constructs themselves. To allow the reader to distinguish between these two kinds of statements, we have found it helpful to establish a typographical convention: Use an initial capital letter for all words in a class name, lower case when referring to things in the domain.

Basis of abstraction: inclusion criteria. Describe the ways in which things in the domain that have been abstracted as a class are alike (that is, inclusion criteria).

> *Customer*
>
> A Customer is an individual or organization that has placed orders for books and other products offered by the store.

Basis of abstraction: exclusion criteria. Establish exclusion criteria if there are things that are *not* abstracted into this class.

> A Customer must have purchased books; a user who simply browses to the site is not considered a Customer until he/she places an Order.

Background information. Sometimes a certain amount of background information enhances the class description.

> Customers remain active for six months after their last order. Active customers receive periodic e-mail reminders of sales and can be eligible for discounts based on how much they have previously purchased.

Technical writing standards. Finally, standard technical writing practices apply to class descriptions: A class description should be written in short declarative sentences using the present tense. Avoid vague or ambiguous terms. There are a number of further examples of class descriptions contained in the appendices. Those we judge most successful preserve the theme of the information as a reflection and abstraction of the reality of the domain.

For many more good examples of class descriptions, see Leon Starr's books [2] and [3].

5.4.3   Attribute Descriptions

Each class description includes short, informative descriptions that tell, for each attribute, how the attribute reflects the real-world characteristic of interest. Some suggestions for preparing the attribute descriptions are given below together with a few examples.

The manner in which we write the attribute description depends on the kind of attribute.

Descriptive attributes. The attribute description for a descriptive attribute states what characteristic, possessed by all things, is being captured in the model by this attribute.

Magnet

desiredCurrent: ElectricalCurrentMeasurement

> Reflects the current expected to be delivered to the magnet. This is in contrast to Magnet.actualCurrent. When actualCurrent equals desiredCurrent (within a tolerance) then the apparatus is stable and the experiment can begin.

Publisher

address: MailingAddress

> The address at which the publisher receives mail. It can be a legal or common-use street address recognized by the post office, or a post office box.

ProductSelection

unitPriceOfSelection: Currency

> Represents the unit price of a product added to an Order at the time the product is selected and added to the order. This attribute is initialized with Product.unitPrice but is kept separately so as to capture the price the customer actually pays even if the actual product price changes.

Naming attributes. The attribute description for a naming attribute should specify the form of the name (if relevant); the organization that assigns, registers, or controls the names (if relevant); and the extent to which the attribute forms a part of a unique name. For example, it is important semantic information that members of the Screen Actors Guild must have unique names.

ScreenActor

screenName: PersonalName

> The name the ScreenActor uses for professional work. Members of the Guild are required to have unique names to encourage "brand identification" for each member. Names are considered different if they differ in any way. Hence, "Fred O. Jones" is different from "Fred Jones."

Referential attributes. Referential attributes provide facts about links. For example, an order may have a customer attribute that refers to the customer who made the order. These attributes are not generally required as this information is implicit in the association. We take up this topic in the next chapter, Chapter 6: Relationships and Associations.

> ### Descriptive Attribute or Referential Attribute?
>
> It is sometimes difficult to decide if an attribute is descriptive or referential because it depends on context. For example, weight is descriptive until you consider a context wider than the earth (e.g., the solar system). Weight then becomes dependent on more than just the object being weighed. The situation is similar with color, once you consider anything other than a standard white light source, or you're attempting to capture specifications of colors in a manufacturing process.
>
> In fact, there are no attributes that are truly "intrinsic"; they just seem that way because the context is held constant.
>
> This observation, due to Conrad Bock, can be turned around: A domain defines a context for your model and only in that context can you determine whether an attribute is descriptive or referential.

5.5   Checking Classes and Attributes

When you start identifying classes in a new domain, you are likely to pick up a few candidates that appear to be classes when, in fact, they are not. Here are some checks that will help you reject these imposters.

All of these checks require a firm grasp on the definition of the class. Each potential instance of a class should have the same characteristics and conform to the same rules as the others. (Interpret "rules" liberally here: laws, organizational policies, laws of physics, custom, and so forth.) In other words, each instance must have the same data and the same behavior as the others.

If a class fails one or more of these checks, you may not have a good abstraction, or you may not have a good grasp of it. Writing down even one sentence to describe the abstraction will clarify your thinking greatly. We strongly recommend you do so as you invent your abstractions, no matter how agile your process.

5.5.1   Subject-Matter Check

Every class has to be a part of the domain at hand. For each candidate class, check it against the mission for the domain. If it does not support the mission, put the class into the domain it does support. For example, a class such as Login Screen more properly belongs in a user interface domain, as it represents a user interface concept and is not intrinsic to the Bookstore domain (the problem of selling books). Review the domain chart as you review the classes in each domain.

5.5.2   Abstraction Checks

Another set of checks examines the abstraction by looking at the class description. Note that problems with these checks could be the sign of a poorly written description as well as a poorly abstracted class.

The OR check. If the inclusion criteria stated in the description use the word "or" in a disjunctive way, you probably don't have a class, but a bunch of conglomerated ideas instead. For example, "A Drawing is an engineering drawing under formal revision control or the pictures my little girl made in kindergarten" is not OK, while "A Drawing is an engineering drawing or sketch under formal revision control" is. Note that in the previous sentence, the word "or" is used conjunctively to bring things together.

The cure is to separate the kinds of things that have been mixed together.

The more-than-a-list check. If the inclusion criteria stated in the description amount only to a list of all the specific things, you probably don't have a good abstraction. For example, describing a Decadent Food[3] as a croissant, a cappuccino, a chocolate pie, a cheesecake, or a cannoli is just a list and provides the reader no basis for deciding whether some other food qualifies. Is a food that begins with "c," such as a cauliflower, also decadent?

Alternatively, "A Decadent Food is an addictive food that has a severely unhealthy effect. Every decadent food has an ecstasy rating and a death index" tells the reader what makes the food decadent.

---

[3] This example is due to Leon Starr, who is fond of decadent things.

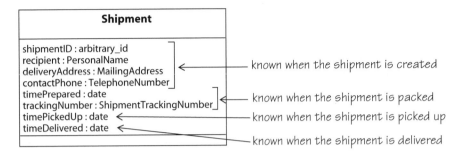

Figure 5.6   *Accumulating Attributes*

5.5.3   **Attribute Checks**

Other checks look at the proposed class attributes. Problems with these checks could identify problems with the individual attribute or problems with the class itself.

Composite value check. Attributes in Executable UML may represent composite values, such as a MailingAddress (street, city, state, postal code) or a complex number (real and imaginary parts), only if the composite is treated as a single value.

If you find that the components of a single value are important to the domain, then abstract one attribute for each component. For example, if the model needs to execute operations based on the city portion of the mailing address, or the area code of a telephone number, then each part should be abstracted as a separate attribute. There is a tension between composite types, such as mailing address, and the composite value check. Whether to represent a composite value as a single attribute or as many attributes depends upon the application of the attribute and its relationship to other values in the domain.

Not-less-than-one check. All attributes must have valid values for each thing, but sometimes an attribute has no value because it is not yet known.

Consider, for example, the Shipment class in Figure 5.6.

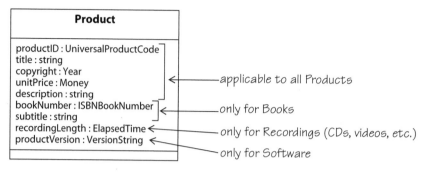

Figure 5.7   *Never-Meaningful Attributes*

The value of the attribute timeDelivered is not known until the shipment's contents are delivered to the customer. In this case, we could choose to extend the domain of the attribute to include none, notKnown, undelivered, or (ugh!) null. But making up an otherwise unused name and extending the domain of the attribute to include it is make-work. Instead, we simply say the attribute has multiplicity 0..1.

These situations, in which an object accumulates attribute values over time, are quite common. (Another example: A Customer's credit line amount is not determined until the customer's Credit Application is approved.) We'll see many such attributes, especially in classes with state machines.[4]

Never-meaningful attributes and nonuniform classes. If, however, a zero multiplicity is trying to indicate "never meaningful," it may indicate an abstraction problem with the class. For example, the store sells more than just books; it also sells videotapes, CDs, DVDs, and computer software. All of these Products have a sale price and are identified by a universal product code (UPC). Books have an ISBN number, CDs, videotapes, and DVDs have a running time, computer software titles have version numbers. Consider a single Product class as in Figure 5.7.

Attributes such as softwareProductVersion and recordingLength are never meaningful for some subset of instances. Having to ask "what kind of

---

[4] The stages of attribute value accumulation are often a good starting point for abstracting the states of a class.

Relational database wizards may recognize this type of factoring as "normalization." Many of the class and attribute checks that we cover in this section are based on relational normalization rules.

This kind of normalization factors out different abstractions so we may examine and understand them. Once we understand the abstractions in our solution, and the patterns of usage for these abstractions at run time, we can select a model compiler that meets our performance requirements. The model compiler may retain the normalized structure of our classes, or it may not.

thing is it" in order to determine if an attribute is meaningful is a red flag that we have a uniformity problem. Remember that every attribute must be meaningful for the typical things *at some time* during the thing's life. The differences between objects are not "details" to be deferred. They are fundamental facts about the domain at hand.

Specialization (see Section 6.5: Generalization and Specialization) is a technique for solving such uniformity problems.

Not-more-than-one check.   In Executable UML, all attributes must be single valued. A Book has multiple Authors; a SoftwareProduct runs on multiple Platforms; an Order has multiple ProductSelections. In such situations, create associations with related classes (see Section 6.1: Associations) and possibly introduce new association classes (Section 6.4: Association Classes).

Sometimes the multiple values of a single attribute are really separate attributes with distinct meanings. Consider a (bad) Shipment attribute called timeList. The attribute description says:

Shipment

timeList: ListOfTimestamps

> Each of the times in the timeList represents the time and date when a specific event in the history of the Shipment occurs: when the shipment is packed, when it is picked up, when it is delivered, etc.

UML requires each attribute to have a multiplicity. Normally, that multiplicity is 1..1, but multiple values are permitted, as well as none (0..*). Executable UML requires that each attribute be single-valued because * multiplicities often hide important abstractions and our job is to find these abstractions.

In this case, abstract separate Shipment attributes: timePrepared, time-PickedUp, and timeDelivered, as in Figure 5.6.

If the "etc." in the description means "there may be more events that we don't know yet," this is really a signal of an incomplete understanding. It may be true that there are multiple events in the history of the Shipment; in such cases, put the time in a separate but related ShippingEvent class.

5.6   Rules, Rules, Rules

The rules of Executable UML are designed for two purposes. The first is knowledge formalization. The rules require factoring of classes and attributes so that each concept is expressed in an Executable UML model at a single level of granularity. Each class and each attribute can be examined and checked, first conceptually ("Is it true that every Order can be described by a dateSatisfied?"), and later in execution. This ensures that we truly understand and formalize the subject matter under study.

The second purpose of these rules is to establish a small set of elements that require compilation into a system. Each new element in Executable UML (multivalued attributes, for example) is a new element to learn, a new element that must be consistent with all other elements, and a new element to implement.

This is a "fuzzy line," of course, but it has to be drawn somewhere. The trick is to make Executable UML rich enough to enable efficient modeling, but simple enough that it can be understood—and implemented cheaply.

5.7 References

[1] Shlaer, Sally, and Stephen J. Mellor: *Object-Oriented Systems Analysis: Modeling the World in Data.* Prentice-Hall, Englewood Cliffs, N.J., 1988.

[2] Starr, Leon: *Executable UML: The Elevator Case Study.* Model Integration, LLC., 2001.

[3] Starr, Leon: *Executable UML: How to Build Class Models.* Prentice-Hall, Upper Saddle River, N.J., 2002.

6

Relationships and Associations

Classes don't exist in isolation; they are interrelated. To formalize our knowledge of a domain, we must identify how the conceptual entities in the domain are associated and reflect these associations as precisely stated *relationships* in the model.

A UML relationship covers associations, generalization, and dependencies. Executable UML defines *associations* between classes, *association classes* that formalize associations, and *generalization*. We do not cover dependencies in this chapter.

We use the term *domain relationship* to describe relationships between things abstracted as classes in the domain under study.

6.1   Associations

Definition: An *association* is the abstraction of a set of domain relationships that hold systematically between different kinds of conceptual entities, abstracted as *classes*, in the domain.

Author WRITES Book
Publisher PRODUCES AND MARKETS Book
Customer PURCHASES Book

The association is stated in terms of the classes abstracted from the domain.

Associations are shown on the class diagram as lines drawn between the two participating classes. The lines on the diagram are labeled with the association names, association ends, and multiplicities.

6.1.1 Association Names

Each association has a *name*. The name is an arbitrary identifier that can be meaningful to the association or can simply be a label, such as R12 for the "twelfth relationship." Executable UML uses relationship names to identify the association unambiguously.

(We call these names *relationship numbers* and we will use them to identify associations and as a discriminator in generalization hierarchies.)

6.1.2 Association Meanings

Each association's meaning is expressed in terms of an *association end*. Not surprisingly, given its name, an association end is a string that appears at the end of an association. The string may be a role or a verb phrase.

Roles. Each of the two classes in an association has a *role*. Write the role names next to the relevant classes as shown in Figure 6.1.

Verb phrases. In some cases it may be difficult to identify a role name that is distinct from the name of the related class. A more meaningful way to state the association is to write its meaning in terms of *verb phrases*. By convention, the phrase is placed next to the direct object of the sentence, as you can see in Figure 6.2.

Using verb phrases has the distinct advantage of providing more descriptive text on the class diagram, and it avoids the search for role names different from the class names, or just leaving the role name blank.

Many UML models you'll see use only role names, and sometimes only one role name at that.

Because one of the purposes of Executable UML is to capture and formalize knowledge, we will use verb phrases in this book.

We use relationship numbers to uniquely identify each association.

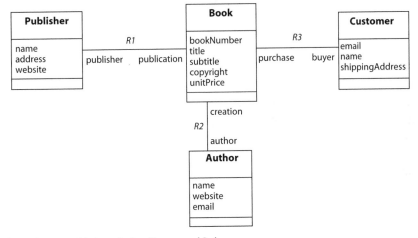

Figure 6.1   *Class Diagram with Association Names and Roles*

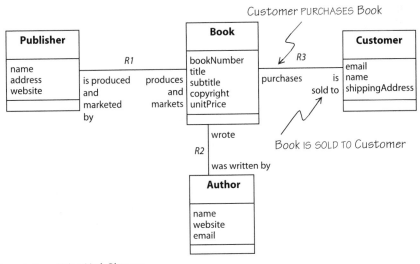

Figure 6.2   *Associations Using Verb Phrases*

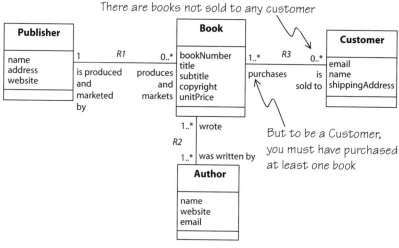

Figure 6.3   *Associations with Multiplicities*

6.1.3   Multiplicity

Associations involving only two objects can be characterized by the number of instances that participate in each instance of the domain relationship. This is represented in UML as a *multiplicity,* a range defining the number of participating instances.

The values for a range can be between zero and an "indefinite number."

Executable UML defines exactly four multiplicities: 1..1, 1..*, 0..1, and 0..*. The first two—the ones that start with one—are *unconditional* (or mandatory, if you prefer) because at least one instance must participate, and the last two—the ones that start with zero—are *conditional.*

In the examples in Figure 6.3, the association between Book and Author is unconditional; one is not an Author unless he has written a Book and every Book has at least one credited Author. (The model ignores the idea of anonymously authored books. If it didn't, we would use a conditional association.)

The Book–Customer association is conditional: A Customer is someone who has purchased books; but, there can be books that no one purchases.

> **How to Model Two**
>
> UML class diagrams allow specific numbers in a multiplicity expression, such as the notion that a piece of paper has exactly 2 sides or a credit card account may have up to four persons (1..4) responsible for the account.
>
> This usage is not recommended for two reasons: First, the related objects may play different roles and should instead be represented by separate associations. For example, the sides of a sheet of paper are related to each other in meaningful ways that may need to be captured. For an extended discussion of this example, see *Executable UML: How to Build Class Models* [1].
>
> Second, the specific multiplicity may be an artifact of some existing practice or restriction, and not fundamental. Thus a simple "many" is actually the most general and most correct solution. What is special about having four people on the credit card account? Either it's arbitrary, in which case we should use multiplicity * instead of 4, or there are rules in the domain that need to be captured.

6.2 Association Descriptions

Just as each class has a description, each association also needs a description to establish its basis of abstraction in the domain. The description of an association should not merely restate the descriptions of the associated classes, but should describe the domain relationship under study.

Describe each association from the point of view of each participating class in an additional block of descriptions in the class description. Hence, the Publisher class description will contain first a description of the meaning of the class Publisher, then a description of each attribute (name, address, etc.), then each association with other classes.

Each association should include the role name or verb phrase, the name of the target class, and the association name, as you can see here:

> *Publisher*
>
> PRODUCES AND MARKETS 0..* Book [R12]
>
> A publisher is responsible for contracting with an author to produce a book and then handles the work of marketing the book to book customers and retailers.

The description should describe the role name or verb phrase. What does it mean to be a publisher in the context of the books? As always, the description should center on the domain under study, not on the model. Hence a sentence such as "The publisher maintains a linked list of books." is anathema.

The description should also justify the multiplicity so that we may understand why a Publisher can exist without Books but why a Book cannot exist without a Publisher. There is no need to restate the multiplicity in the text. Here is an example:

> Every book we sell is produced by some publisher. We do not sell books directly produced by authors. In a few cases an author will sell books directly; in those cases we use the author or the author's company as the publisher.

The description of the association also appears in the description of the other class, in this case the Book:

> *Book*
>
> IS PRODUCED AND MARKETED BY 1 Publisher [R12]
>
> A publisher is responsible for contracting with an author to produce a book and then handles the work of marketing the book to customers and retailers.

Depending on your preference, you can write a single association description that is automatically propagated into both classes (our preference);

write two descriptions (tends to lead to some stilted and redundant writing); write one description with a reference to it from another class (works well if the reference is a hyperlink); or just write a single description (but then the reader doesn't know whether the one that's missing was intended to have been written).

6.3 Checking Associations

The multiplicities of associations must be checked to ensure a complete and correct understanding of the relationship in the domain. To do so, consider the number of possible instances that can participate in the relationship.

6.3.1 Conditionality

As an example, consider the association between senators and senate seats. Each state in the United States has two senate seats, each of which can be occupied by one person at a time. However, a senate seat could be unoccupied due to the death or resignation of a senator. Hence, although a senate seat is *normally* occupied, it is not required that a senate seat is *always* occupied.

The multiplicity of the association between a Senate Seat and a Senator at the Senator end is therefore 0..1.

Contrast this with executive positions in government. A given U.S. state has exactly one governor, elected or acting, at any particular time (because that is how the laws in all the states work). A given person can be the governor of only one state at any time (again, because of law: The governor has to be a resident of the state he governs and he can be a resident of only one state at a time).

The multiplicity of the association between Governor and State is therefore 1..1 at both ends.

The definition of the association imposes *referential constraints* to ensure that the data in the system is consistent with the model and consistent with itself. The referentials integrity constraints require any implementation based on this model to account for the following:

- If a state (or governor) is to be removed from the system, the corresponding governor (or state) must also be removed.
- If a state (or governor) is to be added to the system, the corresponding governor (or state) must be added.

When building a model, you must check the conditionality of associations against the rules and policies in the domain under study.

Exactly how these constraints are enforced is a topic taken up in several places, notably Chapter 11: Synchronizing Objects.

6.3.2   Capturing the Correct Classes and Roles

Consider the associations as shown in Figure 6.3 (page 84):

> Publisher PRODUCES AND MARKETS Book
> Customer PURCHASES Book

Is Book a specification or the actual tangible thing? The association with Publisher clearly has a specification nature, while the association with Customer certainly refers to a particular tangible instance of the purchase made by a Customer. This problem becomes apparent when we try to answer, "Where do I capture the price that an individual customer paid?" or "Where do I put the notion that a customer bought a certain quantity?"

The purpose of modeling is to reveal these subtle and important distinctions before they turn into bugs. Here we have a case in which two different associations with the same class view the class differently. This indicates a uniformity problem with the Book class itself. A solution is to abstract a separate class to represent the instance of the Book purchased by the Customer, as seen in Figure 6.4.

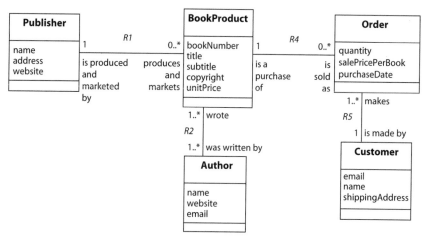

Figure 6.4 *Separate Classes for Book Product and Order*

In Figure 6.4, we replaced the single Book class with BookProduct and Order. One is now clearly the specification class and the other is the tangible thing. The additional class provides other benefits: We can now record the actual sale price of the book, the quantity purchased, and the date of the purchase.

Interaction between multiplicity and class definition. The association between Order and Customer is unconditional: A Customer must have purchased a copy of a Book, and a copy of a Book must be sold to a Customer. This is based upon how we choose to define the classes: A Customer does not come into existence until a purchase is made.

If we instead choose to have prospective customers (who have purchased nothing) loaded into our system, then the multiplicity of the association and the definition of Customer would both be different, as depicted in Figure 6.5.

More specific class names. One way to express the precise meaning of the association is to add adjectives to the class name. For example, we can replace Customer with ActiveCustomer to distinguish those customers who have purchased books from lurkers who might visit the site but never purchase anything.

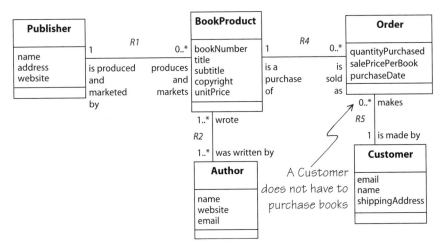

Figure 6.5   *Conditional Associations between Customer and Book Purchase*

By saying ActiveCustomer, we've qualified what it means to be a customer and improved the model. You may be thinking, "Neat trick, but is that how the real world works?" Again, this is good practice for evaluation of the association. A significant part of the analysis process is to determine which things are part of the domain—and which are not. Are any other types of customers included in this domain? How are their characteristics and behavior different from *ActiveCustomers*?

6.3.3   Multiple Associations

Sometimes there can be two or more associations between the same two classes. Each real-world association needs to be modeled individually.

Different roles.   Consider the situation depicted in Figure 6.6.

Figure 6.6   *Multiple Associations between Classes*

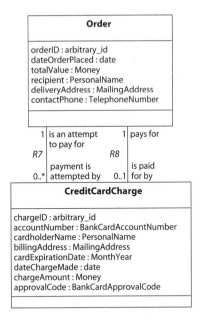

Figure 6.7   *History Pattern*

Each of these associations has a related, but different, meaning. While it is certainly the nominal case that the same Tenant both RENTS and LIVES IN an apartment, we can have people who live in an apartment who are not the tenants officially listed on the apartment's lease. There are other situations: A parent rents an apartment for a child; the principal tenant informally sublets the apartment to others. In all cases, the populations of associated instances do not have to be the same.

Different time. Models may also contain multiple associations between the same two classes when the different associations represent different time scopes. The most common is the current vs. history pattern seen in Figure 6.7, in which one association captures a current transaction and a second association captures a historical set of transactions.

Both associations R7 and R8 are necessary because the store needs to track all the credit card charges, including those that were declined, rejected, or canceled. One association captures the historical information regarding all the charges ever attempted:

Can we model the history pattern in Figure 6.7 with a single association and a boolean attribute paysForBook that captures which one of the attempted charges is the one that actually paid for the book?

CreditCardCharge
chargeID : arbitrary_id accountNumber : BankCardAccountNumber cardholderName : PersonalName billingAddress : MailingAddress cardExpirationDate : MonthYear dateChargeMade : date chargeAmount : Money approvalCode : BankCardApprovalCode paysForBook : boolean

While this approach seems to "save associations," it also hides an important fact inside some conditional logic that distinguishes the one charge instance that pays for the book from all the others. It is better to expose the fact as a separate association on the model.

The purpose of modeling associations is to capture rules in the domain, so don't "save" them.

Credit Card Charge ATTEMPTS TO PAY FOR Order

while the other captures the approved charge that actually pays for the order:

Credit Card Charge ACTUALLY PAYS FOR Order

Finding multiple associations. When we see an association like this one:

does this association mean IS CURRENTLY TRAVELING ON, IS SCHEDULED TO TRAVEL ON, or AT SOME TIME TRAVELED ON?

Since a person can only be traveling on one airplane at a time, IS CURRENTLY TRAVELING ON has multiplicity:

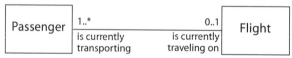

but IS SCHEDULED TO TRAVEL ON and AT SOME TIME TRAVELED ON have a many multiplicity:

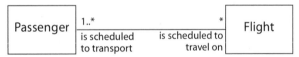

We suggest writing the most descriptive verb phrases for the associations, as well as writing detailed association descriptions. As you write the descriptions and note these concerns, you're doing exactly the right thing in checking the association. Perhaps the multiplicity is wrong, perhaps the association is improperly formed, perhaps the class names are ambiguous, perhaps there are multiple associations hiding behind a single line.

Multiple associations form loops. Note that whenever you have multiple associations between the same two classes, you have a relationship loop and therefore need to model properly the constraints between those associations. Section 8.4: Association Loops discusses this issue in detail.

6.4   Association Classes

In many cases, we find associations that give rise to additional classes. Usually these additional classes have attributes to capture data that's not properly part of either of the two participating classes. Figure 6.8 shows how to model the association with a third class, an *association class,* and place the attributes there.

Definition: An *association class* is an abstraction, as a class, of an association that may have its own attributes, other associations, and behavior.

Strictly speaking, an association class is a reification, not an abstraction. An association is already an abstraction of its links. An association class creates a first-class entity where one did not previously exist, which is reification.

"Reification" means roughly "to make into a thing." Our definition avoids introducing yet another term.

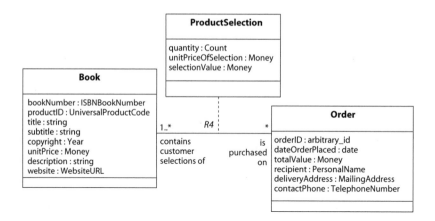

Figure 6.8   *The Association Class ProductSelection*

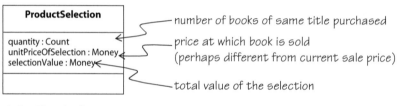

Figure 6.9   *Association Class Attributes*

The instances of the association class are the links between the participating objects. An association class is therefore a class whose instances come into existence when an association between the two principal instances is created. The instance of the association class is deleted when the two principal instances are unrelated.

Definition: A *link object* is an instance of an association class.

Association classes carry attributes. An association class carries attributes that describe the association itself, as shown in Figure 6.9.

Associations to association classes. An association class can participate in associations. Figure 6.10 shows how the Book Purchase is paid for by a Credit Card Charge.

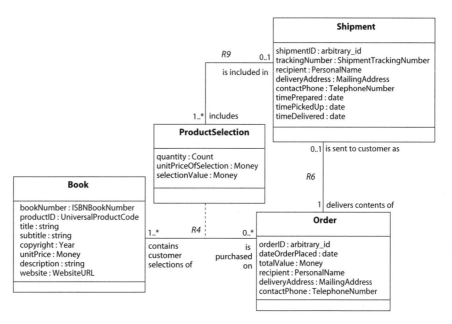

Figure 6.10   *Associations to an Association Class*

Association classes for behavior.   We will also see association classes that exist to model the behavior of associations, especially contention. We take up this topic in Chapter 13: Relationship Dynamics.

6.5   Generalization and Specialization

All of the instances of a class must share common characteristics and common behavior. But we often face things that are somewhat common yet somewhat different.

6.5.1   The Concept of Generalization and Specialization

In Section 5.5: Checking Classes and Attributes, we presented a Product as an example of a uniformity problem. The online store sells more than just books; it also sells videotapes, CDs, DVDs, and computer software. All these products have a sale price and are identified by a universal product code (UPC). Books have an ISBN number; CDs, videotapes, and DVDs have a running time; computer software titles have version numbers. We

BookProduct	**RecordingProduct**	**SoftwareProduct**
productID title copyright unitPrice description bookNumber subtitle	productID title copyright unitPrice description runningTime	productID title copyright unitPrice description productVersion

Figure 6.11   *Separate Product Classes*

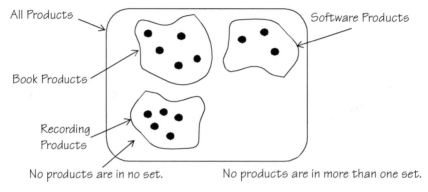

Figure 6.12   *Partitioning of Products into Subsets*

noted a uniformity problem that made a single Product class undesirable and promised to show how to correct the problem.

An alternative to the single Product class is to have separate classes for each type of product, as shown in Figure 6.11. But while this is a more precise attribution, it isn't quite satisfying either. Attributes (and behaviors) that ought to be common are spread across many classes.

The concept of *generalization* allows us to have the best of both worlds when confronted by this type of problem. We can have both a single Product class and individual classes for BookProduct, RecordingProduct, and SoftwareProduct. Figure 6.12 shows how these products may be partitioned into subsets, one for each kind of product.

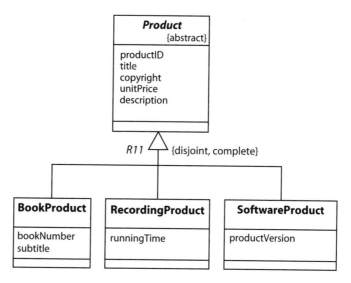

Figure 6.13   *Product Generalization and Specialization*

Figure 6.13 models the Product class as a generalization of BookProduct, RecordingProduct, and SoftwareProduct. This means that the *superclass* Product contains attributes and associations applicable to all of the *subclasses* BookProduct, RecordingProduct, and SoftwareProduct. Likewise, BookProduct is a *specialization* of the Product class. It contains additional attributes and associations that are relevant only to books.

Definition: A *superclass* is a class that generalizes classes in a generalization-specialization hierarchy.

Definition: A *subclass* is a class that specializes classes in a generalization-specialization hierarchy.

Definition: A *leaf subclass* is a subclass that is not the superclass of any other class.

Each superclass and each subclass is a class like any other. It may have attributes and participate in associations. It must have a class description and descriptions for each attribute and association in which it participates.

Inheritance is a related, but different, concept. The *UML Reference Manual* [2] (p. 287) states: "Generalization is a taxonomic relationship among elements. It describes what an element *is*. Inheritance is a mechanism for combining shared incremental descriptions to form a full description of an element. They are not the same thing, although they are closely related." (See also the formal definition of UML in [3].)

The reference manual clearly distinguishes between the two concepts. Executable UML uses generalization and specialization, also called *subclassing*.

Of course, generalization and specialization can be implemented using inheritance, and inheritance can be used as an implementation mechanism in other contexts.

With the preceding in mind, we may now (finally!) define an *object*.

Definition: An *object* is an instance of a class, or an instance of several classes in a generalization-specialization hierarchy.

6.5.2   Mutual Exclusion and its Implications

Executable UML prescribes a strict mutual exclusion principle in defining generalizations: Each instance of a superclass must be one and only one of its superclasses, and each instance of a subclass must be an instance of the superclass.

Definition: An *abstract class* is a class whose instances can be created only in conjunction with an instance of one of its descendant subclasses.

In UML terms, all Executable UML superclasses are tagged {abstract} and all generalizations are tagged {disjoint, complete}. This means:

- Each Product must be one of the subclasses: a BookProduct, Software-Product, or RecordingProduct. This makes the Product class *abstract*, because you can't make an instance of Product that is not an instance of one of its subclasses.
- Each Product must be one or the other of the subclasses. It is not possible to create an instance of a Product that is both a BookProduct and a SoftwareProduct ("disjoint").

We are careful to use "instance" to mean an instance of a class and to use "object" in the object-oriented way to mean an instance of a class potentially combined with instances of other classes in a generalization hierarchy to make a single object.

Hence, the instance of the class BookProduct for a book on Executable UML and an instance of the class Product for the same Executable UML book constitute a single object.

Superclasses in Executable UML are all abstract—you cannot create an object that is only an instance of the superclass without its also being an instance of exactly one of the subclasses.

- The stated subclasses are the only subclasses of Product; there are no other hidden or unknown subclasses ("complete"). Since an Executable UML model is a precise specification, all subclassings are complete.

This approach supports the semantic modeling properties of Executable UML, and abstraction from things in the domain: the several products. Consequently, each product is a member of the superset and exactly one subset. The set partitioning is disjoint and complete as shown by the tag {disjoint, complete}.

6.5.3   Repeated Specialization

A class can be specialized repeatedly, as shown in Figure 6.14. Bank accounts can be subclassed into checking and savings accounts. A checking account can be further subclassed into regular and interest-bearing accounts.

In cases of repeated specialization, all the non-leaf classes are abstract; hence the class CheckingAccount is abstract even as it is also a subclass.

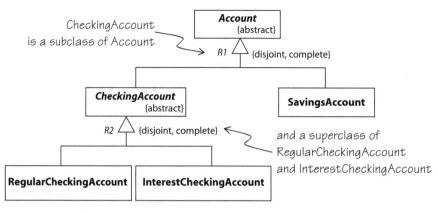

Figure 6.14   *Repeated Specialization*

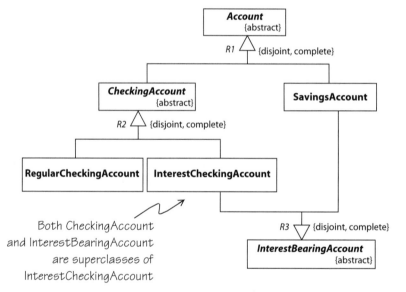

Figure 6.15   *Multiple Generalization*

6.5.4   Multiple Generalization

Consider now the hierarchy of Figure 6.15, in which a single subclass is the subclass of multiple superclasses. In this model, the class InterestCheckingAccount is a subclass of InterestBearingAccount and CheckingAccount. This is perfectly legal. Figure 6.16 illustrates how the accounts are organized into {disjoint, complete} subsets.

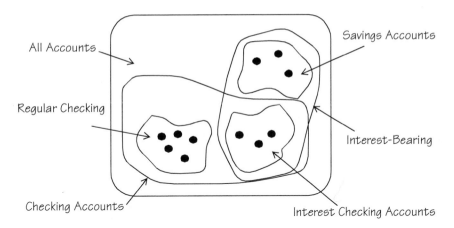

Figure 6.16 *Illustration of Multiple Generalization*

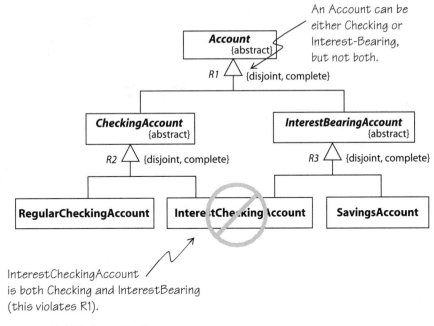

Figure 6.17 *Improper Multiple Generalization*

However, when building these kinds of structures, watch out for "diamond generalization," as illustrated in Figure 6.17, wherein the same instance purports to be a subclass of two superclasses that have the same parent.

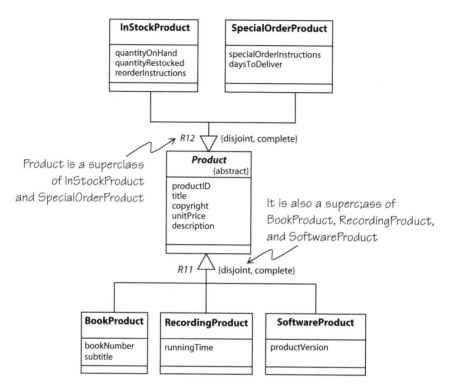

Figure 6.18   *Compound Generalization*

Here we have made the InterestBearingAccount a subclass of an Account. (After all, the InterestBearingAccount is surely some kind of account.) The result of this innocuous change is that an InterestCheckingAccount has a parent CheckingAccount that is a subclass of Account, and a parent InterestBearingAccount that is a different subclass of Account. The mutual exclusion rule forbids this. This situation is quite rare, but it is subtle and can cause a great deal of confusion.

6.5.5 Compound Generalization

In Figure 6.13 we subclassed Product into Book, Recording, and Software. In addition, some of each kind of Product are not actually kept in stock, but are special-ordered from the Publisher whenever ordered by a Customer. This subclassing is separate and distinct from whether the Product

> UML allows Figure 6.18 to be an easier-to-draw version of a single hierarchy, if the association name is the same. That is, if both hierarchies were labeled R13, a Product would be just one of the five subclasses (Book Product, Recording Product, Software Product, In-Stock Product, and Special Order Product) as well as the superclass.
>
> Formally, the relationship number here is called a *discriminator*.

is a Book, Recording, or Software product. Figure 6.18 shows how we can represent this with a distinct generalization-specialization relationship.

We call this a *compound generalization* since the superclass is a disjoint, complete generalization in more than one hierarchy. Each generalization is shown as a separate relationship with its own triangle and collection of subclasses

6.6 Reflexive Associations

Links can exist between instances of the same class, for example, between nodes in a ring network or authors of a book. Associations that have the same class at both ends are known as *reflexive associations*.

Definition: A *reflexive association* is an association between instances of the same class.

Reflexive associations to model sequence. The individual author credits on a book (Authorships) appear in a certain sequence. Each credit may have a role (e.g., editor, compiled by, as told to). We can model this as in Figure 6.19.

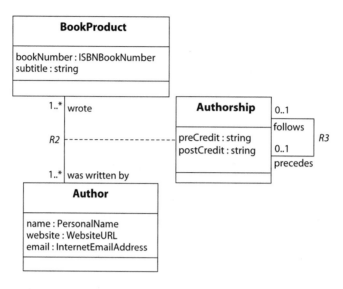

Figure 6.19   *Reflexive Association Modeling Sequence*

Generally these reflexive associations are conditional at both ends: There is a first Authorship that has no predecessor and a last Authorship that has no successor.

In cases where a sequence is a closed loop, the association can be unconditional, as in Figure 6.20.

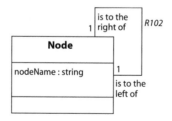

Figure 6.20   *Closed Loop Reflexive Association*

In the network, the nodes form a complete circle in which each node has one other node to the left and one to the right. All instances are equal and participate equally in the IS NEXT TO association.

Using reflexive associations to model hierarchies. Some reflexive associations model hierarchy. Consider a scheme for categorizing products, as shown in Figure 6.21.

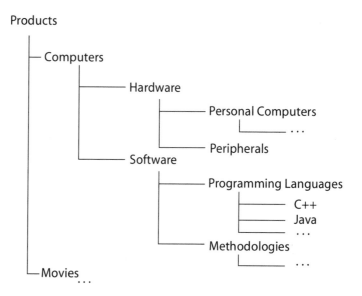

Figure 6.21   *A Category Hierarchy*

Some product categories are not part of any parent category (the root). For example, Product is part of no other category but is divided into Computers, Movies, and other categories. Others are not divided into any child categories. For example, C++ is part of Programming Languages and C++ is divided into nothing (a leaf).

Categories are part of at most one parent category and can be divided into zero or more child categories, hence the association, R14, is one-to-many and biconditional.

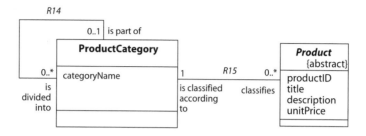

Figure 6.22 *Reflexive Association Modeling the Category Hierarchy*

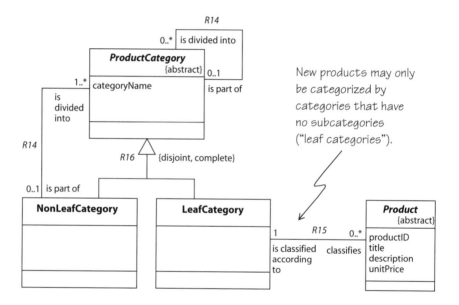

Figure 6.23 *Subtyping ProductCategory*

As modeled in Figure 6.22, any Product can be associated with any Product Category. If, however, we want to associate Products only with leaf categories, we will need to model it differently, as in Figure 6.23.

Here, we've divided the categories into "nonleaf" categories, which must be divided into other categories, and "leaf" categories, which are not divided. In this way, only those categories that are not subdivided into other categories can be used to categorize products.

What started out as a simple reflexive association is now modeled with separate classes for each role. This approach, while requiring more classes, is likely to be more useful and correct as the root, nonleaf, and leaf categories are each likely to have distinct attributes and behaviors that would be too difficult to capture in a single Category class.

6.7 The Class Model

It's a pity that "object-oriented" is such a popular term. It's the domain relationships between things that truly define the rules for a domain. Their formalization as associations of various kinds are often far more interesting than the objects because associations capture the rules in the domain.

Taken together, classes, attributes, relationships, and their descriptions form the class model that is the basis for all subsequent work because Executable UML models define the behavior of instances of classes and associations.

We begin by examining actions on classes, objects, attributes, and links.

6.8 References

[1] Starr, Leon: *Executable UML: How to Build Class Models.* Model Integration, LLC., 2002.

[2] Rumbaugh, James: *The Unified Modeling Language Reference Manual.* Addison-Wesley, Reading MA, 1998.

[3] UML URL: *www.omg.org/cgi-bin/doc?formal/01-09-67*

7

Class Actions

The declaration of a class on a class diagram doesn't "do" anything; the declaration merely states that when we create instances of the class, each object must have the data and behavior declared by the class.

Actions do stuff: They create and delete objects, access attributes and links, make conditional choices, iterate, transform data, and otherwise generally compute. In the course of this book, we shall describe the actions you can specify that make the domain actually do something. In this chapter, we'll describe those actions that affect objects, links, and classes.

Executable UML relies on the *Precise Action Semantics for UML* [1] adopted as an integral part of UML in late 2001. These action semantics provide for the specification of actions, but they do not define an action language syntax.

Presently, therefore, there is no standard syntax for actions, though to specify the actions in an executable model, we have to use something, some concrete syntax. The syntax we use here is a real one, and it executes today [2]. The complete case study models for the online bookstore have been executed using this language, and the case study models are presented in Appendix B.

Why NotJava?

Why not just write Java? Or just use your favorite programming language?

The answer has to do with raising the level of abstraction. To gain access to higher-level abstractions such as data structures and control structures, we gave up the ability to manipulate registers and the stack directly. This conferred independence from the hardware platform, in turn enabling portability of programs from one hardware platform to another.

So it is with Executable UML and the action language. In return for the ability to work in terms of the domain objects directly, you give up pointer manipulation, arrays, lists, and various implementation tricks your language allows. This grants independence from the software platform. Now you can build Executable UML models and have them execute on a distributed system using CORBA, a small footprint embedded chip using C and no operating system, or a complex multi-processor implementation using C++—all without having to change the application models.

To garner these benefits, the action semantics:

- defines statements that are by default concurrent, so that statements that do not share common data can run concurrently.
- defines functional computations separately from the data access logic, so that functional computation does not need to be respecified when a model compiler changes the data structures.
- allows direct manipulation of UML elements only, so that model compilers can safely assume their own rules are not violated.

The action semantics does not specify software structure anywhere. There are no mechanisms to denote persistence, or the manner of an invocation, or distribution, or how data is stored. All this is properly the business of the model compiler.

An Executable UML model specifies the minimum required to show how a domain works in the context of the problem, and that's all.

These requirements, and others, are discussed in detail in *Software-Platform-Independent, Precise Action Specifications for UML* [3].

But this chapter is not about syntax. Accordingly, this chapter does not describe every syntactic element of the language we use (if statements and loops, for example), nor does it describe every syntactic nitty-gritty detail.

To describe syntax, we use conventional syntax description forms, such as <class>, and we use the following typographical conventions for representing action language:

> **Boldfaced** words are keywords or reserved words.
> Capitalized Italics are class names.
> Lowercase *italics* are object references or attributes.

For example:

> **select any** *objectRef* **from instances of** *Class*
> **where** *selected.className == "my Class"*;
>   *// Comments may appear anywhere;*
>   *// we show them below the action fragment*

To define a language is not difficult. Given the standard definition of the semantics that is provided by the action semantics, you could design your own favorite syntax. To illustrate this point, we present two other action languages in Section 7.6: Other Action Languages.

7.1 Object and Attribute Actions

Definition: An *action* is an individual operation that performs a single task on an element of a model.

When we write object actions, we write the action for an arbitrary object. The target of the action is specified at run time, and is generally held in an object reference variable.

Definition: An *object reference* is a value that refers to an object.

An object reference is not the object itself.

Figure 7.1 lists syntax for several object and attribute actions, and several examples are shown in Figure 7.2 .

In the first line, the object reference *newPublisher* refers to the newly created *Publisher* object.

Action	Syntax
Create object	**create object instance** <object reference> **of** <class>;
Write attribute	<object reference>.<attribute name> = <expression>;
Read attribute	... <object reference>.<attribute name> // (in an expression)
Delete object	**delete object instance** <object reference>;

Figure 7.1   Syntax for Several Object and Attribute Actions

```
create object instance newPublisher of Publisher;
     // newPublisher refers to an instance of the Publisher class
newPublisher.name = "Addison-Wesley";
x = newPublisher.name;
     // x gets the value for the name
delete object instance newPublisher;
```

Figure 7.2   Examples of Object and Attribute Actions

The second line sets the attribute *name* to "Addison-Wesley" and the next line reads that attribute and places the result in a variable *x*.

The last line deletes the newly created object.

In the course of this book we will use the action language a great deal, so you will see a plethora of examples, including many extensions to the basic syntactic elements described in this chapter. No need to get carried away here.

7.2   Selection Expressions

Actions can operate on one or more objects in the domain. We use *selection expressions* to select single objects or sets of objects. The result of a selection expression is an object reference set.

Definition: An *object reference set* holds a set of object references.

Concept	Syntax
Class extent	**select many** <object reference set> **from instances of** <class>;
Qualification (one object)	**select any** <object reference set> **from instances of** <class> **where** <where clause>; // similar to SQL
Qualification (many objects)	**select many** <object reference set> **from instances of** <class> **where** <where clause>; // similar to SQL

Figure 7.3   Selection Expressions

```
select many books from instances of Book;
select many newBooks from instances of Book
    where selected.copyright == 2002;
select many notSoNewBooks from instances of Book
    where selected.copyright < 2002 and selected.copyright > 1995;
select many reallyNewBooks from instances of Book
    where selected.copyright > 2025;
if empty reallyNewBooks
    // No such books
```

Figure 7.4   Examples of Selection Expressions and Adjuncts

The *extent* of a class is its current set of objects. (A *set* is a mathematical term that means some number (possibly zero) of distinct elements. A class extent is always a set because the objects of a class are defined to be distinct.)

Figure 7.3 shows actions and concepts related to object selection, and several examples are shown in Figure 7.4. The first statement gets the extent of all books, and the object reference set *books* refers to the current set of books.

To access a subset of the objects in an extent, we specify the criteria that define the subset using a **where** clause in which *selected* refers to the current object, and the dot operator accesses attributes of that object. The second statement in Figure 7.4 returns the subset of all books copyrighted in 2002.

The selection expression may be an arbitrarily complex expression written in terms of the attributes of the class, as shown in the third statement.

```
select many notSoNewBooks from instances of Book
    where selected.copyright < 2002 and selected.copyright > 1995;
for each book in notSoNewBooks
    book.unitPrice = book.unitPrice * 1.10;
    // Whack 'em up by 10%
end for;
```

Figure 7.5   *Example of Iteration*

```
huge = 150000000;
select any richPublisher from instances of Publisher
    where selected.annualRevenue > huge;
```

Figure 7.6   *Examples of Selection Expressions and Adjuncts*

A **select** statement may fail to find any objects. The operator **empty**, applied to an object reference, is true if the (object reference) set is empty, and the **select** statement did not find any objects. The last two statements select *reallyNewBooks* and check whether the object reference set is empty.

When we have a set of objects, we can operate on each instance of that set, as illustrated in Figure 7.5.

All the **select** statements above return many instances by design, as indicated by the **many** operator.

To return a single, arbitrary, instance, use **any,** as illustrated in Figure 7.6. The example picks a single publisher from the many that qualify. The **any** operator assumes that many publishers are huge, but returns only one.

7.3   Link Actions

Just as classes have actions that create and delete their objects, so associations have actions that create and delete their instances, called links.

Figure 7.7 lists a syntax for several link actions, and several examples are shown in Figure 7.8.

Action	Syntax
Create link	**relate** <object reference> **to** <object reference> **across** <association>; // or, when there is a need to disambiguate the association: **relate** <object reference> **to** <object reference> **across** <association>.'<verb phrase>';
Traverse link	**select [one | many]** <object reference> **related by** <object reference> -> <class> [<association>]; // or, when there is a need to disambiguate the association: **select [one | many]** <object reference> **related by** <object reference> -> <class>[<association>.'<verb phrase>'];
Delete link	**unrelate** <object reference> **from** <object reference> **across** <association>; // or, when there is a need to disambiguate the association: **unrelate** <object reference> **from** <object reference> **across** <association>.'<verb phrase>';

Figure 7.7 *Syntax for Link Actions*

```
relate newBook to newPublisher across R1;
relate newPublisher to newBook across R1;
relate newBook to myPublisher across R1.'produces and markets';

select one bookPublisher related by newBook -> Publisher[R1];
select many allPublisherBooks related by newPublisher->Book[R1];
select any anyPublisherBook related by newPublisher->Book[R1];

unrelate newBook from myPublisher across R1;
```

Figure 7.8 *Link Action Examples*

As you would expect, the order of the two object references is immaterial, so the first two statements are equivalent. For clarity, the association end can be included, as illustrated by the third statement. The association end is required to specify the direction of traversal in a reflexive association.

The examples in the second block all show traversals. The dagger "points" to the target class, and the square brackets contain the association name. The **one** after the **select** statement indicates the target of the traversal is a single instance across an association with multiplicity 1 or 0..1. When the association has a "many" multiplicity (1..* or 0..*), use **select many** to get the complete set of related instances or **select any** to get one arbitrary instance.

The last statement unrelates two objects by providing object references and the association name.

7.4   Link Object Actions

An association class acts as both an ordinary class and an association, so an instance of an association class is both an object and a link. An instance of an association class is called a *link object*. Because of this dual nature, all operations on link objects affect both the link and the object at once.

Figure 7.9 shows the syntax for several link object actions, and Figure 7.10 shows several examples.

Action	Syntax

Create link object action	**relate** <object reference> **to** <object reference>
	    across <association>
	    creating <link object>;

Traverse link action	**select one** <object reference> // to the link object
	    that relates <object reference> **to** <object reference>
	    across <association>;

Unrelate action	**unrelate** <object reference> **from** <object reference> **across** <association>;

Figure 7.9   Link Object Action Syntax

relate *myBook* **to** *bookAuthor* **across R2 creating** *authorship;*

select one *authorship* **that relates** *myBook* **to** *myAuthor* **across** *R2;*

unrelate *myBook* **from** *myAuthor* **across** *R2;*

Figure 7.10   *Examples of Link Object Actions*

The first statement creates a link object and returns it as the result of the statement.

The second statement selects a single authorship based on the object references for a book and an author.

The last statement unrelates the link and deletes the link object as a single operation.

7.5   Generalization Hierarchies

An instance of a superclass always requires an instance of a subclass and vice versa. Consequently, the creation or deletion of an object classified as a leaf subclass, which implies all the object's parents, creates or deletes the instance of that subclass and all of its parent classes.

The syntax is the same as that of creating and deleting objects that are not in generalization hierarchies, except that in addition, an object may be a member of multiple hierarchies. Consequently, the object creation must list all the classes of which the object is a member, as indicated in Figure 7.11. Figure 7.12 shows some examples.

Action	Syntax
Create object	**create object instance** *<object reference>* **of** *<class list>*;
Reclassify object	**reclassify object instance** *<object reference>* **from** *<class>* **to** *<class>*;
Delete object	**delete object instance** *<object reference>*;

Figure 7.11   *Creation, Deletion, and Reclassification in Hierarchies*

Some popular programming languages, such as C++ and Java, do not support a reclassification operation directly. Model compilers generate code to simulate the necessary behavior by creating an instance of the subclass and deleting the instance of the previous subclass.

```
create object instance newBook of BookProduct;

newBook.ISBN = "123-456-267-9";
newBook.copyright = "2002";
newBook.title = "Executable UML";
newBook.description = "..."; // Let's be modest here.

create object instance multiBook of BookProduct, StockedProduct;

reclassify object instance newBook
    from StockedProduct to SpecialOrderProduct;

delete object instance newBook; // same as usual
```

Figure 7.12   *Examples of Object Creation in Multiple Hierarchies*

The first line shows creation of an object *newBook*, which is an instance of *BookProduct*, which is in turn a subclass of *Product,* as shown in Figure 6.13 on page 97. To access attributes of the superclasses, access them as you would attributes of any object. The second block of statements initializes attributes of the object *newBook* as defined by the class *BookProduct* and its superclass *Product.*

The third statement block (of one line) creates an object *multiBook*, which is an instance of *BookProduct* and *StockedProduct*, both of which are (multiple) specializations of *Product.* The sole difference between this line and the first is the specification of the multiple leaf classes to which the object belongs. The example is based on Figure 6.18 (see page 102), which illustrates a compound generalization..

Definition: Reclassification is the act of moving an object from one leaf subclass in a generalization-specialization hierarchy to another.

When an object is reclassified, all the old subclass's attributes and associations go away, and new attributes and associations are established for the new subclass. Superclass attributes and associations and the attributes and associations of other subclasses are left unchanged.

> // Make this the shipment for the order.
> (Self, order) | **link** R1.'contains product selected as';
>
> // Copy the delivery information for this shipment from the Order.
> // (The write attribute operator is '>')
> order.deliverToCustomer > self.deliverTo;
>
> // Now copy the remaining information.
> order.(deliveryDestination, deliveryContactPhone) >
>   self.(deliveryDestination, deliveryContactPhone);

Figure 7.13 *Actions in the Shipment State Machine*

7.6   Other Action Languages

The object action language shown here is not the only syntax for object actions. In this section, we'll present two other languages that support the action semantics and compare how these languages present fundamental actions.

7.6.1   SMALL

SMALL[1] is a language invented as a precursor to the action semantics work.[2] Like the action semantics, execution proceeds in parallel[3] for all statements, except where constrained by data or control flow. Consequently, if two statements write the same variable and their order of execution has not been constrained, it is indeterminate which value will be used in subsequent processing.

The key syntactic property of the language is its explicit use of data flow. Reading SMALL is like reading a shell script for UNIX that starts with a data-access operation and connects operations together using pipes. Consequently, assignments and other data flow from left to right, as shown in the example in Figure 7.13.

---

[1] An acronym for Shlaer-Mellor Action Language. One L is gratuitous.

[2] The language was invented by Stephen J. Mellor, based on Peter Fontana's insight that all chains of operations end in a write, or a signal generation. Gregory Rochford and Cortland D. Starrett built a parser to verify the syntax.

[3] The statements proceed in parallel from the developer's perspective. The model compiler can serialize the statements as desired.

Action	Syntax
Create object	\<object reference\> >> \<class list\>;
Write attribute	\<expression\> > \<object reference\>.\<attribute name\> ;
Read attribute	... \<object reference\>.\<attribute name\> | // yields a value piped onward ...
Delete object	\<object reference\> << ;
Reclassify object	\<object reference\> --> \<class list\>;
Class extent	\<class\>(**all)** | // yields a set of values piped onward ..
Qualification	\<class\>(\<**where clause**\>) | // yields a set of values piped onward ..
Create link	(\<object reference\> , \<object reference\>) | **link** \<association\>;
Traverse link	\<object reference\> -> [\<association\>] \<class\>([**one** | **many**]);
Delete link	(\<object reference\> , \<object reference\>) | **unlink** \<association\>;
Create link object action	(\<object reference\> , \<object reference\>) | **link** \<association\> >> \<association class\>
Traverse link action	**select one** \<object reference\> // to the link object **that relates** \<object reference\> **to** \<object reference\> **across** \<association\>;
Unrelate link action	(\<object reference\> , \<object reference\>) | **unlink** \<association\> << \<association class\>

Figure 7.14   *Actions in* SMALL

The syntax is summarized in Figure 7.14.

For an example of iteration over a collection, see Figure 7.15. Here, we select the instances of the Book that have a copyright within the specified dates and access the associated book prices. This collection of values is piped to a separately defined function *Factor*, with a parameter 1.1, and the result is written to the *bookPrice* attribute against the set of *Book*s. The expression *Book( )* in a statement refers to the same set of books that were accessed by the original selection expression, avoiding any potential for data access conflict in the syntactic expression.

> *Book(.copyright < 2002 & .copyright >1995).bookPrice |*
> *Factor(1.1) > Book( ).bookPrice;*
> *// Whack 'em up by 10%.*

Figure 7.15   *Iteration over a Collection in SMALL*

7.6.2   TALL

TALL[4] is a functional language based on the action semantics work. Actions return values that can be used in other actions, and values may be provided as input to several concurrent actions.[5]

An example for the shipment state machine actions is shown in Figure 7.16.

An example of iteration over a collection is shown in Figure 7.17. The syntax is summarized in Figure 7.18.

> *// Make this the shipment for the order.*
> *self -> ("contains product selected as") Order := order;*
>
> *// Copy the delivery information for this shipment from the Order.*
> *self {*
> *   .deliverTo := order.deliverToCustomer;*
> *   .deliveryDestination := order.deliveryDestination;*
> *   .deliveryContactPhone := order.deliveryContactPhone;*
> *}*
> *// Notify the shipping clerk that a shipment is ready to pack.*
> **signal** *ShippingClerk::shipmentReadyToPack;*

Figure 7.16   *Actions in the Shipment State Machine*

> **foreach** *b* **in** *Book [.copyright > 1995* **and** *.copyright < 2002] {*
> *   b.bookPrice *= 1.1;   // whack 'em up by 10%*
> *}*

Figure 7.17   *Iteration over a Collection in TALL*

[4] The name is an acronym for That Action Language. One L is gratuitous.
[5] TALL was designed by Marc J. Balcer, Conrad Bock, and Dirk Epperson.

Action	Syntax
Create object	<object reference> := **new** <class list>**;**
Write attribute	<object reference>.<attribute name> = <expression>;
Read attribute	... <object reference>.<attribute name> // (in an expression)
Delete object	**delete** <object reference>**;**
Reclassify object	**reclassify** <object reference> **from** <class> **to** <class>**;**
Class extent	<object reference set> := <class>;
Qualification	<object reference set> := <class> [<where clause>]; // similar to SQL
Create link	<object reference> -> (<verb phrase>) <class> := <object reference>
Traverse link	**[one	many]** <object reference> -> (<verb phrase>) <class>
Delete link	<object reference> -> (<verb phrase>) <class> **:= null**

Create link object action	<link object> **:=**
	    (<object reference> -> (<verb phrase>) <class>
	        := <object reference>)

Traverse link action	<object reference> // to the link object := <object reference> **<->** <object reference>;
Unrelate action	<object reference> -> (<verb phrase>) <class> **:= null**

Figure 7.18 *Actions in TALL*

7.6.3   Actions and Syntax

We have presented here, albeit briefly, three separate action languages. The languages are fundamentally different, yet they can all be expressed in terms of the action semantics.

We trust that this demonstrates conclusively that syntax is unimportant.

The actions described so far act on objects of classes, attributes, and associations. There are a few other actions that communicate between objects and other domains, which we describe when we introduce those concepts.

Now that we have an action language in hand, we can also employ it to define several additional constraints, the topic of the next chapter.

7.7   References

[1]   UML Action Semantics URL: *www.omg.org/cgi-bin/doc?ptc/02-01-09*

[2]   BridgePoint Object Action Language Manual
      www.projtech.com/pdfs/bp/oal.pdf

[3]   Mellor, Stephen J., Steve Tockey, Rodolphe Arthaud, and Philippe Leblanc: Software-Platform-Independent, Precise Action Specifications for UML. In *Proceedings of «UML 98»*.

8

Constraints

This chapter shows how to describe formally several commonly occurring *constraints*. The constraints are a fundamental part of the semantics of the domain and they may be used to direct and optimize the structure of the implementation.

Definition: A *constraint* is a rule, expressed as a calculation in terms of other classes, attributes, and associations, that restricts the values of attributes and/or associations in a model.

A constraint is executable, defining computed values and providing run-time checks.

8.1   Unique Instance Constraints

Objects may have sets of attributes that are required to be unique.

- a customer's login ID
- a publisher's ISBN code
- an order's order number

> Object orientation endows each object with its own unique identity, the object handle. This handle uniquely identifies an object, but it is implicit and carries no semantic significance. An object's identifier carries semantics—it's a rule about the domain—and is made explicit.

These attributes constitute ways to identify an individual instance. We call each required-to-be-unique set of attributes an *identifier*.

Definition: An *identifier* is a set of one or more attributes that uniquely distinguishes each instance of a class.

8.1.1   Single Attribute Identifiers

To capture this notion of uniqueness in the model, we establish uniqueness constraints. Examples of unique-instance constraints are:

- No two customers can have the same e-mail address.
- Each publisher has a unique ISBN prefix code.
- Each new order is assigned a unique number.

Customer
email : InternetEmailAddress name : PersonalName shippingAddress : MailingAddress phone : TelephoneNumber purchasesMade : Count

Publisher	**Order**
groupCode : ISBNGroupIdentifier publisherCode : ISBNPublisherPrefix name : string address : MailingAddress website : WebsiteURL	orderID : arbitrary_id dateOrderPlaced : date totalValue : Money recipient : PersonalName deliveryAddress : MailingAddress contactPhone : TelephoneNumber

Uniqueness constraints formalize rules in the domain—both rules about the world (e.g., publishers are assigned unique ISBN prefix codes by the publishing industry) as well as rules that we make up (the customer's e-mail address is his login ID and therefore must be unique).

Any kind of attribute can be used to make up an identifier.

The notion of a naming attribute is different from that of an identifier, although naming attributes are frequently used in identifiers. For example, nothing prohibits two publishers from having the same company name if they were established in different jurisdictions, but the ISBN code is required, by policy, to be unique.

context *Customer* **inv:**
    *Customer.***allInstances***( ) ->* **forAll***(p1, p2 |*
        p1 <> p2 **implies**
            p1.email <> p2.email)

Figure 8.1   *Unique Instance Constraint in OCL*

Constraints in OCL. To define a unique-instance constraint formally, we may use the Object Constraint Language (OCL). Figure 8.1 depicts the constraint for the Customer.

The first line defines the context of the constraint, namely the class for which the constraint applies, and the fact that the constraint is a definition of an invariant (**inv**).

The second line iterates over all instances of the class using two free variables, *p1* and *p2*. **allInstances** is a predefined operator that finds all the instances of the associated class, and the dagger symbol (->) indicates that the following operation acts on a collection, in this case, all the instances of the customer.

The third line introduces an implication. For two arbitrary instances of the class, *p1* and *p2*, that are not equal, this fact implies something (on the following line).

The last line states the invariant, namely that the identifying attribute of the two instances must not be the same.

Unique instance constraint idiom. The example in Figure 8.2 forms an idiom.

This idiom is the *unique instance constraint.* The unique instance constraint for the Publisher and the Order follow the same idiom.

> ### OCL–The Object Constraint Language
>
> The Object Constraint Language (OCL) is a fundamental part of the UML, described in Section 6 of the *UML 1.4 Specification* [1]. It is designated as the official way to express constraints on UML models. The semantics of UML themselves are defined using OCL.
>
> The constraints shown in this chapter are written in OCL and in action language. These constraint expressions are written as boolean functions that return true if the constraint is satisfied and false if the constraint is violated.
>
> We hope for and encourage a convergence between OCL and action languages, such that a developer can write a constraint using the same language used for actions and that model compilers will be able to check and to enforce these constraints.

```
context <class> inv:
    <class>.allInstances( ) -> forAll(p1, p2 |
        p1 <> p2 implies
            p1.<identifier > <> p2.<identifier> )
```

Figure 8.2   *Unique Instance Constraint Idiom*

```
select many customers from instances of Customer
    where selected.email == self.email;
return ((cardinality customers) == 1);
    // Only one should match the ID; if more then the ID is not unique.
```

Figure 8.3   *Unique Instance Constraint in Action Language*

Definition: A *constraint idiom* is a general pattern for a commonly occurring type of constraint that can be represented by a predefined tag.

Constraints in action language. The constraints in Figure 8.1 can also be written in action language, as shown in Figure 8.3.

Specifically, this is written as an instance function on the Customer class.

Graphical notation. UML allows the definition of tags. A tag is a string that can be added to any model element, enclosed in braces { }. Figure 8.4

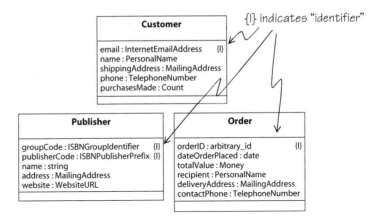

Figure 8.4   *Identifiers on the Class Diagram*

shows how we use the tag {I} on each identifying attribute to denote an identifier.

The presence of the tags is a shorthand for writing the unique instance constraint, so there is no need to explicitly write the OCL or action language.

Contrived identifiers unnecessary. Shlaer-Mellor ([2] and [3]), a precursor to Executable UML, required that every class contain at least one identifier, even if that identifier was an attribute placed in the object solely for the purpose of being its identifier. This practice is not required in Executable UML.

8.1.2   Multiple Attribute Identifiers

An identifier may consist of multiple attributes. For example, publishers have code numbers assigned by "ISBN agencies." The code number is not unique among all publishers, but is unique among publishers in the same ISBN agency group.

Definition: An *identifying attribute* is an attribute that forms part of at least one identifier.

```
context Publisher inv:
  Publisher.allInstances( ) -> forAll(p1, p2 |
    p1 <> p2 implies
      ( p1.groupCode and p1.publisherCode ) <>
        (p2.groupCode and p2.publisherCode)
```

Figure 8.5   *Multiple-Attribute Identifier Constraint in OCL*

```
select many publishers from instances of Publisher
    where selected.groupCode == self.groupCode
    and selected.publisherCode == self.publisherCode;
return (cardinality publishers == 1);
```

Figure 8.6   *Multiple-Attribute Identifier Constraint in Action Language*

The Publisher's identifier comprises two identifying attributes: Publisher.groupCode and Publisher.publisherCode.

The constraint is depicted in Figure 8.5. Or, see Figure 8.6 for the constraint in action language. This action language snippet asserts that the combination of the two attributes must be distinct.

This idiom is another unique instance constraint, this time with multiple identifying attributes. Constraints involving any number of attributes are possible. But since the unique instance constraint is a common idiom, we do not need to write OCL or action language for it; we simply tag the attributes as shown in Figure 8.7.

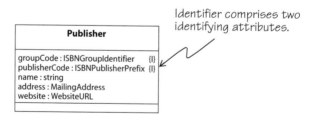

Figure 8.7   *Multiple-Attribute Identifier on Class Diagram*

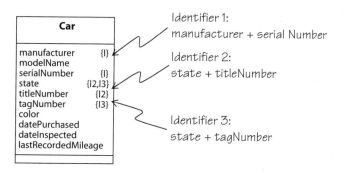

Figure 8.8 *Multiple Identifiers on Class Diagram*

8.1.3   **Multiple Identifiers**

A class may have several identifiers, each of which consists of one or more identifying attributes. In this case, we write several unique instance constraints for the same class.

When there is more than one identifier, use the tags {I}, {I2}, {I3}, and so on. Select a new tag for each new identifier, and tag every identifying attribute in a given identifier with that tag. Hence, each identifying tag ({I}, {I2}, {I3}, etc.) applies to all attributes of a single identifier that defines one of the unique instance constraints.

Furthermore, an identifying attribute may be a part of more than one identifier. For example, a car can be identified by:

- manufacturer + serialNumber
- state + titleNumber
- state + tagNumber

In this example, the state attribute is a part of two identifiers.

A single attribute may be a part of several identifiers, so it may be tagged several times. In our example depicted in Figure 8.8, the tags {I2, I3} are shown for the state attribute of Car.

Search for identifiers. When abstracting attributes of classes, pay special attention to finding identifying attributes. Look for situations in which no two instances may have the same value for an attribute or set of attributes. In some cases, the business may have unique numbering or identifying schemes for many of the things being modeled. These are the identifying attributes, and they constitute a rule in the domain.

8.2   Derived Attributes

Because an Executable UML model captures the information inherent in a domain, redundant attributes are generally frowned upon. However, there are occasions when a clear understanding of a domain is best served by capturing the dependency between attributes explicitly.

Definition: A *derived attribute* is an attribute whose value can be computed from other attributes already in the model.

Figure 8.9 shows two derived attributes, each prefixed by a / (slash).

The attribute ProductSelection.selectionValue can be defined in OCL like this:

```
context Selection inv:
    Self.selectionValue =
        Self.quantity * Self.unitPriceOfSelection;
```

or in action language this way:

```
self.selectionValue = self.quantity * self.unitPriceOfSelection;
```

Executable UML enforces this constraint by prohibiting writing to the attribute totalSelectionPrice and by requiring any model compiler to guarantee the constraint before the attribute can be read.

Derived attribute dependencies can span multiple classes. Figure 8.9 also shows how the class Order allows a customer to purchase several different products in one transaction. Each product is represented as a distinct ProductSelection.

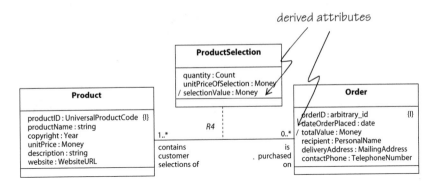

Figure 8.9   *Derived Attributes*

In this example, Order.totalOrderAmount is derived from the sum of all the associated ProductSelection.totalSelectionPrice. Its definition in OCL looks like this:

context *Order* **inv**:
    Self.totalValue =
        Self.Selection.selectionValue ->sum()

This derived attribute definition is written in action language, as shown below.

```
total = 0.00;
select many selections related by self->Selection[R3];
for each selection in selections
    total = total + selection.selectionValue;
end for;
self.totalValue = total;
```

Unlike the identifier idiom, which can be represented by tags, the derived attribute marker (/) indicates the presence of a constraint that must be specified.

> Specifying an attribute as a derived attribute asserts the dependency between the attributes. It does not require the model compiler to recompute totalPurchasePrice every time either quantitySelected or unitPriceForOrder changes, nor to compute the value of totalPurchasePrice only when it is read. Either of those two times, or any time between them, meets the constraint.
>
> This rule gives the model compiler (and the architects programming the model compiler) the necessary flexibility to establish their own desired performance properties.

8.3   Referential Constraints

When we begin abstracting classes and attributes, our candidate classes might include attributes such as

- Book.publisher
- CreditCardCharge.accountNumber
- Order.customerID

Attributes like these are characteristics of the classes, but they also refer to the related classes. It is important, then, that we capture the fact that each such attribute is tied to an association.

8.3.1   Referential Attributes

A *referential attribute* identifies the instance of the associated class.

Definition: A *referential attribute* is an attribute whose value is the value of an identifying attribute in one or more associated classes.

We tag the referential attribute with {R*n*}, where *n* is the number of the association being formalized. For example, the attribute BookProduct.publisher refers to the identifier of Publisher, formalizing the association named R1. See Figure 8.10.

Once there is a referential attribute formalizing the association, there is no need to put in a "backwards pointer" in Publisher. That would be redun-

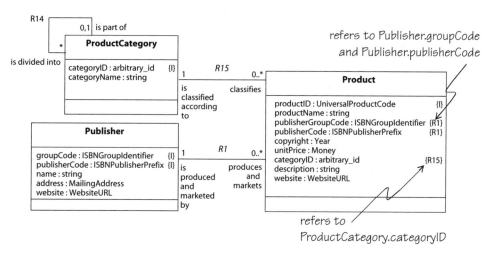

Figure 8.10 *Referential Attributes*

dant, because it formalizes the same fact about R1. (Model compilers can optimize the actual storage scheme for the association based on the pattern of usage of access, not on the placement of the referential attribute.)

Names of referential attributes. There is no requirement that the name of the referential attribute be exactly the same as the identifying attribute of the referred-to class, only that the set of values the referential attribute can take on is the same as a currently existing value for the identifying attribute.

When a class is identified by multiple attributes, an association is formalized using all of the identifier's attributes, though there are some exceptions described in Section 8.4: Association Loops.

Referential attributes not mandatory. For the purposes of knowledge formalization, the existence of the association and its description is sufficient to communicate meaning.

Shlaer-Mellor required referential attributes for all associations, even if it meant inventing identifiers. This practice is not required in Executable UML.

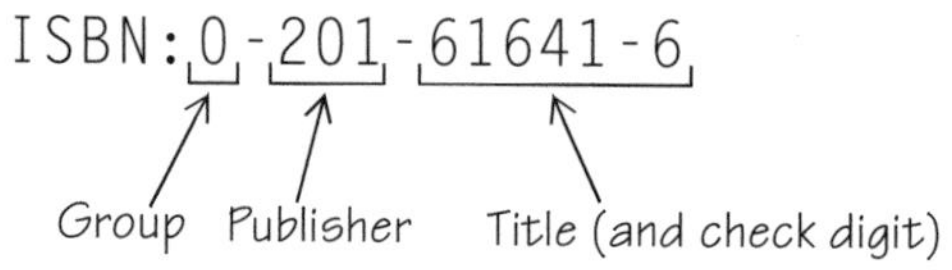

ISBN: 0 - 201 - 61641 - 6

Group   Publisher   Title (and check digit)

Figure 8.11   *Components of an International Standard Book Number (ISBN)*

However, referential attributes are useful in cases where it is easier to express constraints and selection expressions in terms of data (attributes) than associations. The following sections provide some examples of these uses of referential attributes.

8.3.2   Derived Identifiers

A book's ISBN ("International Standard Book Number") is a ten-character string. The first set of characters identify a publication group (a national or regional collection of publishers), those in the second set identify the publisher, and the remaining characters identify the book.[1]

This string actually comprises three pieces of information:

- the group code
- the publisher code
- the title code

The title code itself does not uniquely identify a book across the entire population of books of all publishers in all languages. By itself, it is not an identifier for a book. Rather, the identifier is the concatenation of all three attributes. A multi-attribute identifier is one solution, but given that the domain experts will consistently refer to the ISBN and that selecting instances of books by three attributes is rather messy, we should really make the ISBN of Figure 8.11 into a single attribute identifier.

In Figure 8.12, we represent the ISBN number as a derived attribute, based on the publication group, publisher, and title code, and Figure 8.13 shows the definition of the attribute.

---

[1] Actually, the last character is a check digit, but we'll consider that to be part of the book code.

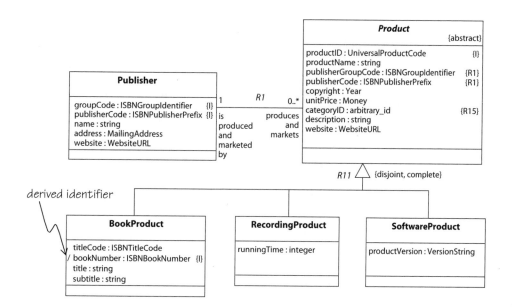

Figure 8.12   *Derived Identifier*

```
select one publisher related by self->Publisher[R1];
self.bookISBN =
    publisher.groupCode
    + "-" + publisher.publisherCode
    + "-" + self.titleCode;
```

Figure 8.13   *Action Language Definition of Derived Attribute bookISBN*

Definition: A *derived identifier* is an identifier that is the derived concatenation of several identifying attributes.

Derived identifiers are commonly used in situations where an attribute is unique within a subset of instances and all the instances in the subset are related to a single instance. In this case, the attribute Book.bookNumber must be unique for all books published by a given publisher in a given language. Two publishers (who have distinct publisherCodes) may each publish a book with the same bookNumber. The bookNumber by itself does not uniquely identify a BookProduct, but the combination of language, publisher, and bookNumber does uniquely identify a BookProduct.

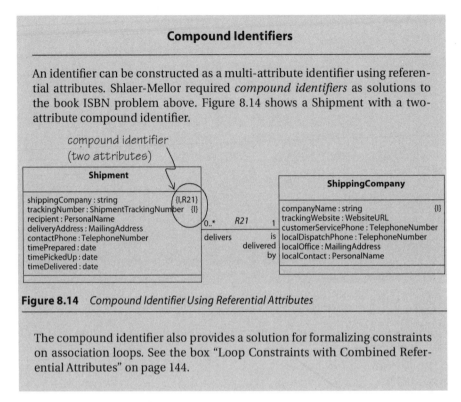

Compound Identifiers

An identifier can be constructed as a multi-attribute identifier using referential attributes. Shlaer-Mellor required *compound identifiers* as solutions to the book ISBN problem above. Figure 8.14 shows a Shipment with a two-attribute compound identifier.

Figure 8.14   *Compound Identifier Using Referential Attributes*

The compound identifier also provides a solution for formalizing constraints on association loops. See the box "Loop Constraints with Combined Referential Attributes" on page 144.

We may then refer to this derived identifier in constraints, referential attributes, and action language. Note that this attribute is both derived *and* an identifier because no two instances could have the same value.

8.4   Association Loops

When we build a model with many classes and associations, it is often possible to trace a path from a class, through other associations and classes, back to the class whence we came. This pattern in the graphic is referred to as an *association loop*.

Definition: An *association loop* is a set of associations that together make up a path from one class, through other classes, back to the same class.

An association loop sometimes has a meaning separate from the sum of its parts, and sometimes it doesn't. Proper analysis of loops enhances our

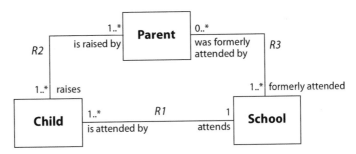

Figure 8.15 *Loop of Unconstrained Associations*

understanding of the problem and the diverse constraints between the associations in the domain.

In this section, we will examine several types of association loops:

- *Unconstrained association loops*, in which the associations mean different things and traversing the associations in different directions leads to different results.
- *Redundant association loops*, in which one association merely restates the same facts (and results in the same instances) as associations already on the model.
- *Constrained association loops*, in which there are specific domain rules and policies such that sets of associations are interrelated. We describe two commonly occurring constrained associations, the equal set constraint and the subset constraint.

8.4.1 Unconstrained Association Loops

An unconstrained association loop is one in which a path from one class to another in the same loop moving in one direction can lead to completely different sets of instances than going in the other direction.

Consider Figure 8.15, for example.

Starting from the Parent class, a given parent formerly attended some number of schools. Moving in the other direction from the Parent class, a Parent raises some number of (school-age) children, each of whom attends school. While it is possible that some students attend the same

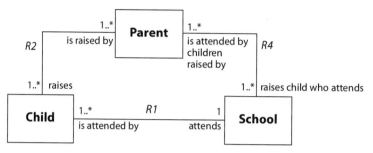

Figure 8.16   *Redundant Association in a Loop*

school their parents formerly attended, it is certainly not a requirement. Any matching associations between the set of schools attended by a parent and the set of schools attended by children of those parents is purely coincidental.

The association loop is *unconstrained* in that examining the set of instances reached by traversing in one direction around the loop does not impose constraints on the set of instances reached by traversing in the other direction.

There are no additional constraints not already described by existing associations, making our job easy. The model in Figure 8.15 is fine as is.

8.4.2   Redundant Associations

If we attempt to model every possible association between classes, some associations may be redundant. Consider Figure 8.16.

The RAISES CHILD WHO ATTENDS association is nothing more than the concatenation of the two other associations and captures no new information. The name of the association even reads like a concatenation of two other associations, and the presence of the Child class in the name of the association is an obvious clue to its redundancy. The association is completely redundant and should not be added to the model.

In such cases, the redundant association, R4, should be removed.

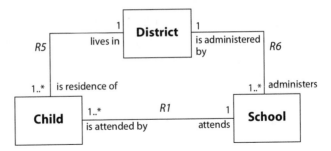

Figure 8.17   *Loop of Constrained Associations*

> *Child*
>
> ATTENDS 1 School [R1]
>
> Each child attends a school. Policy states that the district that administers the school the child attends must be the same as the district in which the child lives.

Figure 8.18   *Description of a Constrained Association*

8.4.3   **Equal Set Constraints**

In other situations, domain rules and policies are such that the two sets of associations yield identical sets of instances but mean different things. Figure 8.17 illustrates the case where it is policy that a child can attend a given school only if the child lives in the same district as that school.

Figure 8.18 shows how the association description incorporates the real business rule "child can only attend a school in the district where he lives" on the Child class. The constraint can be expressed in OCL, as shown in Figure 8.19.

---

context *Child* **inv**
    self.School.District = self.District;

Figure 8.19   *OCL for the Equal Set Constraint*

The same loop constraint can be expressed differently depending on the context of the constraint. In Figure 8.19 and Figure 8.20, the constraint is written from the perspective of the Child class. The constraint could just as well have been written from the perspective of the School:

context *School* **inv**
  self.Child -> **forAll**(*s* | *s.District = Self.District*)

stating, in English:

The children who attend the school must all live in the district that administers the school.

Each loop constraint needs to be written only once. We recommend placing the constraint in the context that makes for the simplest constraint expression.

```
select one schoolDistrict related by self->School[R1]->District[R6];
select one residenceDistrict related by self->District[R5];
return (schoolDistrict == residenceDistrict);
```

Figure 8.20   *Action Language for the Equal Set Constraint*

The constraint can also be written as a boolean function in action language. An example for any instance of Child is shown in Figure 8.20.

When the set of instances selected by traversing a loop in one direction *has to be the same* as the set of instances selected by traversing the loop in the opposite direction, we say that the loop is subject to an *equal set constraint*. In Figure 8.17, the instances selected by traversing from Child to District directly (R5) *has to be the same* as the set of instances selected by traversing via the Child class (R1 + R6), according to the rules and policies of the domain.

This commonly occurring constraint can be written on the class diagram as shown in Figure 8.21.

Equal Set Constraints and Redundant Associations

An equal set constraint differs from a set of redundant associations in that the sets of associations mean different things. This cannot be determined by a mere mechanical evaluation of the models; it requires an understanding of the meanings of the associations, typically gained by writing the association descriptions. So write those descriptions!

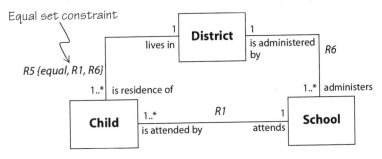

Figure 8.21   *Graphical Representation of an Equal Set Constraint*

8.4.4   Subset Constraints

Consider the following: A parent may be a member of the Parent–Teacher Association (PTA) only of a school attended by the parent's child. For example, a parent with one child attending school A and another child attending school B could serve on the PTAs of A, B, both, or neither, but that parent cannot serve (as a parent) on the PTA of just any school.

This association loop is constrained so that the set of instances selected by traversing from parent to school directly (R7) *has to be a subset* of the instances selected by traversing via the Child class (R2 + R1), according to the rules and policies of the domain, as shown in Figure 8.22.

The association is described in Figure 8.23.

Loop Constraints with Combined Referential Attributes

The loop constraints for fully and partially constrained associations can be written using referential attributes.

In Shlaer-Mellor, identifiers and referential attributes were the preferred way to formalize relationships and to specify relationship loop constraints. This was based on the notion that one association's instance set (the set of corresponding instances) can be completely determined by the values of the other relationships around the loop. In the case of the Child, School, and District model of Figure 8.17, the associations could be formalized using referential attributes, as shown below:

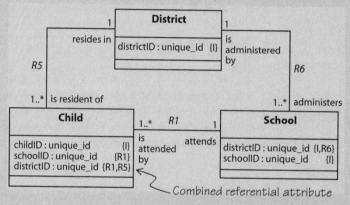

In the Child class, the referential attributes residenceDistrict and schoolDistrict had to be the same. These two referential attributes would therefore be combined into a single referential attribute that formalizes both associations.

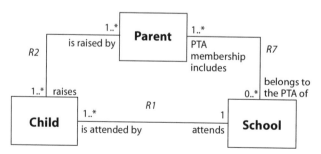

Figure 8.22 *Subset Constrained Associations*

School

PTA MEMBERSHIP INCLUDES * Parent [R7]

For a parent to join the school's PTA, the parent must have children attending the school. However, not all parents of children who attend the school elect to join the PTA.

Figure 8.23 *Description of a Subset Constrained Association*

The OCL is:

Context *Parent* **inv**:
　　Self.School -> exists(Self.child)

and the action language is:

select one *ptaSchool* **related by** *self->School[R7];*
select many *childSchools* **related by** *self->Parent[R7]->Child[R2]->School[R1]*
　where *selected == ptaSchool;*
return *not_empty childSchools;*

Contrast this with the OCL for the equal set constraint. In Figure 8.19, the predicate stated that two sets must be equal; however, in the example above, the derived association is a *subset*. One or both parents may serve, but only if one of their children attends that school. The subset constraint is depicted in Figure 8.24.

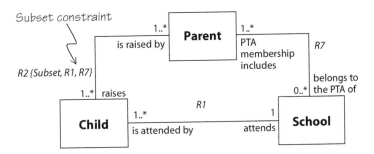

Figure 8.24 *Graphical Representation of a Subset Constraint*

8.5   **Constraints Capture Semantics**

Constraints are critical in formally expressing the rules and policies of a domain such that the rules can be checked in a running system. While the actual mechanisms of constraint enforcement depend on the mechanisms of the selected model compiler, the process of identifying and writing these constraints has substantial value in formalizing the knowledge about a domain.

Model compilers can also use constraints to optimize data storage and data-access operations.

Now that we have a complete model of the conceptual entities, their domain relationships, and constraints, we can move on to describing dynamic behavior.

8.6   **References**

[1] UML 1.4 and OCL URL: *www.omg.org/cgi-bin/doc?formal/01-09-67*

[2] Shlaer, Sally, and Stephen J. Mellor: *Object-Oriented Systems Analysis: Modeling the World in Data.* Prentice-Hall, Englewood Cliffs, N.J., 1988.

[3] Shlaer, Sally, and Stephen J. Mellor: *Object Lifecycles: Modeling the World in States.* Prentice Hall PTR, Englewood Cliffs, N.J., 1992.

9

Lifecycles

So far, we've abstracted classes in terms of their attributes and the associations that hold between those classes. The work that we've done to understand data—the classes, their attributes, their associations, and their constraints—is of tremendous value in understanding the semantics of a domain.

Although we have abstracted classes based on both data and behavior, we have not yet described the detailed behavior of instances of classes and associations.

In the next few chapters, we'll see how to use *state machines* to model the lifecycles of the classes in a domain.

9.1   Concept of a Lifecycle

Each instance of a class generally has a lifetime. Objects are created, they progress through certain stages, and then go away. Their behavior is a progression through various stages over time. These changes over time are known as the *lifecycle* of the object.

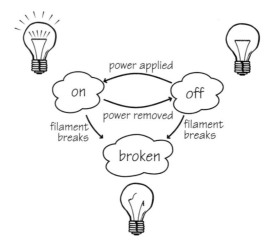

Figure 9.1 *Lifecycle of Light Bulb*

As an example of a lifecycle, let's consider a light bulb. When power is applied, the bulb (if properly installed) goes on. When power is removed, the bulb goes off. Eventually the filament breaks and applying power has no effect.

Figure 9.1 shows a representation of the light bulb's behavior.

This simple pattern of dynamic behavior is followed by all light bulbs throughout their lifetimes.

Figure 9.1 shows how we've abstracted the behavior pattern into a collection of *stages* (on, off, and broken) and a collection of *incidents* (power applied, power removed, and filament breaks) that cause *progressions* from stage to stage.

In this chapter, we show how to use state machines to model lifecycles.[1]

---

[1] Some of this material is drawn from Object Lifecycles. [1]

9.2   State Machine

A lifecycle is formally expressed as a *state machine*, comprising:

- *States.* Each state represents a stage in the lifecycle of a typical instance of the class.
- *Events.* Each event represents an incident or indication that a progression is happening.
- *Transitions.* A transition rule specifies what new state is achieved when an object in a given state receives a particular event.
- *Procedures.* A procedure is an activity or operation that must be accomplished when an object arrives in a state. Each state has its own procedure. Procedures comprise *actions*.

The state machine is represented as a *statechart diagram*, as defined first in [2]. That is, the statechart diagram is a representation of the underlying semantics defined by the state machine.

9.2.1   Example Class with a State Machine

To show how to create a state machine for a class, we'll use an example of a compact, inexpensive microwave oven, the One-Minute Microwaver. We've abstracted a class for the microwave oven:

MicrowaveOven
manufacturer serialNumber lightOn doorOpen powerTubeEnergized cookingTimeRemaining

Its operation can be summarized as:

- This simple oven has a single control button. When the oven door is closed and the user presses the button, the oven will cook (that is, energize the power tube) for 1 minute.
- There is a light inside the oven. Any time the oven is cooking, the light must be turned on, so you can peer through the window in the oven's

door and see if your food is bubbling. Any time the door is open, the light must be on, so you can see your food or so you have enough light to clean the oven.

- When the oven times out (cooks until the desired preset time), it turns off both the power tube and the light. It then emits a warning beep to signal that the food is ready.
- The user can stop the cooking by opening the door. Once the door is opened, the timer resets to zero.
- Closing the oven door turns out the light.

Reading this specification, we see several pertinent incidents that affect the operation of the oven:

- The door is opened.
- The door is closed.
- The control button is pressed.
- The timer counts down to zero ("times out").

These incidents are abstracted as *events*.

Likewise, there are several behaviors that occur in response to these events:

- Turn on the light.
- Turn off the light.
- Energize the power tube.
- De-energize the power tube.
- Set the timer for 1 minute.
- Add 1 minute to the timer.
- Clear the timer.
- Sound the beeper.

These behaviors are abstracted as *actions* in the states' procedures.

We can express this behavior pattern as a statechart diagram. Figure 9.2 shows a statechart diagram for the microwave oven. The states are represented by rounded rectangles, each labeled with an appropriate name for the state. The transitions are shown by arrows connecting two states. Each transition is labeled with the event that causes the transition. The actions that make up each procedure associated with a state are described in the lower compartment of the state box.

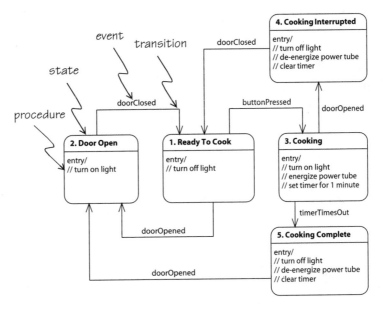

Figure 9.2   *Statechart for the One-Minute Microwave Oven*

9.2.2   **States**

A *state* abstracts a distinct stage in the lifecycle.

Definition: A *state* represents a condition of an object in which a defined set of rules, policies, regulations, and physical laws applies.

Each state is given a name that is unique within this state machine. States are also numbered. The number of the state is arbitrary and does not imply any sequencing to the states. Figure 9.3 shows how the state names and numbers are written in the top compartment of the state box.

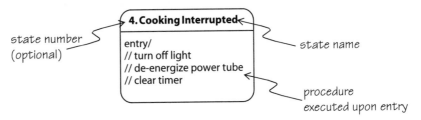

Figure 9.3   *State Box Containing State Number, Name, and Procedure*

An object is in exactly one state at a time. Although we can see from the microwave oven statechart diagram that the door is closed in several states, this does not mean that the microwave is in several states at once. The states Ready to Cook and Cooking are different because they exhibit different behaviors and they respond to events differently.

If your understanding of the domain under study leads you to a need to be in two (or more) states at once, build a new class (or classes).

While it's important to choose good, meaningful state names, the name of the state is just an arbitrary label. The real meaning of the state is in the behavior associated with the state—the procedure executed upon entry to the state, the events that cause transitions into the state, and the events that cause transitions out of the state.

9.2.3   Events

Definition: An *event* is the abstraction of an incident in the domain that tells us that something has happened.

The event is named based on its meaning in the domain. In the case of the microwave oven, we have these meanings for the events: door opened, door closed, button pressed, and time complete.

An event is received by a state machine because something happens to it. Events are always received by a specific object; they are not broadcast. When the door of oven MM-231432 is opened, only that oven detects the doorOpened event; it is not seen by all of the ovens in the world.

Event names and labels. The name of the event is based on its meaning. Each event also has a shorthand label based on the class abbreviation and a number. The order of the numbers is arbitrary and unrelated to the state numbers.

The microwave oven has events:

- MicrowaveOven1: doorOpened
- MicrowaveOven2: doorClosed
- MicrowaveOven3: buttonPressed
- MicrowaveOven4: timerTimesOut

MicrowaveOven
manufacturer serialNumber lightOn doorOpen powerTubeEnergized cookingTimeRemaining
«event» doorOpened doorClosed buttonPressed timerTimesOut

The events received by a class's state machine can be shown on the class diagram as shown on the left.

Place the signals in the bottom compartment with the stereotype «event».

UML does not specifically require that signals be shown on the class diagram, but some people have found it convenient if their tool allows it. We will use this as an illustration only.

Event specification vs. event occurrence. When an event (buttonPressed, for example) appears on a statechart diagram, it represents the concept of a typical but unspecified occurrence of an incident—in this case, any button-press on any microwave oven. This concept should be distinguished from the particular occurrences of a button-press on oven P at 3 P.M., another at 3:10, and a button-press on oven Q at 9 P.M. Both concepts are referred to informally as an event, and the meaning is generally clear from the context. However, when it is necessary to distinguish by means of terminology, we use *event specification* to refer to a typical unspecified occurrence (any button-press on any oven) and *event occurrence* to refer to a particular occurrence (the button-press on oven T at 3:10).

9.2.4   Transitions

Transitions specify what happens—what new state is achieved—when a particular event occurs while in a certain state.

Definition: A *transition* abstracts the progression from state to state as caused by an event.

Each transition is labeled with the event that causes the progression.

There may be multiple transitions out of a state only if they are caused by different events. Figure 9.2 showed that when the oven is in Door Closed state, opening the door transitions to Door Open, while pressing the button from the Door Closed state makes a transition to the Cooking state.

There may multiple transitions into a state, each caused by the same event or by different events. All such events must carry the same data.

The words "queue" and "buffer" appear nowhere in these explanations, nor, for that matter, in the remainder of the book, because an Executable UML model cannot manipulate or make assumptions about queues or buffers. (A model compiler may employ a queue, but that's its business, not ours.)

An object detects an event, and either it triggers a transition or it doesn't. If the event does not trigger a transition, it's gone forever, just as an astronomer who misses an eclipse can't save it until the telescope is set up. In this sense, an event is "consumed" at the moment of detection. See also Section 11.2: Rules about Signals.

Reflexive transitions. An event may cause a *reflexive transition* from one state into the same state. For example, pressing the button on the microwave extends the cooking time by one minute per press. The effect is the same as with any other transition: on entry to the state, the procedure is executed.

See Figure 9.7 and Figure 9.10 for examples of reflexive transitions.

9.2.5   Procedures

Definition: A state *procedure* is an operation executed by an object on entry to a state.

Each state has one associated procedure, which in turn comprises several actions. Actions in procedures can do just about anything.

To minimize distraction, the microwave oven example uses informal descriptions written as comments for the procedure. But the real value in Executable UML is that these procedures can be written formally—they have a defined semantics and they can be executed.

Because all instances of a class share the same state machine specification, the procedures must be defined so that they can be executed by any object.

9.3 State Transition Table

Examination of the statechart diagram for the microwave oven reveals that the model fails to answer certain important questions:

- What happens if we press the button when cooking is complete?
- What happens if we press the button while cooking?
- What happens if we press the button when the door is open?
- Can we close the door when the door is already closed? (Put another way: What happens if we detect the doorClosed event when the door is already closed?)

The statechart diagram shows a set of states, events, and transitions, but the diagram cannot cover all possible combinations. In this section, we'll use an alternative representation[2] of a state machine—the *state transition table* (STT)—to ensure completeness of the underlying model.

9.3.1 Basics of the State Transition Table

A state machine's transitions can be presented in a state transition table as shown in Figure 9.4. In a state transition table, each row represents a state and each column represents an event. The cells are filled in to specify what happens when an object in a given state (the row) detects a particular event (the column).

9.3.2 Discovering New Transitions

Empty cells on the STT represent combinations of states and events that may have been overlooked. Completing these will lead to a discussion among experts as to what features are required, and, one hopes, to a more complete model of the solution.

For example, pressing the button when cooking is complete currently does nothing. There's no entry showing any transition for this combination. Looking back to the specification of the oven, we find that this situa-

---

[2] The underlying *model* is the same, we simply have two representations of it. One representation is graphical but incomplete, and the other is tabular, showing all combinations of states and events. Your tool should maintain the underlying model, not the diagram or the table.

	buttonPressed	doorOpened	doorClosed	timerTimesOut
Ready To Cook	Cooking	Door Open		
Cooking		Cooking Interrupted		Cooking Complete
Cooking Complete		Door Open		
Cooking Interrupted			Door Closed	
Door Open			Door Closed	

Figure 9.4   *State Transition Table Based on Microwave Oven Statechart Diagram*

tion was in fact omitted: It is perfectly reasonable to start the oven again and to transition back to the Cooking state as shown in the revised STT and corresponding statechart diagram of Figure 9.5. (The new transition is shown in italics.)

9.3.3   Discovering New States and Events

In many cases, analysis of a state machine using an STT may lead to new states and new events. In those cases, adding the new states and events will add new rows and columns to the state transition table.

In the last section we asked the question, "What happens if the user presses the button when the door is closed and cooking is complete?" We discovered a new transition. Now let's ask, "What happens if the user presses the button when the door is closed and the oven is cooking?" We decide that if the first button-press added a minute of time (from zero to one minute) and started the oven cooking, then another button-press should add another minute of time to the oven. Generally, if the user presses the button at any time when the oven is cooking, one minute is added to the cooking time. So if the oven has 40 seconds more cooking time to go, pressing the button twice sets the cooking time to 2 minutes and 40 seconds.

To address this, we could simply draw a transition from Cooking back to Cooking as shown in Figure 9.6, but the wrong actions occur when the second button-press occurs. The light and power tube are already on; we

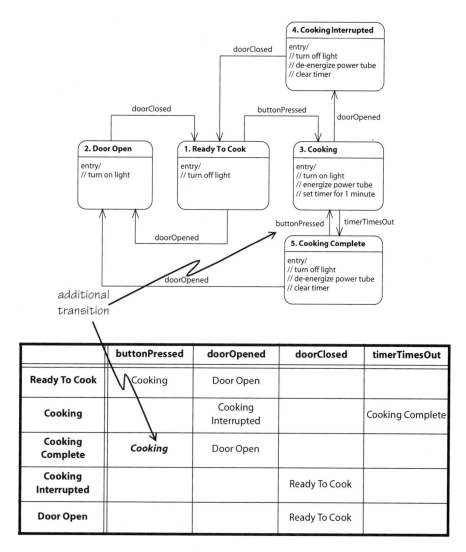

Figure 9.5 *Statechart Diagram and STT with Additional Transition*

don't need to turn them on again. We want to add a minute to the timer; we don't want to set it to 1 minute. We therefore add a new state, CookingExtended, to the statechart diagram.

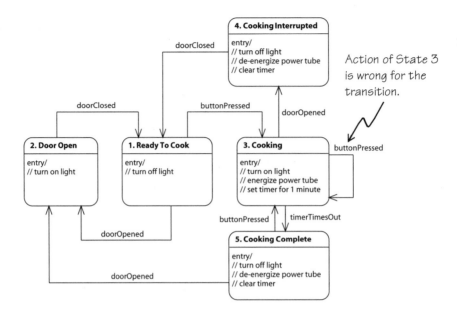

Figure 9.6   *Wrong Transition Added to Extend the Cooking Period*

Of course, you will need to analyze all the cells in those new rows and columns and add new transitions and possibly more states to the model. This also has the effect of adding a new row to the state transition table. Adding a new row to the state transition table adds a new state and some transitions to the statechart diagram. Figure 9.7 shows the combined effect of adding a new state to the statechart diagram and a new row to the state transition table.

The resulting model is "more complex" than before because it has an "extra" state. Yet the model *should* distinguish the various cases because they are different in the domain. A correct state machine has sufficient states to model properly all of the subtleties in the object's lifecycle. The purpose of modeling is to expose detail in the problem—details such as the difference between what happens when the button is pressed the first time and what happens subsequent times.

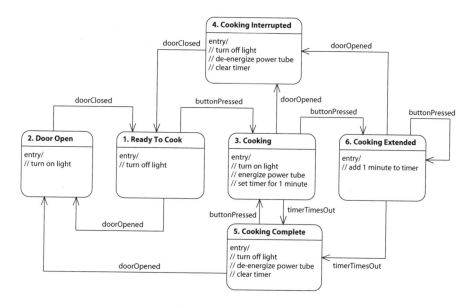

	buttonPressed	**doorOpened**	**doorClosed**	**timerTimesOut**
Ready To Cook	Cooking	Door Open		
Cooking	*Cooking Extended*	Cooking Interrupted		Cooking Complete
Cooking Complete	Cooking	Door Open		
Cooking Interrupted			Ready To Cook	
Door Open			Ready To Cook	
Cooking Extended	*Cooking Extended*	*Cooking Interrupted*		*Cooking Complete*

Figure 9.7   *Statechart Diagram and STT with New Cooking Extended State*

	buttonPressed	doorOpened	doorClosed	timerTimesOut
Ready To Cook	Cooking	Door Open		*Event Ignored*
Cooking	Cooking Extended	Cooking Interrupted		Cooking Complete
Cooking Complete	Cooking	Door Open		
Cooking Interrupted	*Event Ignored*		Ready To Cook	*Event Ignored*
Door Open	*Event Ignored*		Ready To Cook	
Cooking Extended	Cooking Extended	Cooking Interrupted		Cooking Complete

Figure 9.8 *State Transition Table with "Event Ignored" Entries*

9.3.4   Event Ignored and Can't Happen

Not every empty cell in the STT is a missing requirement. In some cases, a particular state-event combination may not cause a transition into a new state. For example, what happens if the cook presses the button on the microwave oven when the door is open? When the cooking is complete? You might say, "Nothing happens." But there are really two different kinds of "nothing." Under some situations, we really want nothing to happen; in other words, the event is ignored. In other situations, the event simply can't happen according to the rules and policies of the domain.

Event Ignored cell entry. When a certain event can happen but causes no effect, the STT cell is filled in as "Event Ignored." In the case of the oven, pressing the button when the door is open has no effect. Figure 9.8 shows the state transition table with Event Ignored entries added. When an event is ignored, the object stays in the same state it is in and *does not* re-execute the procedure. In this way, an Event Ignored is different from a transition to the same state.

Although the event is ignored in the sense of not causing a transition, it has been detected and consumed by the state machine. The event is not held until the object arrives in a state where the event can cause a transition.

	buttonPressed	doorOpened	doorClosed	timerTimesOut
Ready To Cook	Cooking	Door Open	*Can't Happen*	Event Ignored
Cooking	Cooking Extended	Cooking Interrupted	*Can't Happen*	Cooking Complete
Cooking Complete	Cooking	Door Open	Can't Happened	*Can't Happen*
Cooking Interrupted	Event Ignored	*Can't Happen*	Ready To Cook	Event Ignored
Door Open	Event Ignored	*Can't Happen*	Ready To Cook	*Can't Happen*
Cooking Extended	Cooking Extended	Cooking Interrupted	*Can't Happen*	Cooking Complete

Figure 9.9   *State Transition Table with "Can't Happen" Entries*

Can't Happen cell entry. If the event cannot happen when the object is in a particular state, record the fact by entering "Can't Happen" in the cell. The Can't Happen entry is reserved for occasions when the event simply cannot occur according to the rules and policies of the domain. For example, the oven cannot receive a doorClosed event when the oven is cooking. The door is already closed in this state; detecting this event in this state makes no sense. It just can't happen. Figure 9.9 shows the Can't Happen entries added to the table.

Can't Happen combinations should have associated descriptions that state why a particular combination is disallowed. For example, doorOpen can't happen in the Interrupted state because the door is already open.

When filling out the state transition table, focus on the problem domain and not on the particular mechanisms implemented by the software. One *could* always argue that any event could be detected in any state. But if the event makes no sense according to the rules and policies of the domain, treat the combination as Can't Happen.

Event Ignored and Can't Happen entries do not appear in the statechart diagram. The statechart diagram shows only the active allowed transitions. Therefore, the state transition table is necessary for a complete interpretation of the state machine for the instances of a class.

Can't Happen or Shouldn't Happen?

Of course, the microwave oven *could* detect a doorOpen event when the door is already open, and in that sense the event shouldn't happen. But in the reality of the domain under study, the behavior of the microwave, the event really cannot happen. So which is it?

Because the model describes the microwave, it Can't Happen. It is the task of the domain that recognizes signals from the hardware to detect this case and filter it out so the microwave is blissfully unaware of the misbehavior of its internal devices.

9.4   Creating and Deleting Objects

Many classes have instances that are created and deleted over time. We can model creation and deletion of objects in the state machines.

9.4.1   Initial Pseudostates

The semantics of UML state machine instance-creation are as follows: First, an object is created, then the state machine instance is started, then the state machine instance is ready to receive events. The state machine instance is started in its *initial pseudostate*.

Definition: An *initial pseudostate* is the state in which the state machine instance for an object is started.

An initial pseudostate is shown by a filled-in circle, as in Figure 9.10.

Several transitions may emanate from the initial pseudostate, so long as each is caused by a different event, just as with any other state.

9.4.2   Final Pseudostates

A state machine instance and its corresponding object are implicitly deleted when a state machine instance makes a transition to a *final pseudostate*.

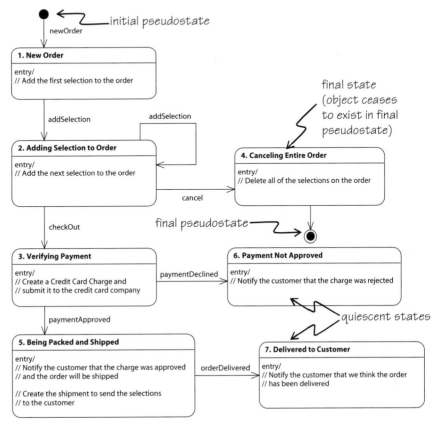

Figure 9.10 *Statechart Diagram for the Order*

Definition: A *final pseudostate* is the state in which an object is deleted.

Final pseudostates are indicated on the statechart diagram by a bulls-eye symbol. The unlabeled transition to the final pseudostate is a *completion event*. As soon as the final state's procedure completes, the instance transitions to the final pseudostate and goes away.

In addition, state machines may have one or more states in which they become quiescent. In a quiescent state, the object continues to exist, but has no subsequent interesting dynamic behavior. While no special notation is used on the statechart diagram, such final states can be identified by their lack of outbound transitions.

The action language that we use in this book has a single statement

generate *<signal>* **to** *<class>* **creator;**

that actually incorporates three individual actions:

- create object
- start state machine instance
- send signal

See Section 10.2: Creating and Deleting Objects for examples.

Examples of each construct are shown in Figure 9.10.

Note that part of abstraction is distinguishing between application behavior and computer behavior. For example, in many financial systems accounts never really go away. Instead they are archived for posterity (or the IRS).

9.5   Forming Lifecycles

Building good state machines takes practice. Here are two reminders to help you avoid traps.

The model is an abstraction. Just as a class diagram doesn't model every fact about a thing as an attribute, so the state machines will capture only those stages and progressions that are relevant to the problem at hand. The light bulb model doesn't include its manufacture, sale, or disposal. These things do happen to a light bulb, but they are (presumably) outside the scope of the problem we're modeling.

Similarly, a light bulb takes time to heat up and is fully on only when the filament has reached a certain temperature. For most problems, this view is overly detailed and fails to abstract unnecessary detail. These decisions depend on the developer's judgment and understanding of the domain.

Capture purpose. If you spot a microwave oven with the door closed and the light off, you don't know whether it contains food ready to eat or not.

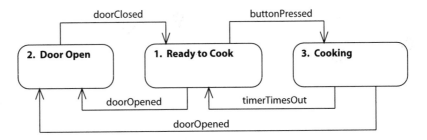

Figure 9.11 *External View of the Microwave Oven*

This is because you don't know the history of states that led to this one. Put another way, you don't know *why* the microwave is exhibiting this behavior.

Modeling only the properties of the oven (light on or off, door open or closed, and power tube on or off) can lead to a model such as Figure 9.11. This model captures a limited snapshot of the microwave oven, where the properties alone established the state.

But our usage of state machines seeks to explain the details of the behavior from inside the class. Their purpose is one of specification: to explain details of behavior so that we can understand why an object needs to behave in a certain way and what actions are required to make it behave properly. This correct use of state machines is called a "clear-box" or internal view. The final model for the microwave oven shown in Figure 9.7 is an example.

9.6   Lifecycles for Classes

Recall the definition of a class.

A *class* is an abstraction of a set of real-world things such that

- All the real-world things in the set—the instances—have the same characteristics ("common characteristics").

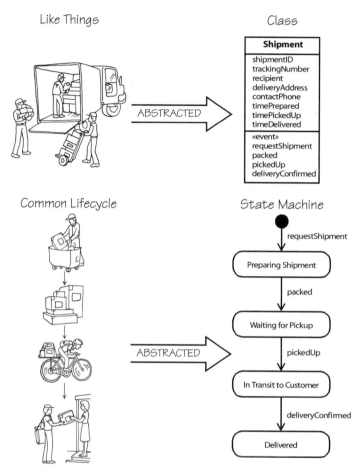

Figure 9.12 *Correspondence between Abstraction as a Class and as a State Machine*

- All instances are subject to and conform to the same rules and policies ("common behavior").

Since all instances of the class must follow the same rules of behavior, when we abstract a group of like things to produce a class, we also abstract their common behavior pattern into a lifecycle typical of the class. The lifecycle provides a formal description of the behavior pattern shared by each of the objects, called a *state machine*, as illustrated in Figure 9.12.

Just as a class has instances, so a state machine also has instances. A state machine instance refers to the execution of a state machine by a particular object. Think of a state machine instance as a private copy of the state machine that is executed by a single object. Each state machine instance is in exactly one state at a time.

9.7 References

[1] Shlaer, Sally, and Stephen J. Mellor: *Object Lifecycles: Modeling the World in States.* Prentice Hall PTR , Englewood Cliffs, N.J., 1992.

[2] Harel, D. "Statecharts: A visual formalism for complex systems." In *Science of Computer Programming* 8, 3 (June 1987), 231–274.

10

Communicating Objects

In Executable UML, we build statechart diagrams and state transition tables for classes and associations to capture their lifecycle behavior. The behavior is defined in actions, grouped together as procedures on the state machines. The behavior is sequenced by signals between state machine instances.

By formalizing behavior as actions in procedures, we make the procedures, the state machines, and so the entire domain model, executable.

Each procedure on a state machine is written using an action language such as that introduced in Chapter 7: Class Actions. This chapter extends these actions to include signaling to existing objects and signaling to cause creation of other objects. Certain rules govern the construction and receipt of the signals and their parameters to maintain consistency of the actions.

For completeness, this chapter describes also the synchronous creation and deletion of objects that have state machines.

Collaboration diagrams help visualize the communication patterns between the several classes, and sequence diagrams illuminate the execution of a single scenario, with known states and attribute values, over time. In this chapter, we show how to use these diagrams, known collectively as *interaction diagrams*, to understand patterns of communication between existing state machine instances and external entities.

10.1   Signals

Objects communicate as a result of state machine instances sending signals. To synchronize the behavior of objects, actions in state machine instances generate *signals* to establish the dynamics of a domain.

Definition: A *signal* is a message that may carry data used by the actions in a procedure of the recipient's state machine instance.

The signaling is asynchronous. Once the signal is sent, the sender goes on about its business. Separately, once the event is detected by the receiver, a transition is made and the receiver executes a procedure. The receiver does not "return" to the sender, though it may choose to send another signal.

10.1.1   Sending Signals

Signal actions send signals to objects. In Figure 10.1, a signal is sent by the shipment and detected as an event by a related order.

An action in the procedure for the shipment generates a signal to the order, where *order* is the object reference of the receiver found by traversing the association R1 from the shipment.

10.1.2   Event Parameters

Definition: An *event parameter* is a data item passed along with an event.

The collection of event parameters on an event can be viewed as an object in its own right created dynamically by the sender.

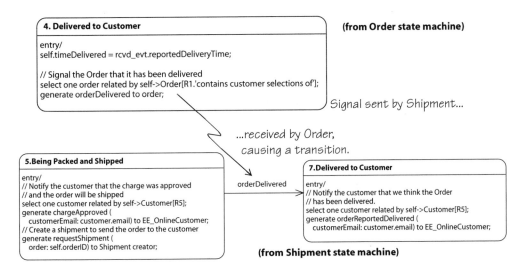

Figure 10.1   *Shipment State Procedure Sends orderDelivered signal to Order*

The actions of the procedure use the values of the event parameters. The parameter values are accessed in the actions conventionally via **rcvd_evt,** which denotes the object that carries the parameters.

Figure 10.2 shows an event and its parameters. In this example, the customer provides information sufficient to check out: the charge card expiration date, the card holder name and credit card number, as well the customer's name, phone number and address. These event parameters are received with the event and accessed in the procedure. Figure 10.2 also shows how parameters are provided to a send (generate) a signal.

All events that cause a transition into a particular state must carry exactly the same event parameters. This rule guarantees that the procedure will have the same parameters regardless of which event caused the transition. This is the same as the general rule in a programming language that requires invocation of a function to have the same signature, regardless of the caller .

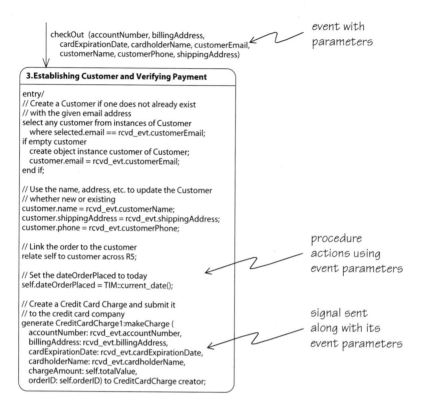

checkOut (accountNumber, billingAddress,
cardExpirationDate, cardholderName, customerEmail,
customerName, customerPhone, shippingAddress)

event with parameters

3.Establishing Customer and Verifying Payment

entry/
// Create a Customer if one does not already exist
// with the given email address
select any customer from instances of Customer
  where selected.email == rcvd_evt.customerEmail;
if empty customer
  create object instance customer of Customer;
  customer.email = rcvd_evt.customerEmail;
end if;

// Use the name, address, etc. to update the Customer
// whether new or existing
customer.name = rcvd_evt.customerName;
customer.shippingAddress = rcvd_evt.shippingAddress;
customer.phone = rcvd_evt.customerPhone;

// Link the order to the customer
relate self to customer across R5;

procedure actions using event parameters

// Set the dateOrderPlaced to today
self.dateOrderPlaced = TIM::current_date();

// Create a Credit Card Charge and submit it
// to the credit card company
generate CreditCardCharge1:makeCharge (
  accountNumber: rcvd_evt.accountNumber,
  billingAddress: rcvd_evt.billingAddress,
  cardExpirationDate: rcvd_evt.cardExpirationDate,
  cardholderName: rcvd_evt.cardholderName,
  chargeAmount: self.totalValue,
  orderID: self.orderID) to CreditCardCharge creator;

signal sent along with its event parameters

Figure 10.2 *Event Parameters Provided to a Procedure in the Order State Machine*

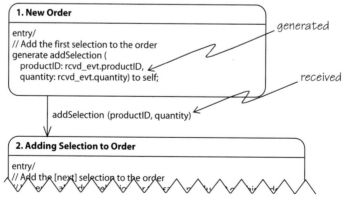

1. New Order

entry/
// Add the first selection to the order
generate addSelection (
  productID: rcvd_evt.productID,
  quantity: rcvd_evt.quantity) to self;

generated

received

addSelection (productID, quantity)

2. Adding Selection to Order

entry/
// Add the [next] selection to the order

Figure 10.3 *Signal to self*

UML uses *signal* to signify an explicit send of an asynchronous message detected as an event by the receiver.

UML uses *event* to signify anything that can be detected by a state machine, regardless of cause. There are several kinds of events defined, including signal events, time events, and change events.

A *signal event* is an event resulting from the receipt of a signal.

Hence, a signal and a (signal) event are really the same thing, but with different names from the perspective of the sender and receiver, respectively.

10.1.3   Signals with Parameters

When a signal carries parameters, the actual parameters are assembled as name/value pairs.

```
generate addSelection (
    productID: rcvd_evt.productID,
    quantity: rcvd_evt.quantity) to order;
```

The parameter name on the left of the colon is the *formal parameter*, and the value specified on right of the colon is the *actual parameter*. By using name-value pairs, the order of the actual parameters is unimportant.

Executable UML requires every parameter to be supplied: If a signal specification is defined to have a certain set of parameters, each time the signal is sent it must carry values for those parameters.

The signal and its parameters are interpreted as a signal event and its parameters by the receiver.

Because signals *are* received as events, event parameters are exactly the same as the signal parameters. All kinds of events on state machines can have parameters, not just signal events, so we shall use "event parameter" preferentially.

10.1.4   Signals to Self

Figure 10.3 shows how a state machine can generate a signal to itself.

UML has the notion of a *completion event* that serves the same purpose as a signal to self. Completion events are always handled first, just like signals to self. Completion events in UML are shown as an unlabeled transition.

With one exception—the transition to a final pseudostate (see Section 9.4.2: Final Pseudostates)—Executable UML labels all transitions. By requiring all transitions to be labeled with events, an omitted event does not cause an unwanted completion event, thereby making Executable UML notationally less error-prone.

This technique can be used to simplify state machines when a single (logical) state needs to be broken into several states, perhaps as the result of some conditional logic.

These signals are syntactically just like any other. However, signals to self are always treated first by the receiver, even if other events are outstanding.

10.1.5 Signals to External Entities

Procedures may need to signal outside the domain to request a particular task to be performed or to provide a notification. Signals can be defined for external entities representing actors, and signal actions can be written in the procedures using these signals:

```
generate requestChargeApproval (...)
    to EE_creditCardCompany;
    // Process a credit card charge
generate chargeApproved (...) to EE_OnlineCustomer;
    // Notify customer
```

These signals to external entities constitute requirements on the domains that communicate with the external entities. It is the responsibility of these domains to satisfy the requirements, not of the domain that generates the signals.

To distinguish external entities from domain classes with similar names, we will (by our own convention) precede all external entities with the letters EE_:

EE_OnlineCustomer
EE_CreditCardCompany
EE_ShippingClerk

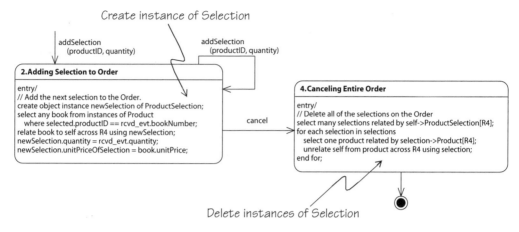

Figure 10.4 *Order Creates and Deletes Instances of Selection*

10.2   Creating and Deleting Objects

Many classes have instances that are created and deleted over time. Actions can synchronously create and delete instances of other classes without state machines, as shown on these states of the Order in Figure 10.4.

The instances of Selection are created and deleted synchronously as part of the procedure. Likewise, the associations between the Order and the Selection are created and deleted directly in the procedures.

10.2.1   Asynchronous Creation and Deletion

Objects can be created and deleted asynchronously by sending signals. A generate signal action **to** *<class>* **creator** performs this function:

> **generate** *requestShipment (order: self)* **to** *Shipment* **creator;**

Figure 10.5 shows how an Order creates a Shipment once its payment is approved.

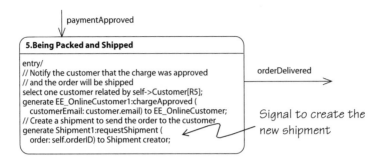

Figure 10.5   *Order State Procedure Signals to Create Shipment*

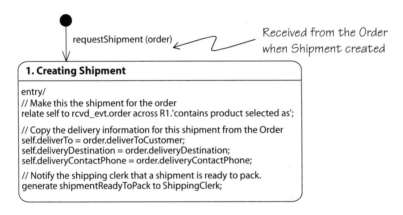

Figure 10.6   *New Shipment is Created, Enters its Initial State, and Executes its Procedure*

Executing the action language **to** *Shipment* **creator**; causes the new Shipment object to be created. The signal requestShipment then causes the transition from the initial pseudostate into the Creating Shipment state, as shown in Figure 10.6. The event parameters are delivered to the procedure and the procedure is executed on the new, object that now exists.

Signaling **to creator** when there is no transition from the initial pseudostate on that event makes no sense: It just cannot be done.

To delete an object, send a signal like any other. If a transition is made into a state with a transition to a final pseudostate, the final transition will be made on completion of the state's procedure, and the object will be gone.

10.2.2   Synchronous Creation and Deletion

Figure 10.4 showed how procedures can synchronously create and delete instances of classes without state machines.

Synchronous creation and deletion can also be used—with care!—when the target object has a state machine. Synchronous creation is realized using the ordinary **create object** action:

> **create object instance** *R2D2* **of** *Robot* **in state** *'Idle'*;

The effect of this action is to create an instance of Robot in the specified state, and, once created, the state machine instance can accept events. The procedure for the initial state is not executed, because there was no transition into the state for this execution.

Similarly, an action can cause the deletion of an object and its associated state machine instance, no matter which state it is in:

> **select one** *shipment* **related by** *self->Shipment[R3]*;
> **delete object instance** *shipment*;

As with initial states, the procedure associated with the state-in-which-the-object-is-deleted is not executed. Consequently, it is the responsibility of the developer to remove all links to the about-to-be-deleted object and carry out any other necessary cleanup.

Use and Misuse of Synchronous Creation and Deletion

While it is good practice to localize behavior in the class that owns the instance, it is not always best practice. Consider the case in which a customer is created, one or more accounts go through their lifecycles until the last account is closed, and then the customer is deleted. The lifecycle of the customer is boring beyond belief: It's created, it passes information along to the account to cause its creation, and then it goes away. All the processing is under the control of the account.

A more effective and less error-prone method is simply to create and delete the customer in the account class. However, do localize the use of this feature to a single creator and deletor wherever possible.

10.3   Visualizing Domain Dynamics

As the number of communicating state machines increases, we need a way to visualize the big picture of the domain dynamics. We use interaction diagrams of two kinds, a collaboration diagram that describes the communications between state machine instances without explicit regard to time, and sequence diagrams that describe objects in specific states over time.

Experienced modelers sketch collaboration and sequence diagrams before formalizing state machines to help organize the dynamics in the domain. Once the state machines have been constructed, the collaboration diagrams can be regenerated from the state machines themselves. The result could be sufficiently horrifying to cause reconstruction of the state machines, or, of course, all could be well.

Similarly, various sequence diagrams can be generated from actual execution traces. By establishing a set of initial states and executing the models from the state machines, an execution trace can be produced. The graphic form of this trace is a sequence diagram. Again, the resulting sequence diagram may be more complex or less regular than desired, and this will cause iteration over the state machines.

This is as it should be: We plan our overall domain dynamics, build the individual state machines according to the plan, evaluate the domain dynamics, and modify them as necessary.

10.3.1   Collaboration Diagrams

The work of creating and processing an Order sends signals to and receives signals from the Credit Card Charge and Shipment state machines. A *collaboration diagram* shows signal communication across links between objects and external entities representing actors.

The collaboration diagramof Figure 10.7 shows overall collaboration in a domain as collaborations between arbitrary instances of classes, where the state machine for each object is represented by a box labeled with the name of an arbitrary instance of classes and their corresponding state machine instances.

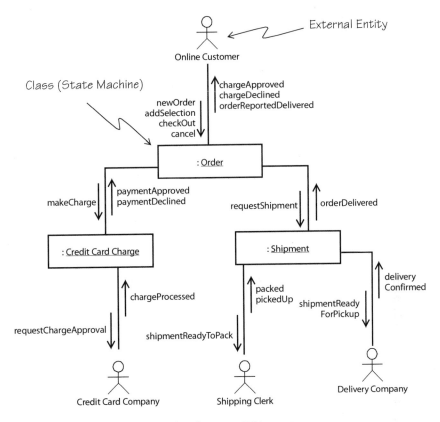

Figure 10.7   *Collaboration Diagram Showing Order, Charge, and Shipment*

The UML syntax for an instance is:

<instance name > : <Class Name>

For example:

Sarzak : Dog

In this case, as in many others, we are concerned with an arbitrary and unspecified object, or, if you prefer, an anonymous object:

: Dog

> UML allows a collaboration diagram to show synchronous method invocations in addition to signals. Because our concern here is communicating state machines, Executable UML suppresses method invocations.
>
> UML uses collaboration diagrams in the context of a single scenario. We have found it valuable to show all the signals between objects, the better to visualize domain dynamics.

It is possible, therefore, to show communication between one instance of an class and another in a particular pattern of execution. The boxes are labeled to distinguish one instance from another.

Each external entity that can generate or receive signals is depicted by a box stereotyped «external entity». Alternatively, an actor symbol suffices.

A collaboration between objects and external entities is shown by one (or more) lines between the participants. A signal sent by one object or external entity and received by another is represented by an arrow[1] from the sender to the receiver. The arrow is annotated with the signal label, name, and the signal parameters. Multiple signals may be associated with a single arrow.

By convention, we omit signals that are generated and received by the same state machine. These details can be seen on the state machine itself.

10.3.2   Concept of a Execution Trace

Definition: An *execution trace* is a sequence of procedures and signals that occurs in response to the arrival of a particular signal when the objects are in specific states and their attributes have specific values.

An execution trace may include activity outside the system: Somewhere along the trace, a signal may be sent to an actor causing the actor to execute some external activity. If the actor responds with a signal, it, as well as the external activity, is considered to be part of the execution trace.

---

[1] UML 1.3 used a single-fleched arrow (sometimes called a half-arrow).
   It means the same thing.

As with use cases, it is helpful sometimes to distinguish between execution traces that are entirely under the control of the system (a single-system interaction), and those that can cross the system boundary (a boundary-crossing interaction).

If a procedure along the execution trace generates more than one signal, the execution trace splits so that two or more legs of the same execution trace are active at the same time.

The definition of the execution trace ("that occurs in response to the arrival of a particular signal when the system is in a particular state") excludes the possibility of one leg *or* another being executed. Because the system is in a known state, at execution time only one choice can be selected.

Each leg of the execution trace eventually terminates. This can happen in one of two ways:

- A state machine enters a state whose procedure sends no more signals. The leg then terminates in this state, and no subsequent activity occurs along the leg.
- A state machine enters a state whose procedure sends a signal to an actor but the actor does not respond. In this case, the activity terminates outside the system.

When a trace enters a state machine that manages contention, the trace may suspend waiting until the resource becomes free. You may choose to regard this as termination of the trace, and begin a new trace for when the resource becomes free.

10.3.3   Sequencing Signals on a Collaboration Diagram

Signals on a collaboration diagram may be numbered to show sequence, as shown in Figure 10.8. The "numbering" scheme forms a tree: 7.1. and 7.2 follow 6, and are concurrent, while 7.2.1 and 7.2.2 follow 7.2 concurrently.

A sequence diagram provides a more graphic view, as discussed in the next section.

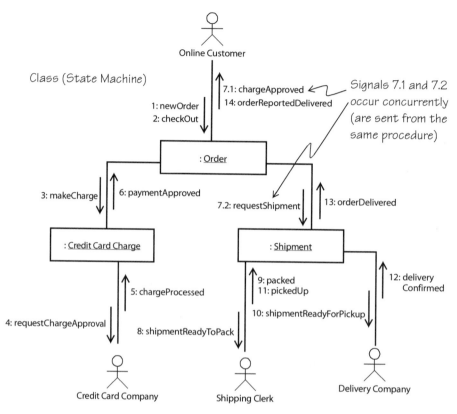

Figure 10.8   *Sequenced Collaboration Diagram*

10.3.4   Sequence Diagram

A *sequence diagram* is a graphical representation of the succession of signals and procedure activations that participate in a particular execution trace.

Figure 10.9 shows a sequence diagram for a successful single-item ordering scenario.

Each column, represented by a dotted line, is an object lifeline. It represents a single object over time. The label at the top of each object lifeline identifies each instance and its class. When only one instance of a class is used in a sequence diagram, we can omit the instance name.

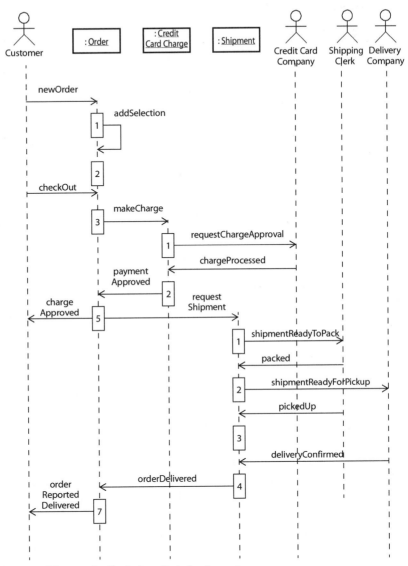

Figure 10.9　*Sequence Diagram for Single-Item Ordering Scenario*

Each object appears separately as the string of states it occupies as it progresses through the scenario; these *activations* are connected by the object's lifeline.

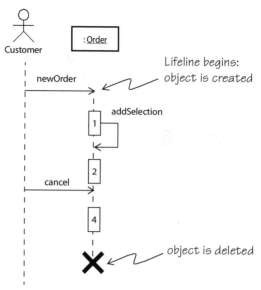

Figure 10.10 *Sequence Diagram Showing Object Creation and Deletion*

Definition: An *activation* is the execution of a single procedure in a state machine instance at some time.

Sources of external signals (actors, such as the customer, the credit card company, the shipping clerk, and the delivery company) are shown as their own columns on the diagram.

The horizontal lines represent signals from one object to another. Each line is labeled with the name of the signal. (To reduce clutter, we do not show lines for the invocation of data-accessor functions of other objects.)

The diagram is laid out along a relative time axis, with the procedures placed on the chart in the order (top to bottom, or vice versa) in which they occur.

Object creation is shown by the presence of the lifeline after the creation signal is received.

Object deletion is shown with a big X at the end of the lifeline, as shown in Figure 10.10.

10.3.5 **Applicability**

Sequence diagrams are most useful as a tool for understanding the interactions between specific objects in a particular context. They are useful to understand some specific scenarios, but not for every possible situation.

After the initial sketches to visualize domain dynamics, manually drawing these beasts—and ensuring they're consistent—is a pain; it's better to derive them from simulations.

Sequence diagrams are also useful to model a particular instance of a use case, with specific values for attributes, starting and ending in specific states. The sequence diagram thus models a particular test case. We take up this topic in Chapter 15: Domain Verification.

Similarly, manually drawing collaboration diagrams is useful to model the desired layering of the state machines, but the collaboration diagram should be generated once the state machines are complete enough to provide useful information.

10.4 **Domain Dynamics**

Executable UML relies on state machines to define processing for a domain. Layering the state machines so they communicate in regular ways and with regular idioms is critical to understanding the domain and how it works.

This chapter focused on declaring the static layering of the state machines, which communicate by sending signals back and forth. The next chapter takes up the topic of defining the rules for the execution of objects.

11

Synchronizing Objects

All[1] the processing that goes on in a domain is the result of executing a procedure in state machine instances.

In Executable UML, every object is in exactly one state at a time, and all objects execute concurrently with respect to one another. An object synchronizes its behavior with another by sending a *signal* that is interpreted by the receiver's state machine as an event. When the event causes a transition in the receiver, the procedure in the destination state *executes after* the action that sent the signal. This is merely cause and effect.

Time is local to each object in Executable UML. There is no global synchronization mechanism and no concept of global time.

This chapter describes the rules for synchronizing objects in Executable UML. We present a summary of the execution rules in gray boxes, and accompanying text describes their implications. Executable UML extends the execution semantics of UML significantly, but consistently.

---

[1] Some processing is activated synchronously by other domains, a topic we address in Chapter 17.

UML places no rules on the model elements that can send or receive signals.

Executable UML uses signals only to synchronize state machine instances, each of which is associated with an object, or, as we shall see later, with a class. State machine instances associated with objects and classes are the only model elements in Executable UML that can send signals and receive events.

Hence, when we say that "an object synchronizes with another object by sending a signal," this is a shorthand for "a state machine instance for an object or a class synchronizes with another state machine instance for an object or a class by sending a signal."

11.1   How to Think about Time

Each concurrently executing object has its own lifeline, which can be synchronized with others by sending signals. This formulation leaves open the question of what "time" on an object lifeline means for each instance.

Consider an object A that sends a signal X to an object C. Once C receives X, it sends a signal Z to B. Object A also immediately sends a signal Y to B. What is the order in which signals arrive at B? Does Y arrive at B first? Or Z?

The Executable UML formalism does not say. There are no rules about the order of receipt of Y and Z, so both of the sequences in Figure 11.1 are legal.

This view of time is similar to Einstein's relativistic view of time. If we transmit a signal to two stars, one which in turn transmits a signal to our second star, it is not known which signal will arrive at the second star first, only that if we send two signals to a single star the signals will arrive in the order we sent them.

The issue extends beyond signal sending to the general question of duration and time. When an instance wants to cause another instance to do something "at three o'clock," how can the two instances agree on when three o'clock actually is? This is a thorny topic in distributed computing and is comprehensively addressed in [1]. Lamport concludes that clock synchronization is not possible, and that each processor can assert reli-

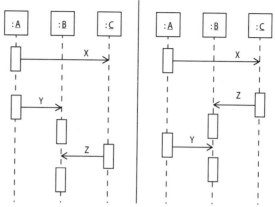

Figure 11.1 *Concurrent Signals*

able statements only about an object lifeline against which it can assign times that do not synchronize with other clocks. In other words, Lamport asserts the Einsteinian view taken by Executable UML.

11.2   Rules about Signals

The following comments refer to the "Rules about Signals" enumerated in the box on page 190.

Specification, not implementation. The primary point to grasp is that these rules are designed to describe required synchronization between objects. This means that when we say that "signals are never lost," we mean that the sender requires the receiver to execute after the signal is sent, and that this is the required order. It is the job of the model compiler to ensure this is so by whatever mechanism it deems appropriate.

No priorities. Similarly, there is no notion of signal priority in these rules, and a modeler cannot arbitrarily accelerate one signal ahead of another. To do so would be equivalent to "going backwards in time."

Sender–receiver instance pair sequencing. We know from Rule 6 that two signals sent from one object to another are received in the order generated. But what happens if signals are outstanding from different senders?

Rules about Signals

1. Signals are never lost: Every signal will be delivered to the object or external entity to which it is directed.
2. A signal is "used up" when it is accepted by an object: The signal then vanishes as a signal and cannot be reused.
3. At some time after a signal is generated, it is made available to the destination object or external entity.
4. When an object completes a procedure, it is now in the new state. Only after completion of the procedure can the object accept a new available signal if any such exist. This is called *run-to-completion.*
5. Multiple signals can be outstanding for a given object, because several objects can be generating signals to a particular receiver during the time the receiver was busy executing a procedure.
6. If a single object generates multiple signals to a receiving instance, the signals will be received in the order generated.
7. If there are signals outstanding for a particular object that were generated by different senders, it is indeterminate which signal will be accepted first.
8. Signals sent to *self* are always accepted before other signals to that instance.

The rule is that there is no rule.

This is analogous to a set of computers sending messages directly one to another. The receiver can distinguish, with certainty, the sending order of messages from the same sender, but the receiver cannot determine the exact ordering of the sending of messages from two different computers. Even time stamping doesn't help because of the problem of synchronizing clocks.

This is precisely the situation described above with the three signals. If the behavior of the recipient is different depending on whether Y arrives at B before Z, and such indeterminacy is undesirable, then the model must be changed to synchronize the signals correctly.

A model compiler may, and probably will, employ mechanisms to resend signals, and it could use priorities on signals. The model compiler is required only to preserve the synchronization built into your executable models.

Rules about Procedures

---

1. Only one state procedure of a given object can be in execution at any time because an object can be in one state at a time.
2. Multiple accessors of an object may execute concurrently, with respect to each other and to state procedures.
3. Procedures in different objects can be executing simultaneously.
4. A procedure takes time, possibly none, to execute.
5. Once initiated, a procedure of an object must complete before another signal can be accepted by the same object. It is the modeler's responsibility to ensure that the procedure will complete.
6. A procedure must leave data describing its own instance consistently. If a procedure updates an attribute of its own instance, it must update all attributes that are derived from the first attribute.
7. If a procedure creates or deletes instances of its own class, it must ensure that any links involving those instances are made consistent with the rules stated on the class diagram (by action or by signal).
8. When a procedure completes, it must leave the system consistent, either by writing data (described in the three rules above) or by generating signals to cause other objects to come into conformance with the data changes made by the sender of the signal.

11.3 Rules about Procedures

The following comments refer to the "Rules about Procedures" enumerated in the box above.

Run-to-completion. The key rule here (Procedures: 4) is called *run-to-completion*. It states that the procedure must complete its execution before the object can recognize another signal directed to the state machine. This is a standard UML rule for execution carried over into Executable UML without change.

It is not literally correct to say that a procedure is "atomic" or "uninterruptable," because other procedures in other objects can, in fact, interrupt and even access data in use by other procedures. This is important because you must design your models to take into account other objects accessing the same data as you.

Propagation. It can take time for the system to become entirely consistent, because it takes time for signals to propagate and procedures to execute.

In the real world, when you receive your bank statement, it is likely that the balance shown on the statement differs from that shown in your checkbook. This is due to the fact that it takes time for checks and deposits to arrive at the bank and to be reflected in the account's balance. The work you go through to verify the statement is correct takes care of this by accounting for uncleared checks and unrecorded deposits.

Inconsistency must be explicitly prohibited in the Executable UML models by synchronization, and by carefully managing data access.

11.4   Rules about Data Access

Because many procedures can execute simultaneously, it is possible for them to access the same object memory at the same time, causing subtle and potentially fatal errors.

Definition: The *data access set* is the set of all data items read, written, or referenced by a single activation.

When the data access sets of several activations intersect, and there is at least one writer, there is the possibility of *data access conflict*. It is the responsibility of the developer to avoid data access conflict. Consequently, there is no substitute for disciplined data access strategies, described below.

Single writers of independent attributes. Good practice generally assures that data access conflict cannot occur or is not relevant. Consider, for example, an object that is the sole writer of its own attributes. The writer updates independent attributes in certain states, and those attributes can then be read consistently by multiple readers.

Dependent attributes. If the attributes are dependent on one another in some way, care must be taken to ensure that data is read consistently. Consider an account that requires the address of a customer expressed as

---

Information Hiding, Encapsulation, Readers, and Writers

Encapsulation is an implementation mechanism used by object-oriented designers and object-oriented model compilers to protect clients from changes in data structure. When we say "multiple readers," this is shorthand for "multiple clients invoking encapsulating functions." We do not mean to violate encapsulation, though the model compiler could choose to do so and we'd never know it!

Encapsulation does not prevent data access conflict, as multiple things are happening at once. An object can be writing its own data at the same time as another object (a client) is re-entrantly invoking the encapsulating function. This is the normal situation in multithreaded environments, and Executable UML is multithreaded in the sense that each object executes concurrently.

Similarly, if there are several writers, they are just clients invoking encapsulating functions, and encapsulation—at the level of information hiding—is not violated. However, encapsulation also covers behavior, and in this case it is fair to say encapsulation has at least been compromised. Hence, it is good practice to localize behavior in a single class, preferably the class that creates the instance.

---

multiple attributes: street and city. It is possible for the street to be read just before the customer updates the address but after the city is updated. This will send mail to the new street address in the old city.

It can be difficult to achieve data consistency for this case in a general way, but it is often easy to do if you are willing to impose some rules on the modeler or on the model compiler. For example, you could require the two attributes to be modeled as one, address, and carry out operations requiring the city or street in a separate domain. Alternatively, you could require the model compiler to impose a transaction over the affected attributes or to lock them. In some cases, the model could guarantee account statements will never be issued at the same time customers' addresses are updated.

This kind of assumption must be documented in the assumptions for the domain, and if necessary, as a requirement on the model compiler.

Do not put a transition on every state in the target state machine to handle an event for reading the dependent attributes; for example, a readAddress event on the Customer.

Do not send signals from one state machine to another to indicate locking of the data. The number of signals can quickly explode and become unmanageable.

A model compiler can easily implement a data locking or transaction strategy uniformly, once you've modeled the required data accesses properly.

Multiple Writers. Similarly, it is the responsibility of the modeler to ensure there is no data access conflict if there are multiple writers; for example, if an order and a credit card charge can both write the total amount of the order. Obviously, this is bad practice, and the model should be changed to ensure a single writer in almost all cases.

11.5   Delayed Signals and Time Events

Executable UML allows for a signal to be sent at some time in the future.

> **generate** *<signal>* **to** *<instance handle>* **delay** *<duration>;*

This action causes the signal to be received after the duration expires. (It is not relevant whether the sender delays sending the signal, or the receiver delays receipt. That decision is properly the domain of the model compiler.)

A delayed signal cannot be manipulated directly by the application, because the delayed signal belongs in the domain of the model compiler, and any such manipulation would constitute domain pollution.

However, there remains a need to refer to a delayed signal, for example, to cancel it:

> **cancel** *<signal>* **from** *<instance handle>* **to** *<instance handle>;*

There can be at most one delayed signal of a given name (an event specification) outstanding for each sender-receiver instance pair at any one time.

Finally, a delayed signal can be caused to be produced at an exact time. The "exact time" is determined by the sender or receiver, according to the wishes of the model compiler.

> **generate** *<signal>* **to** *<instance handle>* **at** *<exact time>;*

This type of signal can be canceled too, using the same *cancel* action.

11.6 Rules, Rules, Rules

This chapter describes the rules for communicating objects in Executable UML. These rules are not optional: The models are executable, and they must have a defined execution semantics.

You gotta have rules.

11.7 References

[1] Lamport, Leslie, and P. M. Melliar-Smith. "Synchronizing clocks in the presence of faults," in *Journal of the ACM*, 32(1):52–78, January 1985.

12

Using Lifecycles

The previous chapters described the mechanics of state machines in terms of statechart diagrams and state transition tables.

This chapter presents some suggestions and techniques for how to go about formulating these models effectively. Here we describe a set of techniques for forming individual lifecycles and refactoring them so they are each simple to understand.

Refactoring statechart diagrams, as well as simply understanding them better, can lead to a need to iterate the class diagram, creating classes for special purposes and to house various kinds of behavior.

12.1 Statechart Diagram Construction Techniques

12.1.1 Modeling Intention

When you come to build the statechart diagram for a class, take the perspective of an object and ask what you need to do to fulfill your destiny. (See [1] for an example of this type of thinking.)

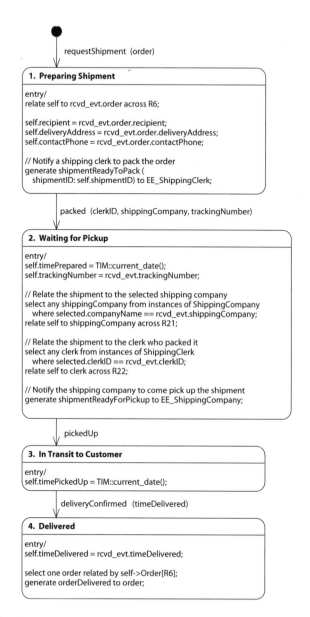

Figure 12.1   *Shipment Lifecycle*

A Shipment, for example, has to make something happen to cause itself to be packed, sent, and delivered to the customer. There's no point in just lying around waiting to be delivered. A Shipment needs to pack itself.

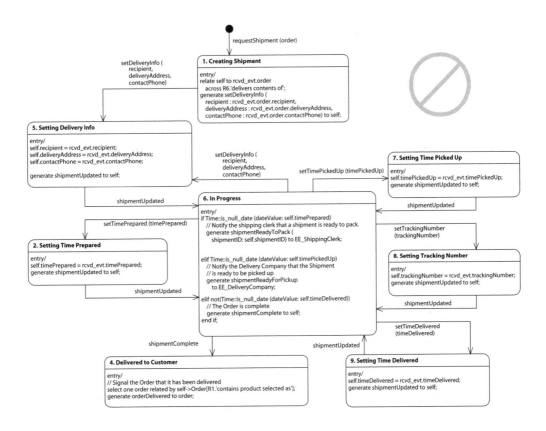

Figure 12.2   *Spider Lifecycle of Shipment*

Once packed, it needs to get picked up by the shipping company and then delivered to the Customer. The shipment drives itself through a sequence of states, as shown in Figure 12.1.

Contrast the lifecycle of Figure 12.1 with an approach that models class behaviors as operations that "get" and "set" related attributes of the class, as shown in Figure 12.2. This model, in contrast to Figure 12.1, does not model a lifecycle, rather it relies on something else to take care of requesting to pack, contacting the shipping company, and so forth. This leads to a "spider" shape, with a central state that waits for requests and a set of legs that respond to each request.

Moreover, this statechart diagram obscures key sequencing issues. There's nothing in the model to determine if a particular operation is valid or not. For example, if we wanted to make sure that we did not set the timeDelivered until the shipment was picked up, we'd need some logic to determine what the state of the object really is, possibly by testing attributes values. This is error-prone, especially if some logic is duplicated in different states.

Alternatively, we may add specific state attributes and then test them. The result in both cases is to encode the state in the logic of the procedures instead of making it explicit. This type of model quickly becomes unmanageable on screen and in concept.

The whole purpose of the lifecycle is to model intention: to capture the desire, on behalf of an object, to get something done.

12.1.2   Modeling Progression

Accumulating attribute values. Many classes that model a request or task accumulate attribute values over time. For example, not all the attributes of the Shipment are set when the object is created.

This does not contradict the rule that every attribute must be meaningful for every object, because every attribute must be meaningful for any object *at some time during the object's lifetime.* In other words, it's perfectly all right for a Shipment to have a trackingNumber that's not yet specified until we get to the state where the shipment is picked up.

The Shipment statechart diagram in Figure 12.1 shows how different attributes of the Shipment are set in different states. Figure 12.3 shows how these attribute values accumulate over time.

Formally, these accumulating attributes have multiplicity 0..1, in contrast to the 1..1 multiplicity of attributes whose values are set at object creation.

State	Accumulating Attribute Values
1. Creating Shipment	shipmentID (set by creation) deliverTo deliveryDestination deliveryContactPhone
2. Waiting to be Picked Up	timePrepared
3. In Transit to Customer	timePickedUp trackingNumber
4. Delivered to Customer	timeDelivered

Figure 12.3   *Accumulating Attributes*

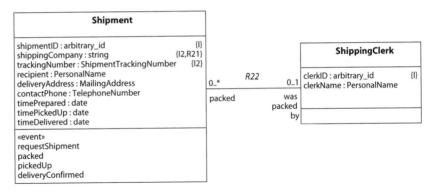

Figure 12.4   *Shipment and Clerk Association*

Accumulating links. This same notion also applies to links: Some conditional associations become meaningful only in certain states. For example, we might have an association between a Shipment and the Shipping Clerk who packed that Shipment, as shown in Figure 12.4.

We create the link in state 2: Waiting For Pickup, as shown in Figure 12.5.

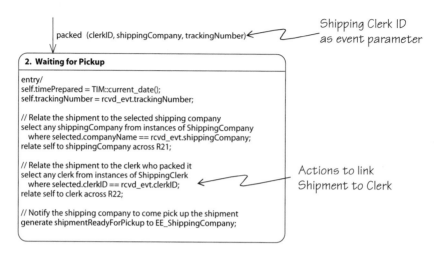

Figure 12.5   *Establishing the Association between Shipment and Shipping Clerk*

12.1.3   Simultaneous Signals

Capture concurrency in the domain in the model. When a shipment is created we may simultaneously request a shipping clerk to pack the shipment and request a tracking number from the shipping company. The shipment can then receive two distinct signals: packed when the shipment is packed and trackingNumberAssigned when the shipping company assigns a tracking number. Figure 12.6 shows how the Shipment model accommodates this concurrency by having two distinct paths, accepting the two signals in either order.

Since we request the packing and the tracking number simultaneously and the operations (outside of the domain) occur simultaneously, we can receive the packed and trackingNumberAssigned signals in either order. The Shipment statechart diagram must be capable of handling both sequences. It does this by having states and transitions such that either sequence of signals (packed, trackingNumberAssigned), or (trackingNumberAssigned, packed) cause the correct behavior of the state machine.

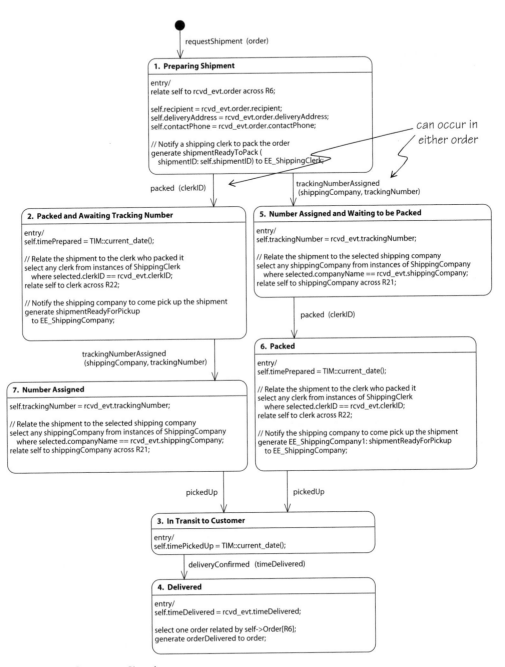

Figure 12.6   *Concurrent Signals*

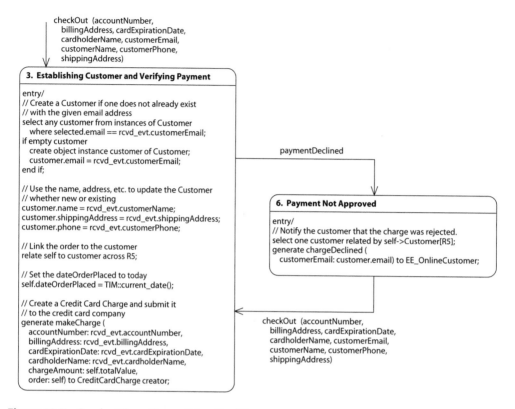

checkOut (accountNumber,
billingAddress, cardExpirationDate,
cardholderName, customerEmail,
customerName, customerPhone,
shippingAddress)

3. Establishing Customer and Verifying Payment

entry/
// Create a Customer if one does not already exist
// with the given email address
select any customer from instances of Customer
   where selected.email == rcvd_evt.customerEmail;
if empty customer
   create object instance customer of Customer;
   customer.email = rcvd_evt.customerEmail;
end if;

// Use the name, address, etc. to update the Customer
// whether new or existing
customer.name = rcvd_evt.customerName;
customer.shippingAddress = rcvd_evt.shippingAddress;
customer.phone = rcvd_evt.customerPhone;

// Link the order to the customer
relate self to customer across R5;

// Set the dateOrderPlaced to today
self.dateOrderPlaced = TIM::current_date();

// Create a Credit Card Charge and submit it
// to the credit card company
generate makeCharge (
   accountNumber: rcvd_evt.accountNumber,
   billingAddress: rcvd_evt.billingAddress,
   cardExpirationDate: rcvd_evt.cardExpirationDate,
   cardholderName: rcvd_evt.cardholderName,
   chargeAmount: self.totalValue,
   order: self) to CreditCardCharge creator;

paymentDeclined

6. Payment Not Approved

entry/
// Notify the customer that the charge was rejected.
select one customer related by self->Customer[R5];
generate chargeDeclined (
   customerEmail: customer.email) to EE_OnlineCustomer;

checkOut (accountNumber,
billingAddress, cardExpirationDate,
cardholderName, customerEmail,
customerName, customerPhone,
shippingAddress)

Figure 12.7   *Resubmitting a Charge Using CheckOut*

12.1.4   Distinct Signals

In the Order statechart diagram of Figure 9.10 on page 163, once a Charge is rejected (the paymentDeclined signal), there is no way to resubmit that charge. In practice, we would like to give the customer the opportunity to retry the charge. Perhaps the customer mistyped the number, or perhaps the link to the credit card company was down. Figure 12.7 shows a simple solution that incorporates a new transition from Payment Not Approved to Verifying Payment triggered by another checkOut signal.

While this solution is adequate, it has some problems. Do we really want the customer also to change the shipping information? Since the check-Out event carries both payment and shipping information, the updated model certainly allows this to happen.

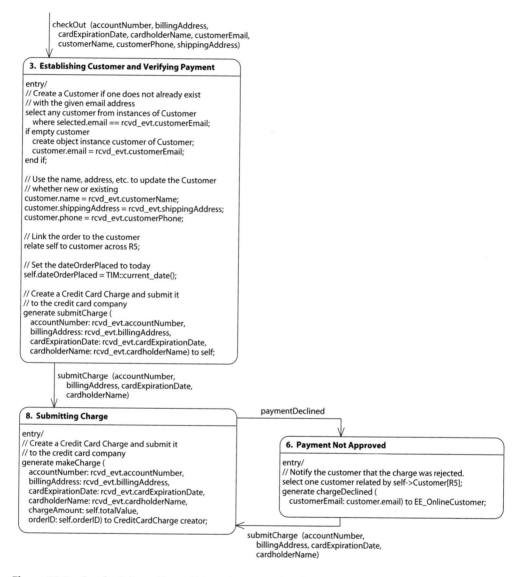

Figure 12.8   *Resubmitting a Charge Using a Separate submitCharge signal*

If the intent is for the customer only to resubmit the payment information, then we should add a new signal, submitCharge. Figure 12.8 shows an updated statechart diagram with this new signal. Checking out an order for the first time carries both shipping and payment information. After the shipping information is set, the state's procedure generates submitCharge to self. The next state's procedure then processes the charge. Subsequent retries of the charge are signaled using submitCharge. By abstracting and using distinct signals, resubmitting the charge cannot have the unintended consequence of changing the shipping information.

12.2   Reworking the Class Diagram

The process of developing statechart diagrams often reveals the need for additional attributes, associations, and even new classes. It can also reveal errors and inconsistencies in an apparently reasonable class diagram.

We cannot emphasize enough that the process of building Executable UML models is incremental and iterative. Systems are developed incrementally, starting from simple models with limited capabilities; additional capabilities are added incrementally. Within each increment, we iterate over the various models. Writing the statechart diagrams and their state procedures may reveal insufficiencies that can best be corrected by reworking the class diagram.

Do not fall into the trap of trying to build the perfect class diagram before looking at the statechart diagrams; and do not treat the class diagram as immutable when working on the statechart diagrams

On the other hand, after several models, you will develop more confidence that your class diagram is correct, and be able to produce good class diagrams before you spend much time on statechart diagrams.

12.2.1   Refactoring Behavior

As you iterate over the models, developing increasingly sophisticated models of a domain, consider opportunities to keep the individual classes simple by refactoring the behavior in one class diagram into separate classes.

The Order as shown in Figure 9.10 on page 163 comes into existence when a Customer selects the first item. Its lifecycle encompasses the entire product selection, purchase, shipping, and delivery processes.

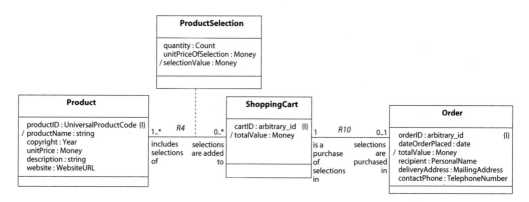

Figure 12.9 *Shopping Cart Class and Related Associations*

We could refactor so that a different kind of Order is not created until the product selections are complete and the payment has been accepted. This requires a separate class that collects the selections and arranges payment: a Shopping Cart. Figure 12.9 shows how the Shopping Cart class relates to the product and to the order.

A Shopping Cart is created when the customer starts shopping. Selections can then be added to the cart. When the customer checks out, the charge is attempted against the customer's account, and an order is created.

This approach leads to a simple Shopping Cart statechart diagram and a simpler Order statechart diagram, as shown in Figure 12.10 and Figure 12.11.

The Shopping Cart is distinct from the Order. The Shopping Cart has Product Selections added to and removed from it. The Order, on the other hand, is not placed until the Shopping Cart is checked out.

12.2.2 Saving Signals in Data

When a state machine instance executes a procedure, the procedure runs to completion before any outstanding signal is processed. Signals are never saved for a later time by the machinery of Executable UML.

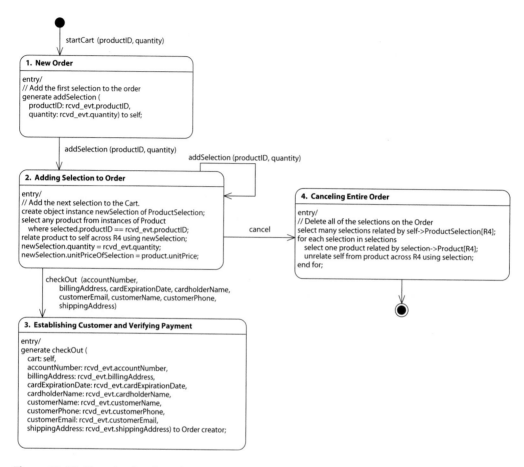

Figure 12.10 *Shopping Cart Statechart Diagram*

In some situations, an object needs to complete a sequence of states before it can process new requests. For each shipment, the shipping clerk should select the books to be shipped, pack the box, seal it, attach the shipping label, and deposit the box at the loading dock. But while the clerk is working on one shipment, other shipments can be created.

In the model, when a shipment is created, it signals the Shipping Clerk shipmentReady so that the clerk can pack and ship the shipment. In every state except Clerk Idle, the clerk is busy and cannot readily respond to the signal.

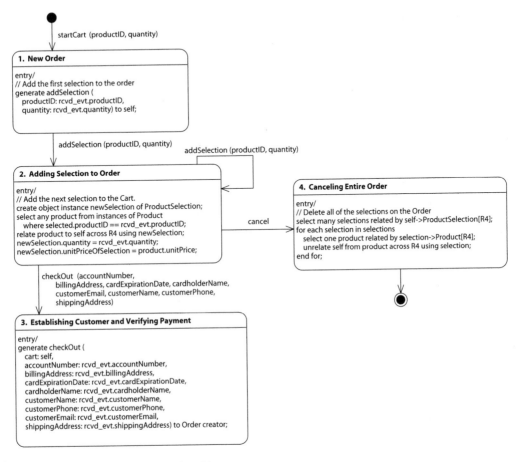

Figure 12.11 *Simpler Order Statechart Diagram*

One option is to add a new transition from every non-idle state to start up a new packaging activity. (This is the cause of those shipments you receive with somebody else's stuff.) Of course, that new packaging activity can also be interrupted, requiring never-ending epicycles of interrupted shipments.

A better solution is for the Clerk to *ignore* the signal in all but the Idle state and then check for any unpacked shipments upon re-entry to the Idle state. Figure 12.12 shows the Shipping Clerk statechart diagram and the state transition table for the signal shipmentReady.

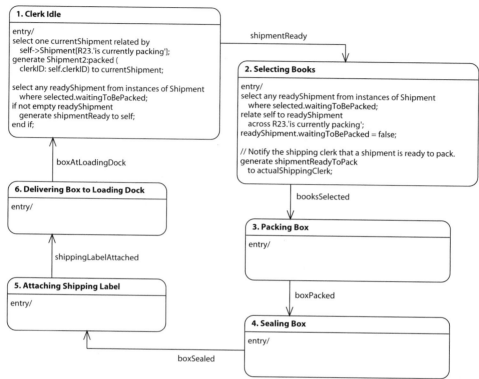

Figure 12.12 *Statechart Diagram and State Transition Table for Shipping Clerk*

	shipment Ready	books Selected	box Packed	box Sealed	shipping Label Attached	boxAt Loading Dock
Clerk Idle	Selecting Books	Can't Happen	Can't Happen	Can't Happen	Can't Happen	Can't Happen
Selecting Books	Event Ignored	Packing Box	Can't Happen	Can't Happen	Can't Happen	Can't Happen
Packing Box	Event Ignored	Can't Happen	Sealing Box	Can't Happen	Can't Happen	Can't Happen
Sealing Box	Event Ignored	Can't Happen	Can't Happen	Attaching Sh. Label	Can't Happen	Can't Happen
Attaching Shipping Label	Event Ignored	Can't Happen	Can't Happen	Can't Happen	Deliv. Box To L. Dock	Can't Happen
Delivering Box to Loading Dock	Event Ignored	Can't Happen	Can't Happen	Can't Happen	Can't Happen	Clerk Idle

The column for the shipmentReady event shows the event ignored in all but the Idle state.

The Shipment not only records information about the shipment, but it also represents the request: The shipment is a trace of the signal sent to the clerk. When created, the shipment sets its own waitingToBePacked attribute to true and signals the Shipping Clerk by sending the shipment-Ready signal. If the Shipping Clerk is idle, it[1] transitions out of the Idle state and starts working. But if the ShippingClerk is not idle, it ignores the shipmentReady, thus continuing to process its current Shipment. Only when the Shipping Clerk completes the current shipment—upon re-entry to the Idle state—does it look for another Shipment to process. Any shipment that has come into existence during the time the shipping clerk was busy will have waitingToBePacked set to true.

We see this pattern most commonly in systems in which there is competition for a resource: many shipments all trying to be packed by a shipping clerk, many movement requests all trying to be serviced by an elevator, and so on.

When an object cannot respond to a signal because it is in the midst of a sequence of states, use a separate class to represent the request. The request then signals the requested object. The requested object is then responsible for checking for more unserviced instances of the request and processing that request.

This is a special case of contention because there is but one shipping clerk and the contention is managed by that single control point, the single shipping clerk. When there are multiple clerks (i.e., multiple servers for a request), there must be some mechanism to manage the contention, which we describe in the next chapter, Chapter 13: Relationship Dynamics, along with more strategies for dealing with such contention issues.

---

[1] The impersonal pronoun "it" is used here intentionally to indicate that we are talking about the Shipping Clerk state machine, not the shipping clerk person.

12.3   References

[1]   Foster, Alan Dean: *Dark Star.* Ballantine, New York, 1974.

The book was made into a film of the same name by John Carpenter and Dan O'Bannon, released in 1974. (Carpenter's idea of special effects back then was to make a spacesuit out of aluminum TV-dinner trays.) The plot involves Bomb #20, which decides, against the wishes of the TV-dinner-tray-clad crew, that it has to fulfill its destiny, namely exploding potential supernovae before they threaten future colonies.

13

Relationship Dynamics

When we formalize a relationship on a class diagram, we capture its static aspects, but we do not capture how the relationship is created or destroyed, nor how it evolves over time. These issues are properly the work of state machines, which are used also to formalize dynamics of relationships between objects.

When an association has an interesting lifecycle, we may abstract an association class and use a statechart diagram to formalize its lifecycle. Because the association class is a class, there is no difference between a state machine for an association class and a state machine for an ordinary, boring class.

Some associations, however, involve some sort of competition for objects representing resources. For each of these, we'll construct a single *class-based state machine* that provides the necessary single point of control for managing the contention.

Class hierarchies can have statechart diagrams at the subclass level, the superclass level, or both. Polymorphic signals can be sent to objects with-

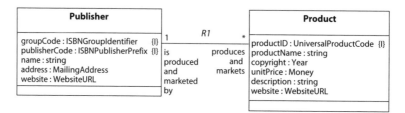

Figure 13.1   *Class Diagram for Publisher and Product*

out regard to their subclass at run time. In addition, objects can reclassify themselves within generalization hierarchies as their role changes over time.

This chapter describes these various forms of relationship dynamics.

13.1   Dynamically Simple Associations

Links between objects are created and deleted over time. There are several approaches to modeling associations. We can

- Create the objects and the link synchronously, and not build any statechart diagrams for the classes or the links.
- Build a statechart diagram for one class or the other, endowing that class with the responsibility of managing creation and deletion of the objects and the link.
- Build a statechart diagram for both classes, assigning the responsibilities for creating and deleting the link between the classes.
- Abstract the association as an association class and use the association class to house the statechart diagram.

13.1.1   Associations without Explicit Lifecycles

Some associations simply exist. In the online bookstore, new products are made available for sale and some products are discontinued. Each product is published by some Publisher. That means that whenever a new product is added, there must be a publisher for that product, as shown in Figure 13.1.

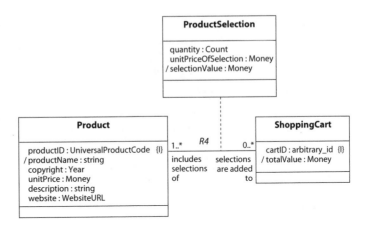

Figure 13.2   *Class Diagram for Product Selection*

The association multiplicity specifies the rules for what must happen when instances of the classes are created and deleted. For example, whenever a product is created or deleted, a link for the Publisher PRODUCES AND MARKETS Product association must be correspondingly created or deleted. If a Publisher is deleted, all the products published by that publisher must be deleted as well.

13.1.2   **Dynamic Associations with Association Classes**

Other associations progress through distinct stages during which different rules and policies apply. These associations are modeled using an association class with a state machine.

The state machine prescribes the behavior of a typical unspecified link. Each link executes this same state machine, and, just as with a class, we use the term *state machine instance* to refer to the execution of the state machine by a particular instance of the association.

The Product Selection association class in the online bookstore, shown in Figure 13.2, has a statechart diagram that receives signals to add a new selection, to change the quantity of an existing selection, and to remove the selection from the shopping cart.

The statechart diagram for the Product Selection is shown in Figure 13.3.

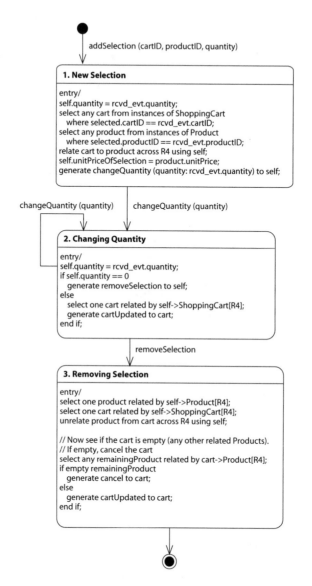

Figure 13.3 *Statechart Diagram for Product Selection*

Since a Shopping Cart must have at least one Product (multiplicity 1..*), when a Product Selection is deleted it checks to see if its deletion would result in an empty cart; if the selection being deleted is the last one in the cart, it signals the cart to delete itself, thereby maintaining the integrity of

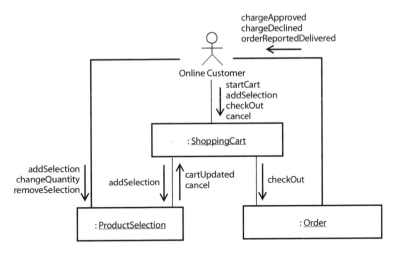

Figure 13.4 *Collaboration between Product Selection and Order*

the association. The coordination between the classes and the online customer external entity is shown in the collaboration diagram in Figure 13.4.

13.2   Associations Involving Competition

13.2.1   Competition in the Domain

For some associations, linking objects involves competition for resources. In the online bookstore, customers do not have to compete with one another to place an order; the store can accept as many orders as it likes.[1] Similarly, the association between publishers and products is not competitive; there is a seemingly unending supply of new books (about UML?), and any publisher's desire to publish a book can be satisfied.

In contrast, consider how shipping clerks select shipments to pack. The Shipping Clerk statechart diagram shown previously in Figure 12.12 on page 210 works correctly if there is a single shipping clerk. When the clerk

---

[1] We have purposely ignored the problem of limited stock and back ordering. All the mechanisms necessary to build those models are covered in this section.

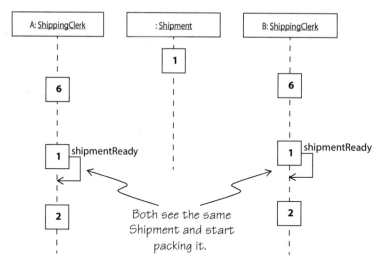

Figure 13.5   *Sequence Diagram Illustrating Contention for the Same Order*

finishes one shipment, he looks for another shipment that is waiting to be packed. If he finds one, he selects that shipment and begins packing it.

If there are several shipping clerks, this simple approach will not work. Because shipping clerks operate concurrently, several shipping clerks could try to pack and ship the same shipment at the same time. Specifically, and you can try this scenario yourself, if two clerks finish at the same time (i.e., two Clerk objects transition to state 1 simultaneously, as shown in Figure 12.12), both will see the same shipment in state 1 and start packing that same order. Figure 13.5 is a sequence diagram illustrating this scenario. Absent any control mechanism, there would be a fight between shipping clerks for shipments to pack.[2]

Having the shipments select a shipping clerk does not solve the problem. The shipments behave concurrently too, and they could also compete for shipping clerks.

---

[2] Yeah, right.

13.2.2 Competition in the Models

We address contention problems of this sort by providing a single control point that serializes competing requests. In the real world, this serialization can be enforced by a variety of mechanisms: a line of customers (a manifestation of a policy requiring that customers be served in order of their arrival) or a person who assigns shipments to shipping clerks based on some other policy, such as the size of the order or the priority status of the associated customer.

In Executable UML, the serialization required to manage competition is accomplished by a single state machine for one of the participants in the competition: an *assigner*.

Definition: An *assigner* is a state machine that serves as a single point of control for creating links on competitive associations.

An assigner resolves contention by selecting and assigning objects for the task at hand. Assigners are typically class-based state machines, though as we shall see, in some cases contention can be managed by an instance-based state machine. A class-based state machine has only one instance, thereby providing the crucial single point of control needed for creating instances of competitive associations.

Just as you may build zero or one instance-based state machine for each class, you may build zero or one class-based state machines for each class.

To model the competition for the shipping clerk, for example, there will be *two* state machines, one that applies for *each* shipping clerk object, and one that coordinates *all* shipping clerks. If, at some time, there are six shipping clerks, then there will be seven state machine instances executing, one for each of the six shipping clerks and one for the shipping clerk class. The shipping clerk and shipment assignment is used as an example used below.

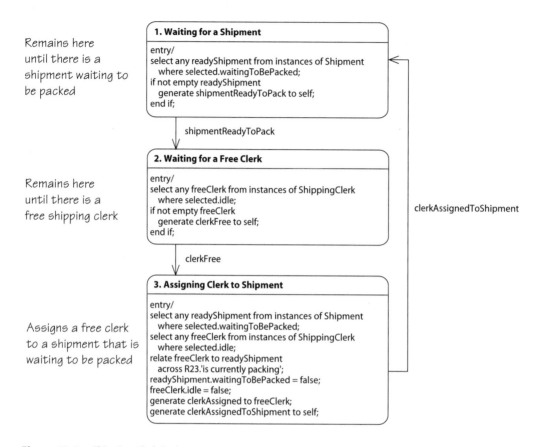

Remains here
until there is a
shipment waiting to
be packed

Remains here
until there is a
free shipping clerk

Assigns a free clerk
to a shipment that is
waiting to be packed

Figure 13.6 *Shipping Clerk Assigner*

13.2.3 An Example

Figure 13.6 shows a fairly common form of assigner. This statechart diagram has two waiting states (states 1 and 2) that correspond to waiting for a shipment ready to be packed, and waiting for an idle shipping clerk. (Executable UML models do not have direct access to the states of the state machines, except in the synchronous create operation.) To know when the two objects are ready, we have added a boolean attribute waitingToBePacked to the Shipment class and a corresponding boolean attribute idle to the Shipping Clerk.

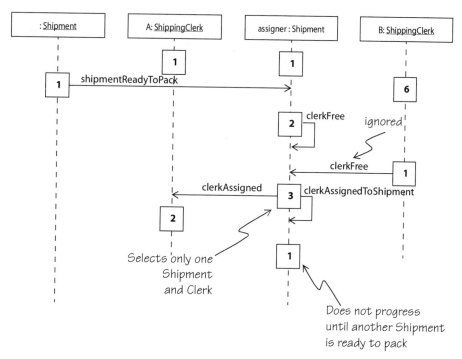

Figure 13.7 *Sequence Diagram Showing an Assigner Managing Competition*

The third state is where the actual association takes place. Only when there is a shipment waiting to be packed and a shipping clerk available to pack it do we enter this third state. According to some policy, the actions select an idle shipping clerk and a shipment waiting to be packed, establish the association, and update the state attributes of the participating classes synchronously so as to avoid reselecting the same object before the idle shipping clerk starts packing.

To understand the operation of the assigner more fully, examine the sequence diagram in Figure 13.7.

Assume the assigner starts in state 1, Waiting for a Shipment, and that the procedure has already been executed. When a shipment is ready to be packed, it requests a shipping clerk by generating the signal shipment-ReadyToPack. The shipment assigner receives this signal and transitions to state 2, Waiting for a Free Clerk.

On arrival in state 2, the assigner executes the procedure. An action determines if there is a free shipping clerk by reading the value of the idle attribute for all clerks. If there is an idle clerk (attribute Clerk.idle true), an action generates a signal clerkFree to itself to cause transition to the third state where the association is made.

Should there be no idle clerks, the assigner waits until it receives an occurrence of clerkFree (the same signal specification), from a shipping clerk recently become idle. This is how the assigner handles both assigning a shipping clerk immediately when one is already idle, and assigning a shipping clerk when one becomes available. Note the similarity to the situation described in Section 12.2.2: Saving Signals in Data: It is the same.

Once the association between the shipping clerk and the shipment is made in state 3, Assigning Clerk to Shipment, the assigner generates a clerkAssigned signal to the selected shipping clerk to go about his business (it could as easily have been the shipment—one of the two has to take charge), and the assigner generates a signal to itself to make a transition into state 1: Waiting for a Shipment. The procedure in this state mirrors the behavior of the procedure in state 2: If there is a shipment waitingTo-BePacked, an action generates a signal to itself to cause transition into the next state, and if not, the state machine waits for a shipment to generate a signal to indicate its readiness to be packed.

The state machine ignores shipmentReady signals while in states 2 and 3, and clerkIdle signals while in states 3 and 1. In both cases, there is a trace of the signal stored as an attribute value in the sending objects, again just as in Section 12.2.2: Saving Signals in Data.

13.2.4   Multi-Instance Contention

Figure 13.8 shows an expanded business with several warehouses, where each warehouse services orders for customers who live nearby.

Obviously enough, we cannot assign any arbitrary shipping clerk to pack a shipment. Instead, we have to assign a shipment to a shipping clerk who works in the right warehouse.

If we created a single assigner to handle all assignments, we'd have the added burden of checking to see whether any ready shipments were at

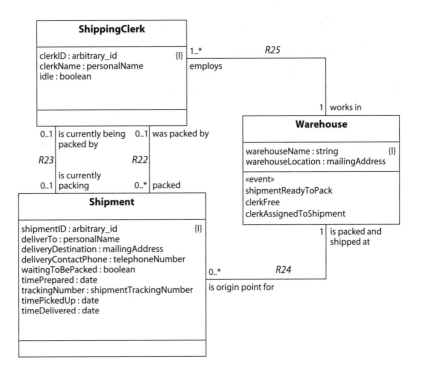

Figure 13.8 *Class Diagram Including Warehouse Associations*

warehouses with idle clerks. A simpler approach is to have one state machine instance per warehouse that manages the assignment.

In this case, we build the contention handling into the warehouse class. There is one state machine per warehouse and the warehouse state machine selects shipping clerks—but only from those shipping clerks assigned to the warehouse. This approach works because the instances of the shipping clerks are partitioned by warehouse, so multiple warehouses cannot compete for the same shipping clerk. The statechart diagram for the warehouse is shown in Figure 13.9.

This statechart diagram replaces the single-instance assigner in the previous section. It is almost identical to the Shipping Clerk assigner, except the selection criteria in each state include a "related by" clause to select only shipments and clerks related to the warehouse.

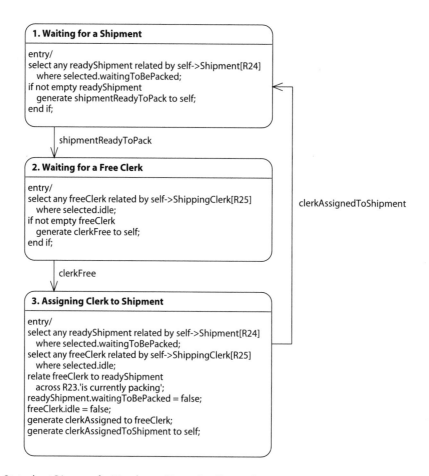

1. Waiting for a Shipment

entry/
select any readyShipment related by self->Shipment[R24]
  where selected.waitingToBePacked;
if not empty readyShipment
  generate shipmentReadyToPack to self;
end if;

shipmentReadyToPack

2. Waiting for a Free Clerk

entry/
select any freeClerk related by self->ShippingClerk[R25]
  where selected.idle;
if not empty freeClerk
  generate clerkFree to self;
end if;

clerkAssignedToShipment

clerkFree

3. Assigning Clerk to Shipment

entry/
select any readyShipment related by self->Shipment[R24]
  where selected.waitingToBePacked;
select any freeClerk related by self->ShippingClerk[R25]
  where selected.idle;
relate freeClerk to readyShipment
  across R23.'is currently packing';
readyShipment.waitingToBePacked = false;
freeClerk.idle = false;
generate clerkAssigned to freeClerk;
generate clerkAssignedToShipment to self;

Figure 13.9 *Statechart Diagram for Warehouse Managing Contention*

If the warehouse had interesting behavior of its own (pretty unlikely in this example), the contention handling could be moved to an association class between the shipping clerk and the warehouse.

13.2.5 Object Selection and Selection Policies

An assigner and its state procedures realize the selection criteria for the associated objects. There is always a policy at work. It could be as simple as selecting an arbitrary object (the shipment–shipping clerk example) or it could be arbitrarily complex. We could, for example, depending on expected quarterly results for the company, choose to ship high-value shipments as soon as possible, or delay them until the beginning of the next quarter. Likewise, we could assign work to clerks in a way that balances the number of shipping jobs processed by each clerk in a shift.

When there is a policy to be followed, the models must have classes and attributes to support the policy; their number and complexity depends entirely on the policy. In all cases, the policy will be localized in the procedure for the state that relates the objects.

The policy supported by an assigner may result in a state machine that is more complex than the three-state form presented so far. Leon Starr's elevator example [1], and the complete online bookstore case study provide additional examples of assigners.

13.3   Dynamics in Generalization Hierarchies

Classes arranged in a generalization hierarchy may also have lifecycles formalized using state machines. Depending on the behavioral differences between the subclasses, we may choose to model separate lifecycles for each subclass or a single lifecycle for the superclass.

13.3.1   Superclass State Machines

Figure 6.13 on page 97 showed how the Product is divided into subclasses for Books, Recordings, and Software. This distinction, however, does not make a difference to the basic lifecycle of a Product. All products are proposed, approved for sale, finally discontinued from sale, and possibly reinstated. Since this basic lifecycle applies to all types of Product, we formalize a single superclass state machine, as shown in Figure 13.10.

13.3.2   Subclass State Machines

Some specializations are created because the different subclasses exhibit different behavior. The bookstore has two different kinds of clerks: shipping clerks who pack and ship customer orders and stock clerks who receive product and stock the warehouse. Different subclasses, as shown in Figure 13.11, are a useful way of modeling these distinct roles.

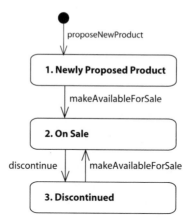

Figure 13.10 *Product Superclass Lifecycle*

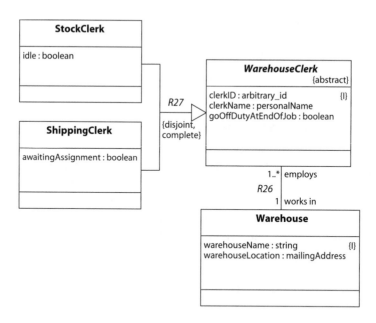

Figure 13.11 *Warehouse Clerk Subclasses*

> ### Multiple Lifecycles and Multiple Hierarchies
>
> It is possible to create a state machine for a superclass and state machines for corresponding subclasses. Similarly, when a class is subclassed into multiple hierarchies, we can create separate state machines for each of these subclasses.
>
> Since all these superclass and subclasses are just classes, they can each have their own state machines, but we have found that in most cases, only one set of state machines is needed.
>
> In other words, don't build multiple statechart diagrams even though you can.

When subclasses are created because the behaviors of the subclasses are different, create separate state machines for each subclass. The state machine of a stock clerk involves activities associated with restocking the warehouse as product arrives from the publishers, while the quite different activities of the shipping clerk were illustrated in the state machine in Figure 12.12 on page 210.

13.4   Polymorphic Events and Polymorphic Signals

When a supervisor tells a clerk to go off-duty, the supervisor does not care whether the clerk is a shipping clerk or a stock clerk. Similarly, when an action sends a signal to an object in a class hierarchy, the sender should not need to know the subclass of the object. Rather, the signal is *polymorphic*.

Definition: A *polymorphic signal* is a signal delivered at run time to a specific state machine for a class in a generalization hierarchy.

In keeping with the distinction between events and signals in UML, we define also a *polymorphic event*.

Definition: A *polymorphic event* is an event that has many potential receiving state machines in a generalization hierarchy.

> ### Rules about Polymorphic Signals
>
> 1. A polymorphic event specification is declared for an abstract superclass, and the corresponding event may be received by any of the superclass's subclasses.
> 2. A polymorphic signal cannot be received by the superclass in which the event is specified, only in the subclasses.
> 3. The polymorphic signal must be able to be received in every branch in the superclass's hierarchy, so that the polymorphic signal occurrence always has a receiving state machine instance.
> 4. At run time, the polymorphic signal occurrence is received as an event by exactly one state machine instance in a given hierarchy.
> 5. If a superclass has repeated specializations, each class in the specialization hierarchy must be able to receive an occurrence of the event.
> 6. If a superclass has multiple specializations, the polymorphic signal occurrence is received by at most one state machine instance in *each* specialization hierarchy.

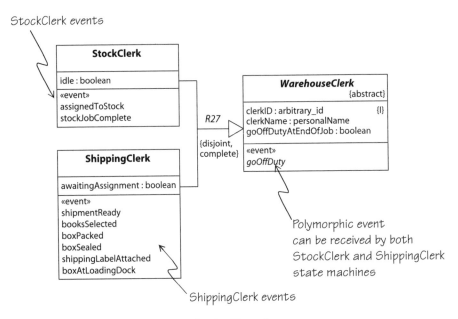

Figure 13.12 *Polymorphic Events in a Generalization Hierarchy*

A polymorphic event is abstracted—and so given a name and a signature—at the superclass level. The signal is then received by the subclass state machine depending on the type at run time. Figure 13.12 illustrates the events received by the different warehouse clerk subclasses and the polymorphic event that can be received by any warehouse clerk, adding the events to the operations compartment for illustrative purposes only.

Each subclass's state machine may respond differently to the same signals, so that, for example, a shipping clerk may be required to complete a shipment first while a stock clerk can knock off immediately.

The sender doesn't have to know the subclass of the clerk. The following action language is perfectly valid because the goOffDuty signal can be sent to any instance of a Clerk:

> **select any** *luckyClerk* **from instances of** *WarehouseClerk;*
> *luckyClerk.goOffDutyAtEndOfJob = true;*
> **generate** *goOffDuty* **to** *luckyClerk;*

The following is not valid, because shipmentReady can be sent only to a shipping clerk, and one cannot determine whether the assignedClerk refers to a stock clerk or a shipping clerk:

> **select any** *assignedClerk* **from instances of** *ShippingClerk;*
> **generate** *shipmentReady* **to** *assignedClerk;*

Signals defined at a subclass level can be sent only to instances of that subclass, while polymorphic signals can be sent to any instance of the superclass.

The rules for polymorphic signals mirror those for polymorphic operations in UML or an object-oriented program. We declare the event in an abstract superclass, and each subclass has to be able to interpret the signal should it arrive at run time.

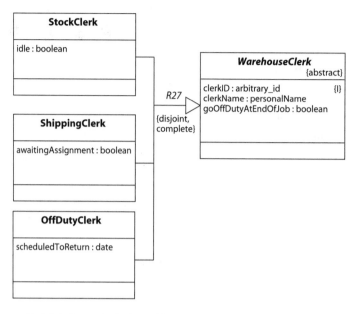

Figure 13.13 *Warehouse Clerk Subclasses, Including OffDutyClerk*

13.5   Reclassification

In the bookstore, the warehouse makes a policy of hiring clerks who can take on several roles, so that the shipping clerk is really just one kind of a more general warehouse clerk. Sometimes a warehouse clerk may be processing shipments, at other times the same clerk may be assigned to restock product, and at still other times the clerk may be off duty.

Because a single clerk can take on several roles during a shift, there must be a mechanism to support *reclassification,* in which an instance of one subclass becomes an instance of a different subclass in the same hierarchy.

Executable UML recognizes the need for reclassification in the context of a generalization and specialization hierarchy when an object playing one role starts to play another role.

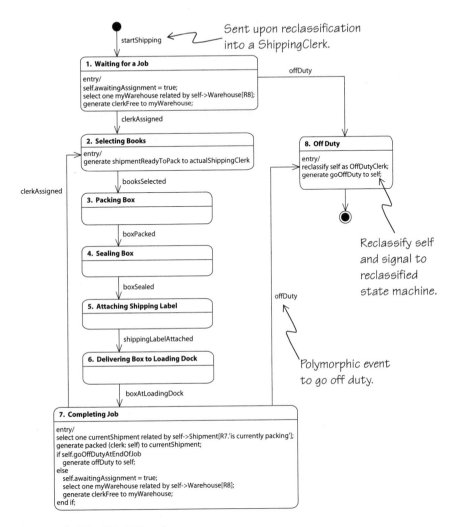

Figure 13.14 *Shipping Clerk (on Duty) Lifecycle*

This fact imposes certain additional rules for formalizing lifecycles as state machines. Chief among these is that each of the stages in the life of the object must fall into one and only one of the subclasses. Since a clerk may now be "off duty" without being assigned to stock or to ship, we need to create a third OffDutyClerk subclass to account for those clerks who are neither stocking nor shipping, as shown in Figure 13.13.

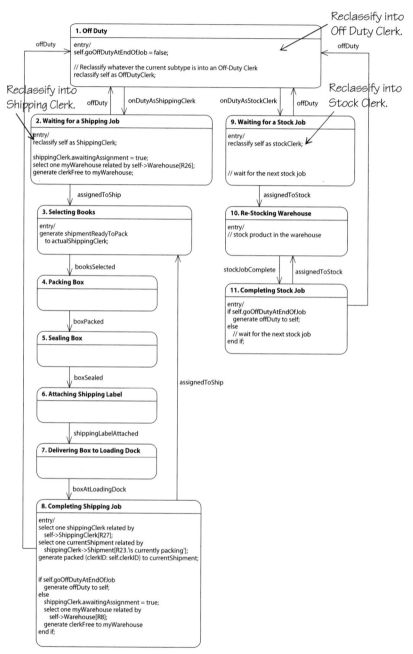

1. Off Duty

entry/
self.goOffDutyAtEndOfJob = false;

// Reclassify whatever the current subtype is into an Off-Duty Clerk
reclassify self as OffDutyClerk;

Reclassify into
Off Duty Clerk.

offDuty

offDuty

Reclassify into
Shipping Clerk.

offDuty   onDutyAsShippingClerk   onDutyAsStockClerk   offDuty

Reclassify into
Stock Clerk.

2. Waiting for a Shipping Job

entry/
reclassify self as ShippingClerk;

shippingClerk.awaitingAssignment = true;
select one myWarehouse related by self->Warehouse[R26];
generate clerkFree to myWarehouse;

9. Waiting for a Stock Job

entry/
reclassify self as stockClerk;

// wait for the next stock job

assignedToShip

assignedToStock

3. Selecting Books

entry/
generate shipmentReadyToPack
   to actualShippingClerk;

10. Re-Stocking Warehouse

entry/
// stock product in the warehouse

booksSelected

stockJobComplete   assignedToStock

4. Packing Box

11. Completing Stock Job

entry/
if self.goOffDutyAtEndOfJob
   generate offDuty to self;
else
   // wait for the next stock job
end if;

boxPacked

5. Sealing Box

boxSealed

assignedToShip

6. Attaching Shipping Label

shippingLabelAttached

7. Delivering Box to Loading Dock

boxAtLoadingDock

8. Completing Shipping Job

entry/
select one shippingClerk related by
   self->ShippingClerk[R27];
select one currentShipment related by
   shippingClerk->Shipment[R23.'is currently packing'];
generate packed (clerkID: self.clerkID) to currentShipment;

if self.goOffDutyAtEndOfJob
   generate offDuty to self;
else
   shippingClerk.awaitingAssignment = true;
   select one myWarehouse related by
      self->Warehouse[R8];
   generate clerkFree to myWarehouse;
end if;

Figure 13.15 *Warehouse Clerk (Superclass) Statechart Diagram Showing Reclassification*

13.5.1   Superclass State Machine

One approach to modeling reclassification is to formalize the whole lifecycle of the superclass. We can create a single Warehouse Clerk state machine that contains all the states of a Shipping Clerk and all the states of a Stock Clerk. This lifecycle also includes an off-duty state where a clerk is neither shipping nor stocking. Figure 13.14 shows this model.

The state procedures in a superclass lifecycle make use of reclassification actions. For the Warehouse Clerk, these reclassifications take place in states 1, 2, and 9.

13.5.2   Subclass State Machines with Reclassification

The single lifecycle shown in Figure 13.14 has many states and incorporates the lifecycles of each of the subclasses. An alternative to building a superclass state machine is to build individual state machines for each of the subclasses. The actions in one subclass's final state cause reclassification.

Reclassification state machines each have initial and final states. Reclassification occurs in the final state of each subclass's state machine. An action in the final state sends a signal to the reclassified subclass.

Figure 13.15 shows a ShippingClerk statechart diagram with reclassification. When the Shipping Clerk comes into existence (the initial pseudostate), it receives a startShipping event. When the Shipping Clerk is signaled to go off duty, it reclassifies into an Off Duty Clerk and signals goOffDuty. The initial and final states of the Stock Clerk and the Off Duty Clerk manage their reclassification in a similar manner.

Now that we have a set of techniques to model classes and relationships between them, we turn our attention to applying these techniques to describe the dynamics of a domain as a whole.

13.6   References

[1] Starr, Leon: *Executable UML: The Elevator Case Study.* Model Integration, LLC., 2001.

14

Domain Dynamics

The statechart diagrams for classes and associations provide a detailed description of the dynamics of each separate component of the domain. In this chapter, we turn our attention to understanding the dynamics of the domain as a whole.

To make the models comprehensible, control should be partitioned across the several classes. The criteria for control partitioning include limiting control in a state machine to single objects and refactoring into new classes and state machines as necessary.

At the macro level in a domain, there are several ways to manage each macro control cycle. In some cases, an actor can push control and the associated parameters to cause the affected state machines to do work, or control and parameters may be pulled by an actor making a request. The macro control cycles must be linked together to form a coherent whole.

Control can be delegated in several ways, principally hierarchically or across a network of state machines. In many systems, the inputs are known to arrive in certain orders, and we may use this knowledge to simplify the state machines and their communications.

This chapter describes these several control strategies to facilitate building clean control schemes for the domain.

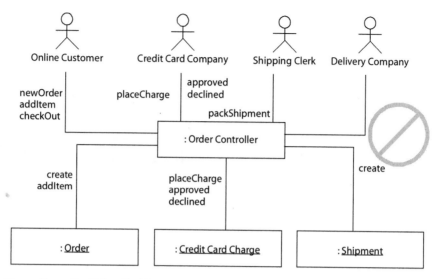

Figure 14.1   *Mongo Controller Object (Bad Design—No Control Partitioning)*

14.1   Partitioning Control

The first rule of partitioning control is you do not make controller objects.

The second rule of partitioning control is *you do not make controller objects.*[1]

A controller object comes about when developers create objects to match use cases. As an example of poor partitioning—actually, no partitioning at all—see the single Order Controller class in Figure 14.1, which controls an entire use case for making and fulfilling an order. All communication goes through the Order Controller, which "simplifies" the collaboration diagram, but leaves the order controller with a very large statechart diagram.

The statechart diagrams of the objects—the real order, the charge, and the shipment—tend to be trivially simple, but that of the controller object is large and complex. These controller statechart diagrams quickly become unmanageable as we incrementally develop the domain.

---

[1] With apologies to Chuck Palahniuk [1].

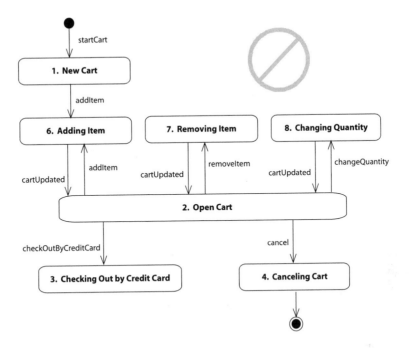

Figure 14.2 *Messy Shopping Cart*

We recommend against a single controller object for this reason.

The single controller is an extreme example of a state machine controlling all the objects in a domain. Controller objects, usually singletons, result in systems that fail to exploit the concurrency in the domain—a disastrous result in these days of distributed systems.

Consider what happens when we extend the online bookstore to allow customers to remove items from a cart and to change the quantity of individual selections. When we add these signals to the shopping cart, we create a complex nest of states and transitions. The signals addSelection, removeSelection, changeQuantity, cancelCart, and checkOut can each be accepted in most of the states of the shopping cart, as shown in Figure 14.2.

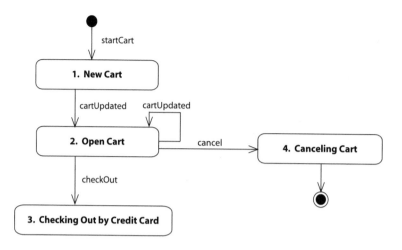

Figure 14.3 *Cleaned-Up Cart*

The cart now exhibits a typical characteristic of complex state machines. Like the single-instance controller, it is a single instance (of the cart) trying to manage multiple instances (of the selections). The solution is to factor out the management of a single selection into a separate Selection statechart diagram. Items are added to the cart by creating instances of Selection; the cart receives only cartUpdated events and does not need to deal with the management of the selection instances. This results in a greatly simplified cart model, as shown in Figure 14.3.

In summary, a domain with good control partitioning exhibits three key characteristics:

- Behavior is partitioned among the classes in a domain: One class does not do all the work, leaving other classes simply to respond to signals and be updated.
- Behavior can be (re)factored to simplify behavior so long as the factored behavior describes some concept in the domain.
- Behavior is partitioned among objects: We generally build state machines to represent the behavior of single objects, not of the class as a whole. (Assigners are sometimes an exception.)

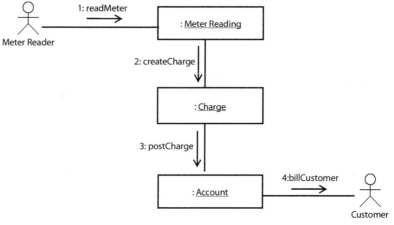

Figure 14.4 *Push Control*

14.2   Control Strategies

In addition to partitioning behavior into the lifecycles of objects, we need some strategies to organize control from a broad perspective. First among these is whether control is "pushed" or "pulled" along a single macro control cycle. In the online bookstore, for example, the checkout of a shopping cart pushes control and the associated parameters forward until the order is shipped or held up on back-order. In contrast, we could have organized control so a shipping clerk attempted to pack a shipment by requesting the next order, thus "pulling" the data toward the shipment.

The online bookstore ordering control cycle naturally favors pushing control, so let's examine a more neutral example.

14.2.1   Push and Pull Control

A power company sends bills to customers based on the meter readings taken at the customers' electric meters. These readings are taken on different days by different meter readers reading meters along different routes.

In a simple model where each meter is billed separately, we can imagine a simple control scheme where a bill is pushed out when a meter is read, as shown schematically in Figure 14.4.

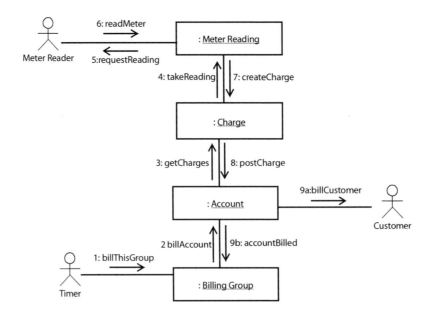

Figure 14.5 *Pure Pull Approach*

But while some customers are billed for a single meter only, other customers are billed for readings taken at several meters. These meters may be along different routes read on different days. A push scheme for the control would require a separate bill per reading, which is not what the customer wants.

In addition, to even out the work in the billing department, bills are produced on fixed days each month according to a billing cycle, which also argues against a simple push approach.

On the other hand, a pure pull approach would create the bills on the accounts' cycle dates. The bills would then request readings of the meters. These requests would then dispatch the meter readers to read the meters. The meter readings would then be posted to the bills. Only when all the readings were collected could the bills be sent, as illustrated in Figure 14.5.

Such an approach might be reasonable if the all the meters were read immediately (e.g., through electronic remote meter reading), but in practice, both bills and readings are scheduled in advance according to billing cycles and meter routes.

We therefore have two macro control cycles: one focused on the meter readings and the other centered around billing cycles.

14.2.2 The Pivot Point

Control can be divided so that it is pushed one way and pulled from another.

Meter readings will be pushed into the system, but only so far as they create charges against the accounts. The charges are then not billed until the account to which they are posted is billed according to its regular billing cycle. Likewise, the account cannot be billed unless there are charges posted to the account from the meter readings.

The *pivot point* is the class at which the flow of control changes from push to pull or vice versa.

Figure 14.6 shows how a meter reading pushes data down to the charges, while the bill pulls data up from the charges to assemble the monthly bill. The pivot point is the class that represents the highest common factor of the data: We break meter readings down into charges and assemble them into the monthly bill.

The best pivot point is that class at which the data can no longer be pushed or pulled usefully to the next step. Hence, the data in the power

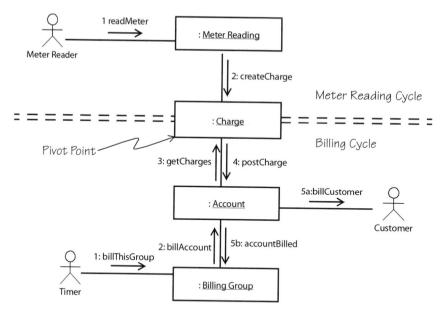

Figure 14.6   *Two Concurrent Cycles with a Pivot Point*

company billing example can be pushed until it is represented as a charge, but it can't be pushed further. This matches the macro cycle of the meter reading. Similarly, the data can be pulled as far back as the charge, but charges can't be created until the meter is actually read. This corresponds to the macro cycle of the billings. Both views support the notion that the pivot point is the charge class.

14.2.3   Finding the Pivot

The concepts of mixed push-and-pull control and the pivot point are important when a domain has multiple concurrent activities that need to rendezvous. In the case of the power company, meter reading and billing occur concurrently in the large, but the production of an individual bill requires the completion of individual meter readings. In the case of the online bookstore, three macro control cycles rendezvous: Customers place orders, product is available in inventory, and shipping clerks prepare shipments.

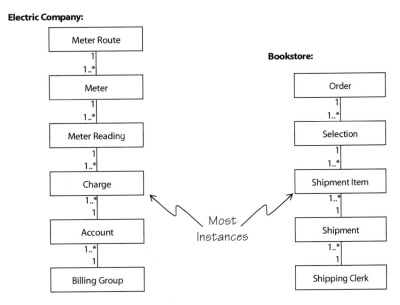

Figure 14.7   *Class with the Most Instances is a Candidate Pivot Point*

To find the pivot point, examine the class diagram for the classes that participate in the collaborations, and use the class that has the most instances as the pivot point. Often the class with the most instances in a collaboration is the one that represents the last useful stage of disassembly into more objects. The next step is to reassemble the many objects into larger units based on some controlling incident.

The left side of Figure 14.7 shows a simplified class diagram for the electric company. (To clarify the assembly and disassembly of the data, the diagram replaces all association classes with simple associations.) Data can be pushed as far as the Charge before the charges need to be accumulated based on the time at which the Billing Groups are sent out. The Charge is the "highest common factor" of Billing Groups and Meter Readings, hence the pivot point for the electricity company is the Charge.

Similarly, for the bookstore, the pivot point is the shipment. The order comprises several shipment items that are in turn assembled into a shipment by a shipping clerk.

In addition to this data assembly/disassembly criterion, assigners factor strongly into the problem of organizing control. When one object in a competitive association is available but the other side is not, control can go only as far as the assigner, so the macro control cycle is terminated.

For example, when a customer places an order, the order and its selections can be pushed only as far as inventory is available. The order is then pulled by the shipment assigner only when sufficient stock is available to create the shipment. Finally, the shipment is pulled by the shipping clerk only when a clerk can be assigned to pack the shipment.

14.3   Delegation of Control

Not all state machines participate equally in the dynamics of a domain. In planning a system of more than a few state machines, we need to delegate responsibilities to the various state machines.

14.3.1   Hierarchical Delegation

Some state machines tell others what to do and get an immediate response. For example, the order tells the credit card charge to make a charge, and the order receives an immediate response indicating success or failure. Similarly, the shipment makes a request to the delivery company and receives a response first to assign a tracking number and then to confirm delivery. These examples of hierarchical control can be seen in Figure 14.8.

14.3.2   Networked Delegation

Hierarchical delegation expects responses from the state machine it controls. By contrast, networked delegation does not require a response from

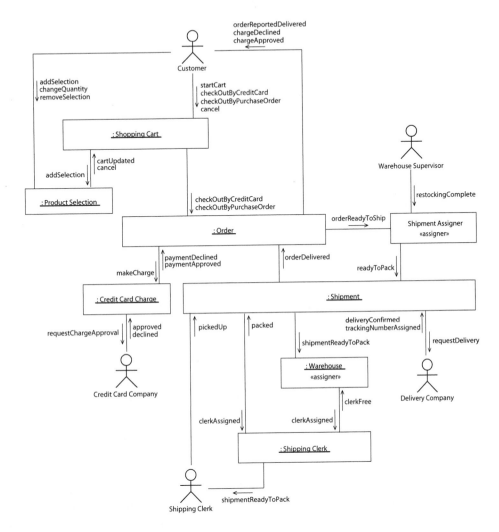

Figure 14.8 *Bookstore Collaboration*

the state machine under control. For example, the order delegates to the shipment assigner to indicate the order is ready to ship. The next thing the order finds out is that the order has actually been delivered. The order does not need to interpose itself, like an interfering manager, at every step.

The precise flow of control is illustrated by the table in Figure 14.9.

The effect of this delegation is that the order statechart diagram does not deal with the details of how the order's contents are packed and shipped. As far as the order is concerned, once the credit card charge is approved, the order is on its way until its delivery is confirmed.

Another example of networked delegation is the sequence that notifies the delivery company to pick up the shipment, but the shipping clerk actually records that the shipment was picked up.

Deciding whether to use hierarchical delegation or networked delegation, or for that matter, deciding who is in charge, is not always an easy task. However, there are no wrong answers. The best approach is to sketch something out and see which is simpler. The diagrams are also planning tools for organizing the state machines in a domain.

14.3.3 Distributing Control in Associations

An especially knotty situation occurs when two classes are apparently at the same level of control. In the examples above, it's clear the shipment is subordinate to the order and the charge and that the selection is a part of the shopping cart, so the shopping cart cannot complete until all the selections are made. But it's not at all clear a clerk should seek out customers, rather than having customers seek out clerks. To use another example, should the cow demilk itself or the milk decow itself? [2]

The answer is neither. The best way to model this situation is to construct an association class, Milking, between the cow and the batch of milk and have the association class manage the control. After all, it is the milking that has the behavior. In some sense, the cow and the milk are unwilling participants.

Similarly, in the case of the customer and clerk, we build an association class, Service, that manages the association. In this case, there is also contention for clerks if we empower the customer, and for customers if we pay the clerks' commission, as described in Chapter 13: Relationship Dynamics.

---

[2] This delightful example is due to Meilir Page-Jones [2].

Activity	Signal
The Order signals the Shipment Assigner that it is ready to be packed and shipped.	orderReadyToShip
The Shipment Assigner selects the available inventory, creates a Shipment, and adds the ShipmentItems to it.	readyToPack
The Shipment signals the Warehouse that a shipment is ready to pack.	shipmentReadyToPack
The Warehouse selects a shipping clerk and assigns the clerk to pack the Shipment.	clerkAssigned
The Shipping Clerk packs the box and signals the Shipment.	packed
The Shipment notifies the Delivery Company that a shipment is ready for pickup.	requestDelivery
The Shipping Clerk records that the Delivery Company has picked up the Shipment.	pickedUp
The Shipping Company reports that the Shipment has been delivered.	deliveryConfirmed
The Shipment signals the Order that it has been delivered.	orderDelivered
The Order notifies the Customer that the Shipment has been reported delivered.	orderReportedDelivered

Figure 14.9 *Activities and Signals*

14.4 Input Conditioning

Partitioning control into concurrently executing state machine instances requires their synchronization, but this can introduce more complexity than was removed by the original partitioning of control.

Consider, as an example, the synchronization between the selection and the shopping cart. Broadly:

- Creation of a selection requires the prior creation of a cart.

- Several selections can be made at once because objects execute concurrently, requiring interselection coordination.
- After checkout, no more selections can be made, which requires coordination with the cart.
- Cancellation of the order must prohibit further selections.

The difficulty is that these rules are not trivial to enforce in the general case. Worse, in reality, the customer is actually only doing one thing at a time, so preventing all this concurrent behavior is a waste of time.

14.4.1 Input Sequencing

Realistically, the customer is going to be doing only one thing at a time and will do those things in a particular order: create a cart, make a sequence of selections, and check out. As long as the inputs are presented this way, the statechart diagrams will remain simple.

We can construct the models for the bookstore domain subject to the assumption that the signals are presented in this general order. This assumption is a requirement on the domain(s) that provide(s) the signals, in this example, on the user interface domain. By making these sets of assumptions–requirement pairs across the bridges between the domains, the problem of sequencing is pushed out of the application domain and down to the domains that provide the signals. This is feasible only because the customer will do only one thing at a time.

The assumption can be formalized by constructing an activity diagram for the use case (Figure 14.10), showing the order in which the application domain accepts the signals. The activity diagram assumes that each activity terminates before the customer is able to start the next one. Should these sequencing assumptions not be realized, the state machines will not operate as hoped.

Any server domain that provides the signals according to the order specified on the activity diagram will work: a web GUI, a Windows GUI, a command-line interface, or an XML document parser. The application domain does not say how the signals are obtained, only the order in which they must be provided.

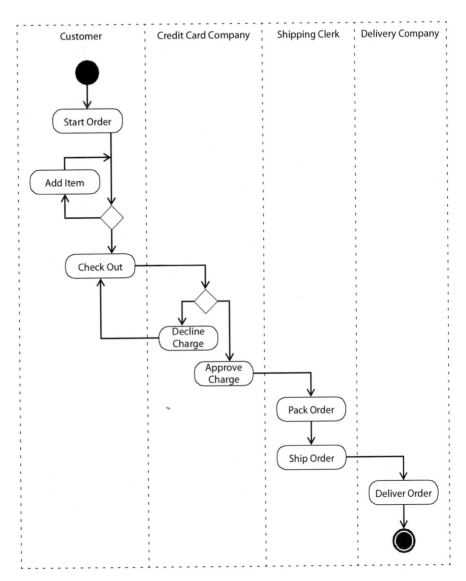

Figure 14.10 *Activity Diagram Showing Input Sequencing*

14.4.2 Distributing the Inputs

The inverse of sequencing the inputs to simplify the state machines is the distribution of the inputs from a form or other user interface mechanism across multiple state machines.

It is not unusual for a form to provide values that describe several classes, such as Selection.quantity and Charge.chargeNumber. Intuitively, these inputs arrive at once with a single signal directed to a single state machine. The receiving state machine passes on unused data items as signal parameters to other state machines, which may in turn pass on further data items to other state machines. The overall pattern is to single-thread the signal through the several state machines, effectively sequencing them—unnecessarily. In addition, the state machines are unnecessarily coupled by the signal parameters that must be passed on through state actions. Note, for example, how the checkOut signal to the Order carries shipping information that is simply stored in the Order until the charge is approved.

An alternative approach is to distribute a set of signals to the state machines that use the associated signal parameters and thereby reduce the coupling. Once the form is accepted, all the signals become available to all the state machines, and there is once again a synchronization problem.

The solution is the same as above: Condition the inputs so that each signal is completely processed before the next is accepted. This rule becomes an assumption placed on the bridge to the user interface, which can readily meet the requirement by treating acceptance of the form as a sequence of signals, each treated as a single system interaction. The pattern for that interaction is also defined by the activity diagram in Figure 14.10.

14.5 Distributed Dynamics

To build halfway decent UML models (executable or not), you have to have a plan for distributing the dynamics. Failure to do so leads to "controller objects" that require change every time anything changes in the requirements. A more robust approach distributes dynamics according to a limited set of idioms such as those presented here.

14.6 References

[1] Palahniuk, Chuck: *Fight Club.* WW Norton and Company, 1996. "The first rule of Fight Club is you do not talk about Fight Club. The second rule of Fight Club is *you do not talk about Fight Club.*"

[2] Page-Jones, Meilir: *Fundamentals of Object-Oriented Design in UML.* Addison-Wesley, Boston, 2000.

15

Domain Verification

The models we have built *are* the application, or some fragment of it. After we've done all this work to create these Executable UML models, complete with constraints and executable actions, it only makes sense that we actually execute these models to ensure they produce the desired behavior.

There are different kinds of verification that can be applied to the models. *Static verification* is the kind of checking a modeling tool does. A tool that understands the semantics of Executable UML can check to make sure that the models are constructed properly—classes have attributes, attributes have types and constraints, states have procedures, procedure action language compiles correctly, and so forth.

This chapter focuses on *dynamic verification*—the process of running actual test cases against the models, just as you would test a Java or C program. After all, the models are executable, so most of the techniques you already know about how to write and run software tests apply equally.

While this chapter appears near the end of the book, remember that domain verification is an ongoing process throughout the life of a project. Just as we recommended developing models incrementally, we recommend testing the models incrementally as well.

This chapter provides a starting point for understanding how to establish test vectors from use cases and from the models, how to execute them automatically, and how to link unit test cases together to make system tests. For a more complete treatise, see a book that focuses on testing.

15.1   Finding Unit Tests for a Single Use Case

Rather than trying to take on a whole use case, we can deal with it piece by piece, one activity at a time. Each activity is defined in terms of a set of preconditions, a single initiating signal, and a set of postconditions.[1]

There may be several possible paths through each use case, such as Add Item to Order, because a use case is a specification of a set of possible behaviors. Each path is determined by combinations of system state and values for signal parameters, and each potential path through the use case is a *scenario*.

Definition: A *scenario* is the planned execution of a use case with ranges of values for signal parameters, initial states for state machine instances, and ranges of values for attributes of objects, so that there is only path through the model.

A scenario is the basis for each test case we want to execute, and each actual execution of a scenario is a test case.

To determine each test case, we must establish the system state and signal parameter values for the objects that distinguish the different scenarios.

To determine the objects that potentially participate in a scenario, use the collaboration diagram and the statechart diagrams to trace through the scenario informally and determine what state machines need to be considered and how many different instances of each are required.

In Add Item to Order, depicted in Figure 15.1, we have an arbitrary unspecified instance of an Order, a product with a quantity on hand,

---

[1] Unit tests apply to single-system interaction use cases, while system tests apply to activities grouped into larger use cases. We can use activity diagrams to show interactions between use cases at any level.

Add Item to Order (orderNumber, productID, quantity)

Add Item to Order adds a quantity of a given product to an existing order. The quantity requested must be capable of being satisfied from the stock on hand.

Preconditions:

- An Order identified by orderNumber exists; it is not expired and it is not yet checked out.
- The product identified by productID is stocked by the store.
- The quantity is a number greater than zero and less than the stock on hand of the product.

Postconditions:

- The Order is not empty, is not checked out, and is not expired.
- The quantity on hand of the product identified by the productID is reduced by the quantity selected.
- The product is included in the order with the given quantity.
- The total value of the order is increased by the unit price of the product times the quantity selected.

Figure 15.1   *Use Case Add Item to Order*

---

and—depending on the scenario—some number of selections. Herein lies a problem: There are several scenarios for a use case, and we generally determine which scenarios actually exist as we trace through what we believe to be a single scenario.

Happily, the preconditions help narrow the choices. For example, Add Item to Order has a precondition that the quantity on hand is greater than zero and less than stock on hand. Were that precondition missing or more loosely defined, there could be several scenarios: one for quantity less than zero, one where the quantity requested is greater than the stock on hand, and another when the quantity requested can be satisfied.

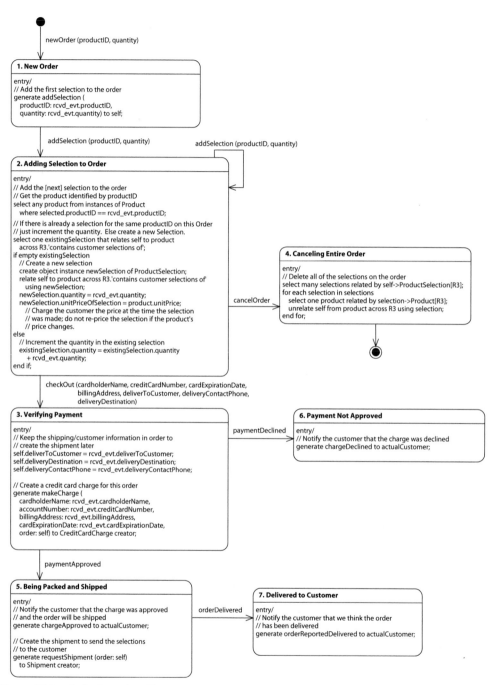

Figure 15.2   *Order Statechart Diagram*

In general, whenever a value is tested so it falls into several ranges, as above, each possible outcome leads to a different path and, therefore, to a different scenario.

Another source of scenarios is the current state of the objects involved. To establish the initial state for state machine instances, examine the state-chart diagram to find the state that meets the preconditions. In the Order statechart diagram in Figure 15.2, the precondition "The order... is not expired and is not yet checked out" can be satisfied by exactly one state, Adding Selection to Order.

(For the purposes of this chapter, the example is drawn from the version of the bookstore models as presented at the end of Chapter 10: Communicating Objects. The principal classes used in this example—Product, Order, and Product Selection—are shown in the class diagram in Figure 15.3. These models do not include the separate shopping cart or the assigner. The creation and execution of test cases against the complete set of bookstore models is left as an exercise to the reader.)

For the test case to be useful, we must also establish the expected result and verify that the models exhibit the desired behavior. The formal expression of the test case with specific values and expected outcomes is a *test vector*.

Definition: A *test vector* is a combination of system state, parameter values for an initiating signal, and an expected outcome by which we know whether the test passed or failed.

The test vector is the basis for automated testing. By specifying and inject-ing a test vector for each scenario and executing it with a verifier, we can ensure that each test case really does correspond to a use case, which we trust is a valid representation of some requirements.

For the example use case, Add Item to Order, there are two choices for the state of the system:

- only one related product selection
- many related product selections

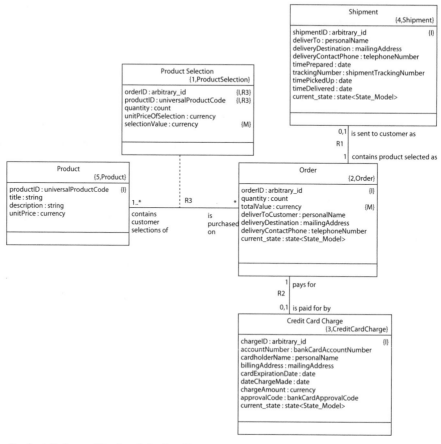

Figure 15.3   *Product, Order, and Product Selection Classes*

and two choices for parameters of the initiating signal:

- product not already selected for the Order
- product already selected for the Order

Consequently, there are four distinct scenarios—the product of the combinations of these choices. Using specific values for the use case described above, we can summarize the four test vectors in the Figure 15.4.

The preconditions state what is required in order to get the expected results from the system. Such positive tests are important but are by no means a complete set of test cases. It is just as important to have negative

Scenario	Product Selection	Signal Parameters	Result
1	product A, quantity 4	product B, quantity 3	4 units of A 3 units of B
2	product A, quantity 4	product A, quantity 3	7 units of A
3	product A, quantity 4 product C, quantity 1 product D, quantity 2	product B, quantity 3	4 units of A 3 units of B 1 unit of C 2 units of D
4	product A, quantity 4 product C, quantity 1 product D, quantity 2	product A, quantity 3	7 units of A 1 unit of C 2 units of D

Figure 15.4 *Four Different Test Vectors for a Single Use Case*

tests that test the models to verify their behavior when some of the preconditions are *not* satisfied. After all, some real-world conditions are unanticipated and so will not meet the preconditions.

By testing values that don't match the preconditions, we can determine whether the models handle errors appropriately. We can also identify new requirements on the models and identify assumptions (requirements on lower-level domains) that can simplify the models.

These additional choices can be combined with other choices to create more test cases.

For Add Item, we can additionally test the following:

- a quantity of zero or less
- a quantity greater than the stock on hand
- an order that has already been checked out but payment was declined (state Payment Not Approved)

Error testing can quickly get out of hand and become overwhelming. In addition, it is sometimes not even possible to predict the expected output! Use your judgment on which tests to build and consider the value added by each new test.

The result of this work is some number of test vectors that can be executed.

```
// Precondition: The product already exists.
create object instance productA of Product;
productA.productID = "881273";
productA.unitPrice = 29.95;
productA.quantityOnHand = 20;


create object instance productB of Product;
productB.productID = "384793";
productB.unitPrice = 34.95;
productV.quantityOnHand = 62;
```

Figure 15.5   *Creating Instances of Product*

15.2   **Test Execution**

The entire testing and verification process of a domain can be automated. Each test can be set up, run, and verified automatically so that we can run tests frequently—ideally with every change. We can also add new test cases as we change the models.

First, we show how to establish a unit test for a single activity in a use case. For each test vector, we need to establish the initial state of the model, accept the external signal that signifies the use case, and execute to see what happens. We then evaluate the outcome to see if it is correct.

The state of the system that must exist prior to the test is defined in terms of a set of objects, the values of their attributes, their current states, and any required associations. Examining the preconditions in Figure 15.1, we need:

- An order.
- A product to add to the order. There must be sufficient quantity on hand to fill the order.
- One or more associated selections already associated with the order. Each selection must be associated to a product.

Write action language to set up the test state of the system. It is easiest and most direct to create Product objects synchronously with arbitrary, but reasonable, attribute values, as shown in Figure 15.5.

```
// Precondition: The order is not empty.
// Precondition: Product A is the only product in the order.
create object instance order of Order in state "Adding Selection to Order";
create object instance existingSelection of ProductSelection;
relate order to productA across R3 using existingSelection;
existingSelection.quantity = 3;
```

Figure 15.6   *Establishing the Initial State*

There now exist two instances of the product unimaginatively named A and B.

To execute test vector 1 from Figure 15.4, we must establish the initial state. The precondition of this activity requires designating Adding Selection to Order as the initial state for the scenario, as shown in Figure 15.6. (Even though state 1, New Order, can accept the same signal, it is self-directed and will have already caused a transition to state 2.)

Next we identify the external signal that initiates the test case and define the parameters to it. The signal parameters include:

- A reference to an existing open order (the one required by the state of the system above).
- A reference to an existing product (again, one required by the state of the system).
- A quantity to add to the order. This value needs to be less than the quantity on-hand of the product.

So we generate the signal addSelection:

generate *addSelection (productID: productB.productID, quantity: 3)* **to** *order;*

Each procedure may send other signals. The verifier processes signals until there are no more signals outstanding, leaving the system in a new state that should match the postconditions in the use case.

This process creates an execution trace that can be visualized using a sequence diagram, which shows the new states, as shown in Figure 15.7.

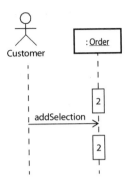

Figure 15.7 *Sequence Diagram for Add Selection Activity (Very Simple!)*

Check also that attributes have the correct values, associations are correct, and that any expected outbound signals have been sent. For this test case:

- A product selection should be associated with the order and the product referenced in the initial signal.
- The quantitySelected in the product selection should match the quantity in the initial signal, plus any amount already selected.
- All derived attributes (e.g., the totalValue of the order) should have the correct value.

Result-checking against externally specified values can also be coded in the test case. In some cases we may need to record the old value of an attribute (e.g., the order's original value) to check it against a new or changed value (the order's value with the new product added to it). Figure 15.8 shows how we could check the results of the test case.

If all the assertions are true, the test vector passes. The test case may also clean up objects and/or restore the system back to a known state so that other test cases may be run.

Test vectors can be checked automatically. We have abbreviated checking the test vector to a single (nonstandard) assert statement in the logic above. To find out more about test vector generation and injection—a whole body of knowledge in itself—see, for example, [1] and [2].

```
// Assume we have set these local variables before sending the initial signal:
oldProductQuantity = productB.quantityOnHand;
selectionQuantity = 3; // used on the test case
oldValue = order.totalValue;

// Make sure the order is not empty and contains a selection for the product.
select one selection related by order->ProductSelection[R3]
    where selected.productID == productB.productID
    and selected.quantitySelected == 3;
assert (not empty selection);

// Quantity on hand is decreased by quantity added to the Order.
select one product related by selection->Product[R3];
assert (product.quantityOnHand = (oldProductQuantity - selectionQuantity));

// Total value of the Order is increased by the value of the product.
assert (order.totalValue =
        oldValue + selectionQuantity * productB.unitPrice);
```

Figure 15.8   *Checking the Results of the Test Case*

15.3   System Tests

A unit test verifies a particular outcome from a single activity. System tests, on the other hand, verify the proper execution of a use case that may involve multiple system interactions by multiple actors. Figure 15.9 shows all the activities in the Order Merchandise use case.

System tests share many of the same characteristics of unit tests: Both begin by establishing the state of the system based on preconditions, both have execution traces started by an initial signal, and both terminate with results that can be verified against postconditions.

The principal distinction is when the execution trace ends. For a unit test, the trace ends when there are no more signals to process, but for a larger use case, the conclusion of one activity merely means that there are more activities to be done. For example, when the customer checks out the order (one activity), that is followed by another activity by the credit card company either to accept or to decline the charge.

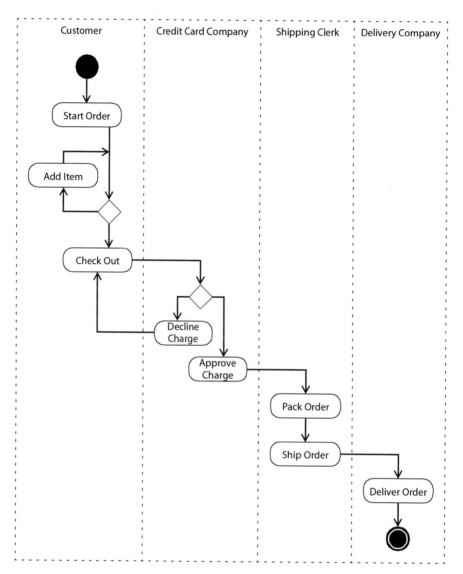

Figure 15.9 *Activity Diagram for the Use Case Order Merchandise*

A system test should therefore chain together the activities that make up the use case. It does this by recognizing the completion of one activity and then initiating the subsequent activities.

Recognizing completion of an activity means there are no more signals to process. This could mean that the activity has produced outbound signals or that the trace has transitioned into a state that generates no signals.

Once activity completion is recognized, the test must verify the correct execution of the activity and, depending on the outcome of the test, initiate the subsequent activity.

Generally, it should not be necessary to do any work to set up the state of the system for the next activity, as the postcondition of one activity should match up to the precondition for the subsequent activity.[2] To build distinct scenarios for system tests, identify different combinations of state-of-the-system conditions and initial signal parameters.

Additionally, a use case's activity diagram may show several different subsequent activities for a given activity. For example, after each Add Item, the customer can either add another item or check out. Different scenarios can yield the one-item order, the two-item order with different products, the two-item order with the same product, and so forth.

System tests are executed much like unit tests, except the test script has code to recognize the completion of one activity and to initiate the next activity automatically. For example, when the credit card charge is created, we send in a signal that either approves or declines the charge.

---

[2] However, to ensure that the system test checks as many threads of execution as possible, it is typically necessary to work backwards so that the preconditions associated with the later actions can be associated with postcondition/precondition pairs of objects earlier in the process, so that a downstream feature must be compatible with an upstream feature. If there is no possible upstream pre/post path to downstream pre/post paths, this is a feature interaction problem—a requirement defect. In some cases, there is significant complexity required to identify such defects.

Separately, depending on the full input space of the inputs, there may be partial spaces of the input space for which reachability can be achieved, but not all. Reachability analysis requires more than just checking simple values and operations (e.g., Boolean, Enumerations). [3]

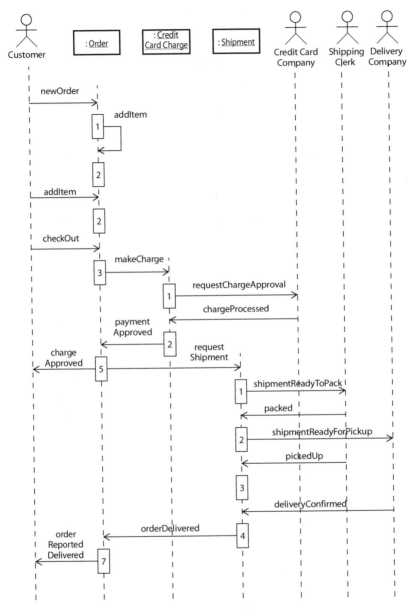

Figure 15.10 *Sequence Diagram for Multiple-Item Ordering Scenario*

The result of a system test can be documented on a collaboration or sequence diagram such as the one in Figure 15.10. A model verifier tool should generate these diagrams. Though they provide a good visual overview of an execution trace, they are incredibly painful to draw by hand.

15.4   Finding Test Cases from the Models

The purpose of the use cases is to gather requirements as a basis for abstraction. As you abstract the domain solution from the user's language used in the use cases, they may no longer be directly mappable to the models. Because the models are the final description of the system, we recommend against polishing the use cases and against spending time and effort making the use cases match the models exactly.

The test cases we build now *are* polished use cases that are built on the basis of the new information we gathered as we abstracted information, and constructed the models. Although the connection between the original use cases and the test cases is less straightforward, the reverse abstraction back from the test cases to the use cases is surely easier than the abstraction process that built the original models.

In turn, this reverse abstraction suggests another approach to finding test cases. Rather than work from the use cases inward to the models, we can work from the models outward to the corresponding scenarios.

Consider, for example, a statechart diagram for the Order in state 2, Adding Selection to Order. This state responds to a signal to add a selection. There are two possibilities: Either the selection already exists, or it doesn't. Each of these different execution traces corresponds to a scenario. The scenario is built from the model, rather than from the originating use case.

This process of building the test cases from the models can be automated. Tools of this type generate test vectors comprising initialization information, a signal to start things off, and a description of the final configuration of the system. This can be used to automate the entire test sequence for regression testing.

15.5   The Verification Gap

For the models to be useful, they must meet the requirements on the domain. Hence, we need to test the models against use cases as the best expression of the requirements. Each test case is a "polished" rendition of its originating use case.

Agile processes rightly propose the construction of test cases before writing code. The same applies to models: You can construct a series of test cases for the models just as you would for code.

Writing test cases first and executing them as soon as there is a model reduces the "verification gap"[3] between the model and its validation. Closing this gap is, we believe, a major contribution of executable models.

Final thought: Keep your brain turned "on" while creating and running tests. The procedures outlined here are not absolute. The tests must be an independent verification of the models; build tests to meet the real requirements.

15.6   References

[1] T-Vec Technologies, Inc. URL: *www.t-vec.com*

[2] Balcer, Marc, Bill Hasling, and Tom Ostrand: "Automatic Generation of Test Scripts from Functional Test Specifications." In *Proceedings of the 3rd Symposium on Software Testing, Analysis, and Verification*, pages 210–218, December 1989.

[3] The footnote text comes from Mark Blackburn, one of our reviewers.

---

[3] This term is due to Terry Bollinger.

16

Model Management

A large domain can be divided into several subsystems, each of which is simply a smaller, more manageable part of a domain.

16.1 Dividing Large Domains

Many domains can be quite large, with dozens or even hundreds of classes. Subsystems provide a way to partition a large domain so that people and groups can work with manageable chunks of the problem.

Definition: A *subsystem* is a part of a domain containing classes, relationships, state machines, and their procedures.

Figure 16.1 shows how the online bookstore domain can be divided into three subsystems: Product Specification, Ordering, and Shipping. Each subsystem contains a cluster of closely related classes.

The package diagrams in this chapter are not official UML package diagrams. The UML has a notation for representing only those packages and package relationships that are directed dependencies, such as the way in which one Java package has classes that inherit from classes in another package.

Subsystem relationships in Executable UML are peer-to-peer. Consequently, the package diagrams are drawn without arrowheads on the connecting lines.

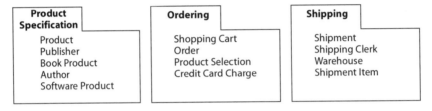

Figure 16.1   *Subsystems and Classes*

16.2   Subsystems and the Class Diagram

Each class belongs to exactly one subsystem. Draw a class diagram for each subsystem.

Of course, classes are related to classes in other subsystems. For example, the Shopping Cart in the Ordering subsystem is associated with the Product in the Product Specification subsystem.

When a class in one subsystem has an association with a class in another subsystem, show the imported class using only the name of the class with either an annotation "imported from <subsystem name>," or a stereotype «imported», as shown in Figure 16.2.

Place the association in only one of the subsystems; do not also create the Product–Shopping Cart association in the Product Specification subsystem. That would be redundant. Describe the association between the

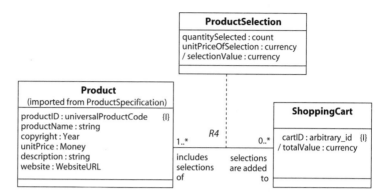

Figure 16.2   *An Imported Class on a Class Diagram*

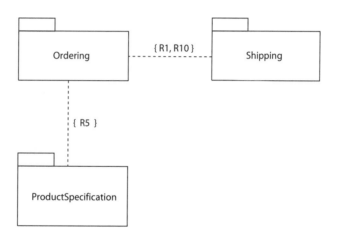

Figure 16.3   *A Package Diagram Showing Spanning Relationships Between Subsystems*

classes in different subsystems in the same manner as described in Section 6.2: Association Descriptions.

All the associations between classes in different subsystems can be summarized on a package diagram, as shown in Figure 16.3. To depict the relationship between subsystems, show a bidirectional dependency between the subsystems and label it with the names and numbers of the associations that span the subsystems.

Subsystem	Prefix	Number Range
Ordering	O_	101 – 199
Product Specification	P_	201 – 200
Shipping	S_	301 – 399

Figure 16.4   *Subsystem Prefixes as Naming and Numbering Conventions*

Naming and numbering conventions. One technique for organizing the classes and relationships in different subsystems is to use subsystem prefixes for class numbers, class names/abbreviations, relationship numbers, and signal names. See Figure 16.4 for an example.

16.3   Collaborations between Subsystems

Similarly, when a class has state behavior, there are collaborations between classes in different subsystems.

When a class in one subsystem collaborates with a class in another subsystem, we show the imported class on the collaboration diagram using only the name of the class, with either an annotation "from <subsystem name>," or a stereotype «imported», as shown in Figure 16.5.

The external entities (e.g., Customer, Warehouse Supervisor) are not part of any subsystem. They represent the explicit interface points to the domain.

To depict the collaborations between subsystems, show directional dependencies with the names of the signals, as illustrated in Figure 16.6.

16.4   Adjusting Subsystem Partitioning

Subsystems are a management convenience. Generally, the classes in a large domain are organized in closely related clusters. These clusters may be based on functional areas (product specification, ordering, shipping), user roles (customer, shipping clerk, credit manager), and so forth.

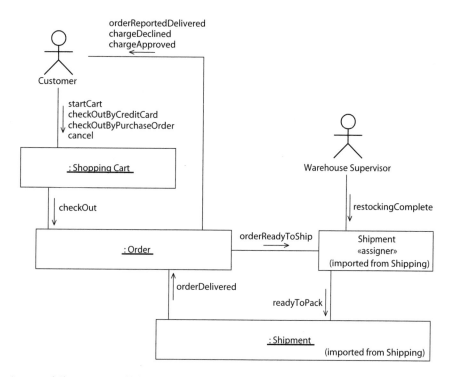

Figure 16.5 *Imported Classes on a Collaboration Diagram*

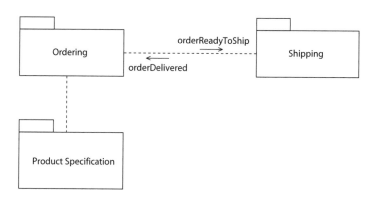

Figure 16.6 *A Package Diagram Showing Spanning Collaborations Between Subsystems*

Assign classes to subsystems based on a logical organization of the work to model a domain. Change the subsystem partitioning when a subsystem becomes very large, a class diagram becomes difficult to read, or the number of spanning relationships and collaborations becomes excessive. Classes can easily be reassigned to different subsystems, subsystems can be split, and subsystems can be combined.

16.5 Model Management

For a project of any real size, model management—and management of the work on the models—is a problem. The combination of domains (to identify the major subject matters in the system) and subsystems (as constituents of each domain) allows us to divide the system into more manageable parts.

The diagrams described here are completely derived from the underlying class diagrams and statechart diagrams. At least some things are easy!

17

Joining Multiple Domains

We partitioned a system into several domains so we could understand each one, but to build a system we need to define how they join together to make a system. This chapter shows how to approach the process of modeling other domains and how to together link individual domains' models.

There are two primary mechanisms for linking domains, both of which may be used in a particular system. One approach is explicit, if anonymous, linkages and invocations, such as inheritance or bridge operations. The second style is implicit, whereby we specify separately from both domains, a set of join points between elements in each domain. This latter style is akin to that used in aspect-oriented programming.[1]

The next, final chapter describes how to compile the several domains into a system using a model compiler.

---

[1] This approach is designated "implicit" because it appears in neither of the domain models. Obviously, everything has to be somewhere.

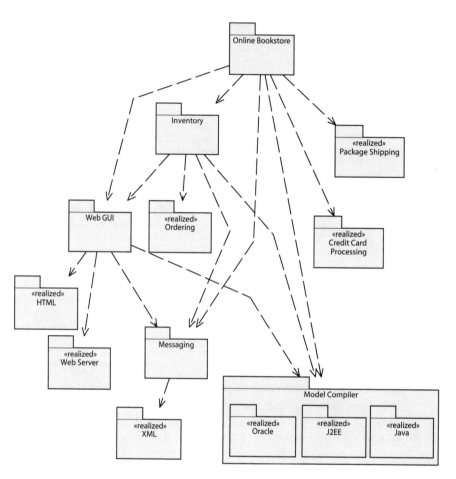

Figure 17.1   *Domain Chart for the Online Bookstore*

This chapter and the next provide only an overview of the process—the subjects of bridging domains and building model compilers are really the subject of books yet to come. These books will focus on the "translatable" part of Executable and Translatable UML, and they will describe mapping techniques for model-driven architectures (MDA).

17.1   Kinds of Domains

The domain chart in Figure 17.1 shows the various subject matters required to build the system. Each domain can be modeled using Executable UML, and the techniques described so far apply uniformly to each domain, though we have focused in the examples on an application, the online bookstore.

17.1.1   Application User Interface

In addition to the application domain, it is common to model the application user interface, a generic name given to the domain that captures the rules for how the user interface is utilized. On the domain chart, this is labeled Web GUI to indicate that we expect to use a web-based application user interface. We distinguish between the application user interface that captures the layout of menus for the application and the technologies that provide the widgets for realizing that user interface, such as HTML and a Web server.

An example of a small portion of the application user interface is shown in Figure 17.2. Note that this model is both more general than a particular application (there's nothing about Bookstore things in it) and not specific to a particular implementation technology—it could be implemented using HTML in a browser, Java Swing components, an ActiveX control, or other technologies.

17.1.2   Generic Service Domains

Some domains represent services in a form more generic than the application and potentially reusable throughout the application and on entirely different applications.

Consider the problem of stocking product inventory in the bookstore. As product is shipped, the inventory count decreases. At some predetermined point, an order is sent to the publisher for more.

Now suppose we also want to track the boxes, tape, packing material, and labels used during shipping. Just like the products, these items are consumed and reordered when the quantities on hand drop below a certain

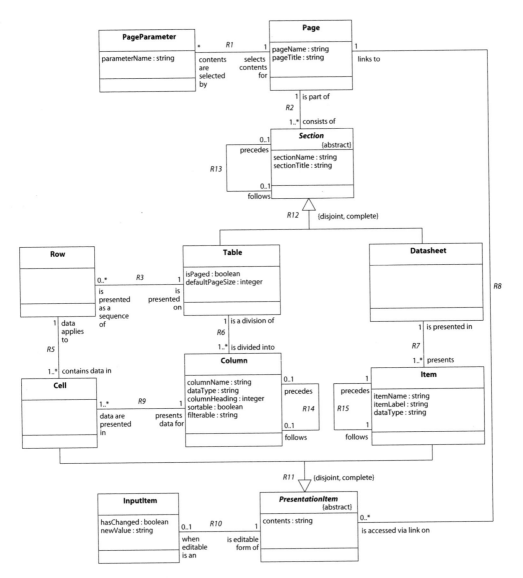

Figure 17.2 *Example of a Web GUI Domain*

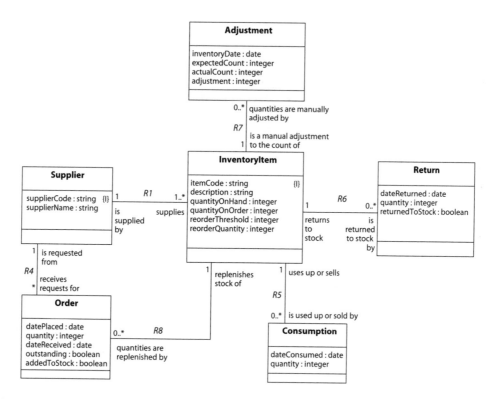

Figure 17.3 *Class Diagram for the Inventory Domain*

predetermined level. We could add this capability to the bookstore models by adding new classes and state machines.

But a more appropriate solution is to abstract an entirely new domain, Inventory, and to make use of that domain's services while modeling both product inventory and shipping.

Figure 17.3 shows a class diagram for an Inventory domain. Again, notice that this domain is more generic than the application itself. By using an Inventory domain in our system, we can model the bookstore application assuming that some domain will provide the services of tracking quantities of products and automatically reordering stock when the quantities on hand fall below the reorder thresholds.

17.1.3   Realized Domains

Some domains may already be realized as code and do not require further modeling. These include the implementation technologies that are used to realize other domains (e.g., HTML, Java, XML), external systems (e.g., the credit card and package-delivery companies' systems), and third-party components (e.g., the Web server).

Definition: A *realized domain* is a domain supplied as code.

On the domain chart, denote each of the realized domains with a «realized» stereotype.

To build the system, all domains must be modeled or realized.

17.2   Anonymous Explicit Bridges

A link to another domain is effected by actions that generate signals or synchronously invoke defined operations on an external entity. The domain to which the external entity refers remains anonymous.

17.2.1   External Entities

Each domain's models include a number of external entities. External entities are not domains themselves; rather, they act as anonymous proxies to other domains. This notion of anonymity is important: There are times when a domain requires something of some other domain—for example, the bookstore needs signals to initiate activities—but the models of the bookstore domain need to be independent of the methods by which those signals originate.

External entities are represented on the collaboration diagrams as boxes with the «external entity» stereotype or as the UML symbols for actors, stick figures. The collaboration diagram in Figure 17.4 shows the external entities that interact with the bookstore.

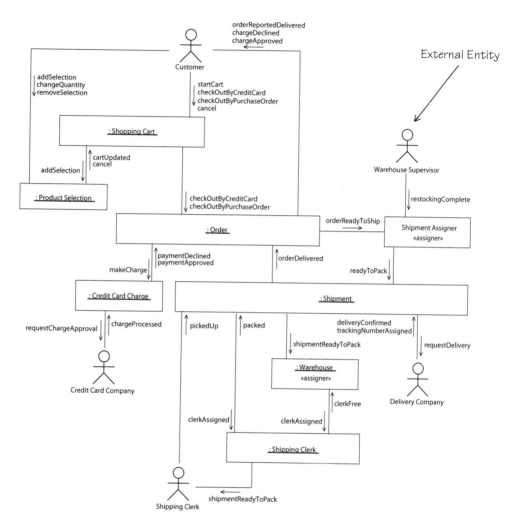

Figure 17.4   *Bookstore Collaboration*

17.2.2   Signals from External Entities

External entities can receive and generate signals. For example, the external entity Customer sends a signal checkOutByCreditCard to the ShoppingCart to check out the cart. We have already seen how signals from external entities initiate activities in the domain.

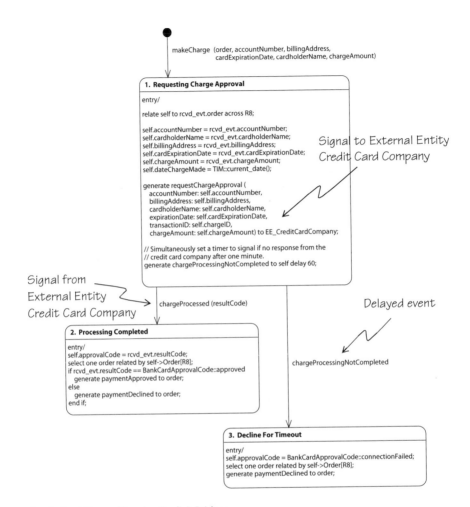

Figure 17.5   *Credit Card Charge Showing Explicit Bridges*

generate *requestChargeApproval(*
  creditCardNumber: rcvd_evt.accountNumber,
  cardExpirationDate: rcvd_evt.cardExpirationDate,
  chargeAmount: self.chargeAmount,
  cardholderName: rcvd_evt.cardholderName,
  billingAddress: rcvd_evt.billingAddress) **to** *CreditCardCompany;*

Figure 17.6   *Generating a Signal to External Entity CreditCardCompany*

The bookstore models show only that some Customer requests to check out the Shopping Cart. It does not say *how* the Customer did this—the Customer could do it by clicking a button on an HTML form, pressing a key on a touchtone phone, or the Vulcan mind-meld. From the perspective of the bookstore domain, it only matters that the Customer must *somehow* signal the Cart to be checked out.

(If while reading the last paragraph you have a strange sense of *déjà vu*—that you read something strikingly similar back in Chapter 3: Domains and Bridges—you're right. This is how we maintain domain separation.)

17.2.3   Signals to External Entities

The procedures can also send signals to external entities. For example, in the online bookstore, once the customer checks out, an attempt is made to charge the card. In the Credit Card Charge model shown in Figure 17.5, the procedure of state 1 generates a signal to the Credit Card Company external entity using the syntax shown in Figure 17.6.

We use signals to external entities whenever the domain requires that a particular service be performed by another domain. In this case, the bookstore requires that some other domain determine whether a particular credit card charge can be approved so that an Order can be processed. Other such explicit signals to external entities notify the Delivery Company that a Shipment is ready to be picked up, notify the Shipping Clerk that an Order is ready to pack, and notify the Customer whether a charge was approved or declined.

17.2.4   Bridge Operations

Signals are asynchronous: An action procedure that sends signals completes after the signals have been sent. The consequences of those signals—the actions of the receiving states' procedures or external entities—take place concurrently or subsequent to the completion of the sending procedure.

There are other times when a procedure requests a service from another domain as part of the procedure. For these situations, a procedure action synchronously invokes a *bridge operation* on an external entity.

```
taxAmount = SalesTax::computeSalesTax (
    purchaseAmount: order.totalAmount,
    purchaseAddress: order.deliveryAddress);
```

Figure 17.7   *A Bridge Operation Calling an External Package*

Definition: A *bridge operation* is an operation defined on an external entity and implemented in another domain.

Like external signal generation, a bridge operation is associated with an external entity. The external entity defines the name of the operation and its signature.

For example, suppose that the bookstore uses an external package to compute sales tax on orders. The calculation is not part of the bookstore domain but is provided by some other domain. Define an external entity to represent the sales tax package (SalesTax) and compute the tax synchronously using a bridge operation, as seen in Figure 17.7.

Bridge operations may return values. In the example above, the bridge computeSalesTax returns a Currency value of the sales tax.

17.2.5   Synchronous or Asynchronous Bridging?

External signals and bridge operations both involve activity outside the domain under study. A bridge operation is synchronous—the invoking action waits for completion of the bridge operation. An external signal is sent and the receiving domain does its work independently of the sender. When to use one or the other?

The general rule is that the actions of state procedures should not require an immediate result within the domain. For example, a request to approve a credit card charge must wait for the bank to approve or decline the charge, and we model this asynchronously. On the other hand, a sales tax calculation that can be carried out as soon as the request is made can be modeled synchronously.

Why don't we just make the bookstore Product a subclass of Inventory Item?

We could. But that, like inheritance, would make the bridge between the two domains explicit.

The concept of domain partitioning is to keep subject matters and their models separate. A model compiler might use inheritance as a mechanism to implement a join between two domains, but that is not a requirement.

Explicit bridging is an object-oriented approach. Implicit joins are an aspect-oriented approach.

17.3 Implicit Bridging with Join Points

The explicit bridges—asynchronous signals to and from external entities and bridge operations—represent the absolutely required coupling between the bookstore domain and the rest of the system. Collectively, the explicit bridges represent the requirements made by the bookstore on other domains in the system.

Explicit bridges, however, represent only some of the interfaces between the bookstore domain and the rest of the system. Most of the bridging in the system is implicit. There is no explicit mention, not even anonymously, of how one domain links to another to be seen anywhere in the models.

17.3.1 Rationale for Join Points

Consider, for example, how the user interface connects to the bookstore domain. While the explicit bridges show certain signals from the Customer and the Shipping Clerk, there is nothing showing how the user interface gets the data to display on the screens.

We could add explicit bridges—for example, a signal from the Shipping Clerk external entity to get the current list of pending Shipments. But that approach has two problems. First, it would make the Shipping Clerk state machine much more complex. Second, it would introduce an unnecessary and inappropriate coupling between the bookstore and a user interface domain.

Bookstore	Inventory
class Publisher	class Supplier
class Product	class InventoryItem
class ShipmentItem	class Consumption

Figure 17.8   *Correspondences between Bookstore and Inventory*

Bookstore	Inventory
Publisher.publisherCode	Supplier.supplierCode
Publisher.publisherName	Supplier.supplierName
Product.title	InventoryItem.description
Product.productID	InventoryItem.itemCode
Product.quantityOnHand	InventoryItem.quantityOnHand
ShipmentItem.quantityShipped	Consumption.quantity
ShipmentItem->Shipment.timePrepared	Consumption.dateConsumed

Figure 17.9   *Correspondences between Attributes*

Bookstore	Inventory
create Publisher	create Supplier
create Product and associate to Publisher	create Inventory Item and associate to Supplier
discontinue Product	discontinue Inventory Item
create ShipmentItem	create Consumption and associate to Inventory Item

Figure 17.10   *Correspondences between Behaviors*

Definition: A *join point* is a correspondence between domains that are created and maintained separately from the models of the two domains involved.

We present the examples of join points informally, using tables and graphical callouts to show the correspondences. The detailed mechanisms for realizing these bridges depend on the model compiler.

17.3.2 Class–Class Joins

Classes in one domain may have counterparts in another domain. Consider the Inventory domain in Figure 17.3. The bookstore Products are instances of InventoryItem. Each time a Product is Shipped—the Shipment Assigner creates a new instance of a Shipment Item—a Consumption is created for the Inventory Item. Figure 17.8 shows how we can summarize the correspondences.

With such a class-to-class join, an object in one domain corresponds to an object in the other domain.

Figure 17.9 shows correspondences between attributes, while Figure 17.10 shows correspondences between behaviors.

These behavioral correspondences are implicit. Rather than writing signals to and from external entities and bridge operations directly in the bookstore models, we formally declare the correspondences listed above as part of the bridge between the two domains.

The real advantage of the Inventory domain now becomes clear: When a Shipment Item is created (a Consumption is created), that Consumption checks the quantity remaining in inventory and automatically reorders product. The whole issue of maintaining sufficient inventory in stock has been pushed down to the Inventory domain, simplifying the bookstore domain models.

17.3.3 Class–Instance Joins

Other bridges are a bit more complex. Consider how certain user interface screens are populated. Unlike the bridge between Bookstore and Inventory, there is not a direct class-to-class mapping. There are no classes in the Web GUI that neatly correspond to classes in the Bookstore. The sets of classes in the two domains are quite distinct.

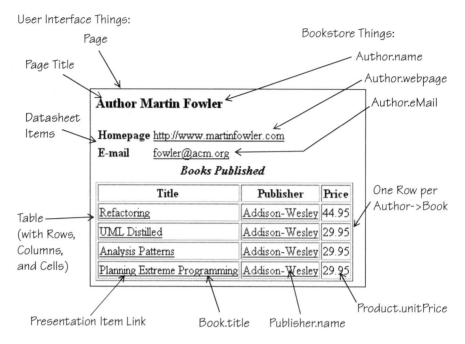

Figure 17.11 *Example UI Screen and Corresponding Bookstore Attributes*

However, there are correspondences at the attribute level, as illustrated in the Author Detail screen of Figure 17.11. The *structure* of the screen can be represented in terms of User Interface domain (see Figure 17.2) things: a Page, a Datasheet with two Items, a Table with three Columns, and PresentationItems that link to other Pages.

But the *content* of the screen can be represented in terms of Bookstore domain things: an Author (name, homepage, e-mail), Books (title and price), and Publisher (name).

Each user interface Page is different. Each has Presentation Items that correspond to different things in the bookstore. We cannot just say, as we did with the Inventory, that all instances of one class correspond to instances of another class. Instead, we need to write correspondences at the level of *instances* of things in the User Interface domain.

Figure 17.11 graphically illustrates the correspondences between User Interface things and Bookstore things in the context of a single object of a UI Page. The Page consists of sections: one datasheet and one table; the datasheet has two Items; the table has four columns and one row per Book written by the Author.

The effect of declaring this bridge is that whenever the Author Detail screen is displayed for a given author, the data for that screen is obtained from the application domain. We can define bridges like this for each of the screens displayed by the bookstore. For pages with editable fields and buttons, we can additionally map the buttons and fields to application signals and signal data.

The result is that the UI activity does not unnecessarily complicate the application domain models. The UI domain is also kept more generic than the application.

17.4   Bridging to the Model Compiler

Model compilers make extensive use of implicit bridging. The model compiler itself provides the engine for executing the models. Each of the Executable UML elements we have defined in this book is bridged implicitly. For example, when we say:

```
select any shipment from instances of Shipment
    where selected.waitingToBePacked;
generate readyToPack() to shipment;
```

both the **select** statement and the **generate** statement bridge implicitly to the chosen implementation in the selected model compiler. The **generate** statement, for example, could be implemented as a function call to a class or by adding a signal message to a queue. We, the modelers, don't know which one, and we don't even need to say explicitly that someone has to take care of making this mapping.

Similarly, the model compiler, by dint of its decisions about data organization and access schemes, knows how to turn the select statement into a call to an encapsulating function or to a SQL query on a database.

18

Model Compilers

This final chapter tells you what to do with your Executable UML models. The short answer is that you compile your Executable UML models into an implementation. No rearranging. No adornment. No elaboration.

A longer answer is that you must choose how to compile your Executable UML models based on the performance requirements and the environment of your application. From this information, you can select a model compiler that meets your needs, compile the models, and deliver the running system.

A programming language compiler generally produces a decorated syntax tree or a stream of tokens from which code can be generated. A model compiler generally accesses a repository that captures the underlying semantic representation of an arbitrary model. The model compiler comprises a set of mechanisms that animate the fundamental constructs of Executable UML, and a set of rules that weave these constructs together with the application.

We describe two complementary approaches to establishing which model compiler to use, one based on understanding the environment into which the application must fit (the rate at which requests arrive, for example), and another based on our knowledge of how software goes together to make a coherent system (the resulting performance of the chosen approach for putting the software together).

You can buy an existing model compiler as a "design-in-a-box." Alternatively, you can modify an existing model compiler or even build your own from scratch.

A model compiler is a realization of the more general idea of an application-independent software architecture. This chapter briefly explores this concept, points to some related literature, and describes an approach for modeling software architectures.

18.1   Compiling the Models: The Bookstore

The online bookstore case study we have developed throughout the book can be compiled and executed. That's the whole point.

However, there are many possible implementations. For example, we could choose to use a Web service written in Java running on an EJB Web server that uses XML messages to communicate, with a relational database for persistence. Alternatively, we could build a set of active server pages, using an ActiveX DLL written in C++ with an API for receiving messages and an object-oriented database for performance reasons. We could even use Perl scripts and a pile of files.

Any one of these implementation choices is valid—if we can make it work—and the choice we make will in no way change the Executable UML models we have built. There is complete domain separation between the model compiler domain and the bookstore application domain. All we need is an *Executable UML model compiler*.

Definition: An *Executable UML model compiler* compiles an Executable UML model into a runnable implementation.

A model compiler comprises a set of mechanisms that manages and localizes the run-time system, and a set of rules for how to weave the Executable UML models together.

18.1.1   Mechanisms

Mechanisms are library-like components that require no specialization: ways to manage a class extent, intertask communication functions, warm-standby logic, and the like. This library of mechanisms is determined by the model compiler, and the mechanisms contained therein fit together to make an Executable UML virtual machine.

The model compiler must therefore provide an implementation mechanism for each of the elements of Executable UML. For example, Executable UML has elements called "classes," "attributes," and the like. A model compiler provides an implementation for each of those elements. One implementation could be a class and private data members in C++; another could be a struct and a set of functions in C. It is possible to implement the functionality of a class in silicon. Each of these is a valid implementation.

Similarly, Executable UML has active elements such as "signal" and "action," and the model compiler must provide an implementation for these too. Hence, a call to a SignalTaker function could implement a signal synchronously within a single task, as could the sending and receiving of a particular kind of message between tasks. A procedure can be implemented as a function or subroutine, and so on.

The model compiler must include mechanisms to

- create, store, and retrieve data
- execute procedures and their actions
- generate signals and receive events
- establish delays and determine absolute time

The model compiler can implement these mechanisms any way it chooses: hardware, software, or wetware. The resulting implementation will have certain performance properties depending on the decisions made about concurrency, tasking, number and type of processors, use of memory, and so on.

18.1.2   Archetypes

The rules for weaving the Executable UML models together are stated as *archetypes*.

Definition: An *archetype* is a fragment of data access and text manipulation logic that states formally how to embed an Executable UML model into text.

The text produced by an archetype is often recognizable by a person—and by a compiler—as a programming language. This means an archetype can be written to target any language, C++, Java, Smalltalk, or even COBOL.

The text produced by an archetype need not be a traditional programming language as such. An archetype could generate Java byte code, completely bypassing the Java compiler, or an archetype could generate assembly code. Archetypes can be written to target hardware description languages such as VHDL or RTL. In fact, archetypes can be written to generate anything from passive metrics on the size of the models to document macros to—if you know the syntax of the language—Klingon.

The text produced by the model compiler need not be human-readable. Once the text is generated, compile it and run it. There is no reason to read it, and certainly no reason to change it. If there is a problem with the resulting code, change either the domain model or the model compiler. Changing the output of a model compiler is just as insane (and very occasionally justifiable) as changing the output of a Java compiler. Don't even think about it.

The archetypes access a repository containing arbitrary Executable UML models. The structure of the repository is defined by a *metamodel*.

Definition: A *metamodel* is a model of a language expressed using a modeling language.

For example, the model of Executable UML is expressed using Executable UML. This model of Executable UML is the so-called metamodel.

The metamodel contains classes such as Object (abbreviated O_OBJ) and Attribute (O_ATTR) with an association R102 between them. It also contains classes for state machines (SM_SM) and Events (SM_EVT) associated

Models, Metamodels, and Metametamodels

The model of Executable UML (i.e., the metamodel) is a model like any other. There is no difference in the meaning of class for the class Product and the class Class. They're both just classes, and one just happens to be describing itself.

The term "metamodel" is useful to distinguish between the model of the bookstore, say, with classes Book, Product, Selection, and so on, and the model that captures the bookstore model, which is to say the metamodel. We can construct useful sentences such as "The class Book is captured in the metamodel as an instance of the class Class whose name is Book." In this case, "meta-" is being used appropriately as a *relative term* to distinguish between the two models. Using "model" instead of "metamodel" would be confusing, more confusing even than saying "an instance of the class Class."

However, when we come to discuss the metamodel itself, some writers talk of metaclasses and meta-attributes and meta-associations and metathis and metathat. The result is an overload of metawhatever that adds no value whatsometa-ever.

What happens when you build a metamodel, as you quite reasonably might, of the metamodel? Do you get a metametamodel with metametaclasses and metameta-associations? Sadly, the answer is Yes. And metametameta? Let's not go there.

by R502. The instances in the metamodel capture the entire semantics of the application, including and especially the action language.

The instances of these (meta)classes capture the classes, attributes, state machines, and events in the bookstore applications, so that an archetype language can traverse these instances.

18.1.3 Archetype Language

An archetype language is a combination of data-access language and string-processing language. It's part data access because we need it to access the repository, and part string manipulation because the outputs are strings that may require some work, such as stripping spaces or applying a capitalization convention. An example is depicted in Figure 18.1.

```
.for each object in O_OBJ
public class ${obj.name} extends StateMachine
    private StateMachineState currentState;
.select many attributes related by object->O_ATTR[R105]
.for each attribute in attributes
    private ${attribute.implType} ${attribute.name};
.end for
    .
    .
    .
.select many signals related by object->SM_SM[R301]->SM_EVT[R303]
.for each signal in signals
    protected void ${signal,name} () throws ooaException;
    .
    .
    .
.end for
}
.emit to file ${obj.name}.java
.end for
```

Figure 18.1   *Highlights of an Archetype that Creates a Java Class*

In the archetype language, every line that does *not* start with a period is just text. The output is exactly the same as the input, so if you write Java, you get Java.

Each line that starts with a period is a command to the archetype language processor. The **.select** statement accesses a repository containing a meta-model populated with instances from the model. A statement such as

> **.select many** *attributes* **related by** *object->O_ATTR[R105]*

selects all the attributes related to the instance handle *object* across R105. The result is a set of attributes for the class (called attribute in the example) for which we are generating code. This set may then be iterated over, thus:

> **.for each** *attribute* **in** *attributes*
>   private ${attribute.implType} ${attribute.name};
> **.end for**

```
public class ProductSelection extends StateMachine {
    private StateMachineState currentState;
    private Count quantity;
    private Currency unitPriceOfSelection
        .
        .
        .

    protected void addSelection () throws ooaException;
    protected void changeQuantity () throws ooaException;
        .
        . .
}
```

```
public class Shipment extends StateMachine {
    private StateMachineState currentState;
    private PersonalName deliverTo;
    private MailingAddress deliveryDestination
        .
        .
        .

    protected void readyToPack () throws ooaException;
    protected void packed () throws ooaException;
        .
        . .
}
```

Figure 18.2 *Java Class Created by Applying Figure 18.1 Archetype to the Bookstore Models*

Once data from the repository is accessed, it can be substituted onto the output stream using ${...}, as shown above. The result is a list of attribute types and their names, each terminated with a (clear text) semicolon.

The metamodel and the archetypes go "all the way down" to the action language. We are not creating frameworks for handcoding actions, but compiling the entire executable model into a target language. But this is not a job for amateurs.

The result of applying the archetype to a portion of the bookstore model can be seen in Figure 18.2.

By modifying the mechanisms or the archetypes, you have complete control over the generated code.

18.2   Model Compilers and the Software Platform

Many systems are deployed today using Executable UML and an appropriate model compiler. Among these systems we count:

- telecommunications switches
- pacemakers
- intermodal transportation logistics
- telephone billing
- stock trading
- automotive navigation systems
- copiers and fax machines

The list is long and growing, as you would expect.

Each model compiler compiles an Executable UML model to a specific target implementation: a software platform. The relationship between a model compiler and a software platform is analogous to the relationship between a language compiler and its hardware platform.

Programming language compilers abstract away details of the hardware platform so that a programmer can express what needs to be done without reference to hardware platform issues, such as register usage and the organization of physical memory. In addition, the language compiler provides the run-time system that manages and localizes these issues.

Similarly, model compilers abstract away details of the software platform such as how data is accessed, tasking structures, and concurrency, so that a modeler can express what needs to be done with reference to them. In addition, the model compiler provides the run-time system that manages and localizes these issues.

Executable UML doesn't include notation to capture these issues for the same reason a programming language doesn't include register allocation or memory organization mechanisms: It would defeat the whole purpose. However, we can use the existing notation of Executable UML to capture the *concepts* of tasks, processors, and concurrently executing units in terms of classes, associations, and attributes between them.

But now we need to select a model compiler, one that compiles to a software platform appropriate to the system. There are two complementary ways to tack down a woolly phrase such as "appropriate to the system," and they depend on the concept of a fit between a context and a "form," the entity under construction.

18.3 Fit

Before the (building) architect Christopher Alexander influenced the software community with his book *A Pattern Language*[1], he also influenced thinking on requirements with an earlier book, *Notes on the Synthesis of Form*[2]. In this book, Alexander described design problems thus:

> [E]very design problem begins with an effort to achieve fitness between two entities: the form in question and its context. The form is the solution to the problem; the context defines the problem. In other words, when we speak of design, the real object of discussion is not the form alone, but the ensemble comprising the form and its context. Good fit is a desired property of this ensemble, which relates to some particular division of the ensemble into form and context.

For the (software) architect, the "context" is certain critical properties of the system as a whole that determine the structure of the "form," the generated code for the system.

One approach is to proceed from the outside in, by examining the context: the manner in which the system's environment impinges on the system. A complementary approach is to proceed from the inside out, by understanding the form: the various dimensions of a software platform, such as data-access schemes, persistence, concurrency, and distribution.

A telephone switching system, for example, is highly asynchronous and concurrent: Each call is made independently of others; calls take place concurrently with no interference except for contention for resources; and access to long-term persistent storage, for the routing of the calls, is random. These are critical properties of the environment, and they can be established without reference to the specific semantics of the application.

The implementation must necessarily be distributed. A concurrent implementation, appropriately allocated, would minimize unnecessary coupling between calls. Some $\log(n)$ algorithm for data access would equalize data-access times, and so on. A model compiler that optimized for these properties would be ideal.

As another example, consider another highly asynchronous and concurrent application, telephone billing. This application has the additional property that no transaction can be lost: Once a transaction begins, it must complete successfully or roll back any intermediate stored data and try again.

A model compiler that included automatic transaction-safety and rollback would be ideal for this system's characteristics.

Now consider a pacemaker. This application has a loosely periodic nature that can be expressed asynchronously using timed signals to assume the responsibility for detecting the nonoccurrence of certain periodic events, such as a heartbeat. There is no need for concurrency, nor a distributed network of computers. Rather, the goal is to minimize the computing hardware required so it can be implanted in the body.

A model compiler that optimized memory usage and executed on a single chip without concurrency would be ideal for this situation.

The Executable UML models for the telephone switching system could be compiled using the model compiler optimized for transaction safety, but the implementation would be unnecessarily inefficient. Similarly, the telephone billing system could be compiled using the single-tasking model compiler, but this solution would not provide sufficient concurrency.

The goal is to select a model compiler (the form) that fits the way in which the environment impinges on the system (the context).

18.4 Buying, Modifying, and Building a Model Compiler

Of the three example model compilers above, two can be bought off the shelf. A transaction-safe system with rollback is available from Kabira Technologies [3], and a model compiler for the pacemaker is available from Project Technology, Inc. [4].

There has to be agreement on a standard Executable UML. This project is under way. Once completed, expect exponential growth in the market for model compilers, so much so that one day soon you will be able to pick a model compiler off the shelf whose form fits your context perfectly.

In the interim, we cannot expect even the growing number of model compilers always to meet your needs. It is worth recalling, however, the discussion on reasons why early software engineers were reluctant to use programming language compilers. (See "Layers of Abstraction and the Market" on page 3.) One frequent argument was that the problem at hand was "special" and so complex that it couldn't possibly be compiled into efficient code. Our experience indicates that a small suite of model compilers can address a surprisingly large range of problems.

An approach to understanding performance requirements is to focus effort on those areas most likely to be of concern. Christopher Alexander also said in [2]:

> It is common practice in engineering, if we wish to make a metal face perfectly smooth, to fit it against the surface of a metal block which is level within finer limits than we are aiming at, by inking the surface of this standard block and rubbing our metal face against the inked surface. If our metal face is not quite level, ink marks appear on it at those points that are higher than the rest. We grind away at these high spots...

Hence, any characterization of performance properties for a system should focus only on those areas likely to cause difficulties, rather than on a complete catalog of all possible data requirements and threads. In any case, successful systems change, adding data and functionality. Any architecture must be robust enough to handle such changes.

A winning strategy is to try out a model compiler and determine just how far off the performance is. After profiling the performance of the model compiler on a representative sample of the application, we may determine that the model compiler needs modification.

18.5   Modeling the Model Compiler as a Domain

The subject matter covered by the model compiler domain is the subject matter of software system design. Any model compiler must provide implementations of the Executable UML formalism, no matter how indirectly. The model compiler will incorporate conceptual entities specific to the nature of the architecture: Pipes and Filters in a pipes-and-filters architecture; Classes, Operations, and Instances in an object-oriented architecture.

The model compiler domain is susceptible to being understood by modeling. It is entirely appropriate to model the model compiler using Executable UML. Or to put it another way, you can analyze your system design.

The notion of assumption and requirement pairs applies equally to the application and the model compiler domains.

- The functional requirements for the model compiler are simply to execute any domain expressed using the Executable UML formalism.
- The model compiler can be understood completely separately from the semantics of the application.
- No amount of analysis of the application will tell you that you need Classes or Pipes in the architecture. The model compiler developer chooses what goes into the model compiler.
- The primary driver of the model compiler's structure is the performance requirements of the various clients.
- Similarly, the various clients' capability requirements drive the model compiler's. The fact that the client requires a facility means that it need not be modeled in the client. (This is the idea, "Don't put design ideas into your application analysis.")

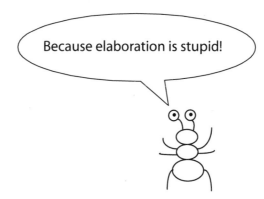

Our thanks to Leon Starr for lending us the ant and his smart-ass remark.

18.6   References

[1] Alexander, Christopher, Sara Ishikawa, and Murray Silverstein:
     A Pattern Language: Towns, Buildings, Construction
     Oxford University Press, Oxford, UK, 1977.

[2] Alexander, Christopher: *Notes on the Synthesis of Form.*
     Harvard University Press, Cambridge, Mass., 1970.

[3] Kabira Technologies URL: *www.kabira.com*

[4] Project Technology, Inc. URL: *www.projtech.com*

A

Glossary

The bracketed numbers following each definition indicate the page number on which the term is defined or first used.

A

abstract class
> An abstract class is a class that cannot be directly instantiated. An instance can be created only in conjunction with an instance of one of its descendant subclasses. [98]

action
> An action is an individual operation that performs a single task on an element of a model. [111]

activation
> An activation is the execution of a single procedure in a state machine instance at some time. [184]

actor
> An actor is a role played by an external entity that requires something from the system in one or more interactions with the system. [42]

archetype
An archetype is a fragment of data access and text manipulation logic that states formally how to embed an Executable UML model into text. [294]

assigner
An assigner is a state machine that serves as a single point of control for creating links on competitive associations. [219]

association
An association is the abstraction of a set of domain relationships that hold systematically between different kinds of conceptual entities, abstracted as classes, in the domain. [81]

association class
An association class is an abstraction, as a class, of an association that may have its own attributes, other associations, and behavior. [93]

association loop
An association loop is a set of associations that together make up a path from one class, through other classes, back to the same class. [138]

attribute
An attribute is the abstraction of a single characteristic possessed by all the entities that were, themselves, abstracted as a class. [64]

B

bridge
A bridge is a layering dependency between domains. One domain makes assumptions, and other domains take those assumptions as requirements. [35]

bridge operation
A bridge operation is an operation defined on an external entity and implemented in another domain. [284]

C

class
> A class is an abstraction from a set of conceptual entities in a domain so that all the conceptual entities in the set have the same characteristics, and they all are subject to and behave according to the same rules and policies. [58]

constraint
> A constraint is a rule, expressed as a calculation in terms of other classes, attributes, and associations, that restricts the values of attributes and/or associations in a model. [125]

constraint idiom
> A constraint idiom is a general pattern for a commonly occurring type of constraint that can be represented by a predefined tag. [128]

core data type
> A core data type is a fundamental datatype from which other domain-specific datatypes can be defined. [65]

D

data access set
> The data access set is the set of all data items read, written, or referenced by a single activation. [192]

derived attribute
> A derived attribute is an attribute whose value can be computed from other attributes already in the model. [132]

derived identifier
> A derived identifier is an identifier that is the derived concatenation of several identifying attributes. [137]

domain
> A domain is an autonomous, real, hypothetical, or abstract world inhabited by a set of conceptual entities that behave according to characteristic rules and policies. [30]

domain-specific data type
> A domain-specific data type is a definition of the set of legal values that can be assigned to attributes in a domain model. [65]

E

event

> An event is the abstraction of an incident in the domain that tells us that something has happened. [152]

event parameter

> An event parameter is a data item passed along with an event. [170]

Executable UML model compiler

> An Executable UML model compiler compiles an Executable UML model into a runnable implementation. [292]

execution trace

> An execution trace is a sequence of procedures and signals that occurs in response to the arrival of a particular signal when the objects are in specific states and their attributes have specific values. [180]

F

final pseudostate

> A final pseudostate is the state in which an object is deleted. [163]

I

identifier

> An identifier is a set of one or more attributes that uniquely distinguishes each instance of a class. [126]

identifying attribute

> An identifying attribute is an attribute that forms part of at least one identifier. [129]

initial pseudostate

> An initial pseudostate is the state in which the state machine for an object is started. [162]

J

join point

> A join point is a correspondence between domains that are created and maintained separately from the models of the two domains involved. [286]

L

leaf subclass
A leaf subclass is a subclass that is not the superclass of any other class. [97]

link object
A link object is an instance of an association class. [94]

M

metamodel
A metamodel is a model of a language expressed using a modeling language. [294]

O

object
An object is an instance of a class, or an instance of several classes in a generalization-specialization hierarchy. [98]

object reference
An object reference is a value that refers to an object. [111]

object reference set
An object reference set holds a set of object references. [112]

P

polymorphic event
A polymorphic event is an event that has many potential receiving state machines in a generalization hierarchy. [227]

polymorphic signal
A polymorphic signal is a signal delivered at run time to a specific state machine for a class in a generalization hierarchy. [227]

procedure
A state procedure is an operation that is executed by an object on entry to a state. [154]

R

realized domain
A realized domain is a domain supplied as code. [280]

reclassification
> Reclassification is the act of moving an object from one leaf subclass in a generalization-specialization hierarchy to another. [118]

referential attribute
> A referential attribute is an attribute whose value is the value of an identifying attribute in one or more associated classes. [134]

reflexive association
> A reflexive association is an association between instances of the same class. [103]

S

scenario
> A scenario is the planned execution of a use case with ranges of values for signal parameters, initial states for state machine instances, and ranges of values for attributes of objects, so that there is only path through the model. [254]

signal
> A signal sequences state machine instances. A signal may carry data used by the actions in the recipient's procedure. [170]

state
> A state represents a condition of an object in which a defined set of rules, policies, regulations, and physical laws applies. [151]

subclass
> A subclass is a class that specializes classes in a generalization-specialization hierarchy. [97]

subsystem
> A subsystem is a part of a domain containing classes, relationships, state machines, and their procedures. [269]

superclass
> A superclass is a class that generalizes classes in a generalization-specialization hierarchy. [97]

T

transition
> A transition abstracts the progression from state to state as caused by an event. [153]

U

use case

A use case specifies an interaction between the system and one or more actors together with the activities performed by the system. [43]

use case postcondition

A use case postcondition represents what must be true when the use case has completed. [54]

use case precondition

A use case precondition denotes a relevant, verifiable property of the system that is required to be true before the use case is performed. [53]

B

Case Study

This appendix contains the Executable UML models for the online bookstore domain. Why did we pick an online bookstore? We could have picked something like heavy equipment leasing or transport logistics or train scheduling. (And we have some truly fascinating models for these domains.) But those would have required significant work to learn the domain. On the other hand, most of you have already bought something online. Perhaps that's how you bought this book! So we can start with something easy.

You'll note that the models are very simple. Many seemingly reasonable features (such as the ability to cancel an order) have been omitted. We did this for three reasons:

- Simplicity and clarity: We did not want to obscure the models with too much application complexity. (But there's enough complexity to show how we deal with real issues.)
- Exercises to the reader
- Incremental development: We wanted to show how Executable UML is appropriate for incremental projects—you do not have to develop the whole domain all at once.

These models can be downloaded from www.executableumlbook.com.

B.1   Subsystem ProductSpecification

The ProductSpecification subsystem contains those classes that describe the organization of products offered by the bookstore.

The class diagram for this subsystem is shown in Figure B.1.

Product

A Product is an item available for sale by the online store. The online store currently offers books (hardcover and paperback), CDs, tapes, videotapes, and DVDs (all classified as "Recordings"), and computer software.

Attributes

    productID: UniversalProductCode

> The UPC code of the product. These are provided by the manufacturer based on a coding scheme established by a consortium of manufacturing organizations.

    productName: string

> The official name of the product. Since some kinds of Product have the same title for a number of different products (e.g., the VHS videocassette and the DVD of the same movie have the same title), this is a derived attribute.

    copyright: Year

> The copyright date for the product as it is listed on the product. If a product has more than one copyright date, we record the most recent copyright date.

    unitPrice: Money

> The price at which the product is sold to customers. Note that this price can change over time. Each time a customer makes a product selection, the "unit price per selection" for that selection is set to the unit price currently in effect for the product. In that way, even if there are price changes, we keep track of the actual price at which an item was sold at the time it was sold.

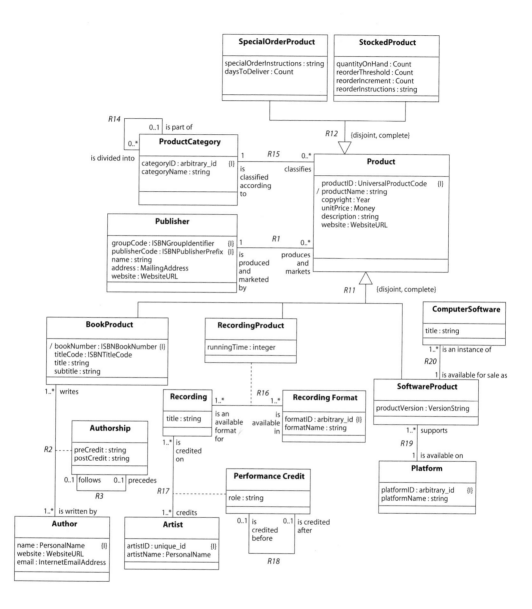

Figure B.1   *ProductSpecification Subsystem Class Diagram*

description: string

> A short description of the product, usually provided by the publisher as part of its marketing program.

website: WebsiteURL

> A website associated with the product. Many authors now create websites to provide supplemental information related to their books, including downloadable software and utilities. Similarly, recordings and software products also have their own websites.

Associations & Relationships

R1

IS PRODUCED AND MARKETED BY 1 Publisher

> A publisher is responsible for contracting with an author to produce a book and then handles the work of marketing the book to customers and retailers.

> Every book we sell is produced by some publisher. We do not sell books directly produced by authors. In a few cases an author will sell books directly; in those cases we use the author or the author's company as the publisher.

R11

IS A SUPERCLASS OF BookProduct
IS A SUPERCLASS OF RecordingProduct
IS A SUPERCLASS OF SoftwareProduct

> The bookstore offers three basic types of publications for sale: books, recordings, and computer software. Products are divided into these three different subclasses because each subclass has distinct attributes and associations that are not meaningful for all products. For example, Books have Authors, but computer software is generally not credited to an Author. However, software is offered to run on a particular Platform (e.g., Macintosh), but books do not require a particular configuration of hardware and software.

> (Note: eBooks are somewhere in between—they run on computers like software but have Authors like Books. At present, the bookstore is classifying all eBooks as Books. This is made

reasonable by the fact that all eBooks that we offer follow a single standard format that is platform-independent.)

R12
IS A SUPERCLASS OF SpecialOrderProduct
IS A SUPERCLASS OF StockedProduct

To provide a broad appeal, the bookstore often offers products for sale that are not actually kept in stock. Generally, rare, expensive, or low-volume items are listed as special order items.

A stocked product may become a special order product if it is discontinued by the publisher. Discontinued products are generally not widely available. Likewise, a popular special order product may be converted into a stocked product. The decision to migrate a product between stocked and special order is made by the marketing department.

R15
IS CLASSIFIED ACCORDING TO 1 ProductCategory

Each product offered for sale is assigned to a particular category that most reasonably characterizes the content or subject matter of the product. Categories provide a way to find similar products or to find products more specialized or more general in nature.

Product categorizations are sometimes provided by the product's publisher, but the final decision as to a product's category rests with the bookstore's marketing department.

R4
SELECTIONS ARE ADDED TO 0..* ShoppingCart

Each time a customer makes a selection, the customer's cart is linked to the corresponding selection, creating an instance of a ProductSelection.

Publisher

A publisher is an organization that is responsible for producing and marketing ("publishing") books and other products sold by the store.

Attributes

groupCode: ISBNGroupIdentifier

> A code that identifies a country, area, or language area partici-
> pating in the ISBN system. Each group has an agency that is
> responsible for assigning unique codes to publishers within
> its group.

> The group code, together with the publisher code, uniquely
> identifies a publisher anywhere in the world.

publisherCode: ISBNPublisherPrefix

> Each publisher is assigned a unique code (one or more digits)
> that is used to uniquely identify the publisher in an Interna-
> tional Standard Book Number (ISBN).

> The U.S. ISBN Agency (www.isbn.org) is responsible for the
> assignment of the ISBN Publisher Prefix to those publishers
> with a residence or office in the U.S. that are publishing their
> titles within the U.S.

name: string

> The common name of the publisher, e.g., "Addison-Wesley" or
> "Prentice-Hall."

address: MailingAddress

> The address at which the publisher receives mail. It can be a
> legal or common-use street address recognized by the post
> office, or a post office box.

website: WebsiteURL

> The publisher's public website, if one exists.

Associations & Relationships

R1

PRODUCES AND MARKETS 0..* Product

> A publisher is responsible for contracting with an author to
> produce a book and then handles the work of marketing the
> book to book customers and retailers.

> Every book we sell is produced by some publisher. We do not
> sell books directly produced by authors. In a few cases an

author will sell books directly; in those cases we use the author or the author's company as the publisher.

Author

An author is an individual who is credited with writing or contributing to a book.

There are no good mechanisms for ensuring that two people with the same name who write different books are represented as different authors.

Attributes

name: PersonalName

> The name of the author as presented on the book.

website: WebsiteURL

> The author's personal website, if available. This is distinct from the publisher's website and the book's website.

email: InternetEmailAddress

> The author's personal e-mail address.

Associations & Relationships

R2

WRITES 1..* BookProduct

> Books are generally written by Authors. Some books, however, do not have any authorship credits. For that reason, this association is conditional: Book IS WRITTEN BY 0..* Author. However, every Author has written at least one book.

Authorship

An Authorship is an individual credit for writing or otherwise contributing to a book. Many people may contribute to a book in different ways; each Authorship identifies the person and his or her role (preCredit and postCredit) on the book.

Examples: Foreword By Ivar Jacobson ("Foreword By" is the preCredit) Grady Booch, editor (", editor" is the postCredit)

Attributes
preCredit: string

> The wording that precedes the name of the author on an Authorship, e.g. "Foreword by."

postCredit: string

> The wording that follows the name of an author on an Authorship, e.g., Grady Booch, editor.

Associations & Relationships
R3

PRECEDES 0..1 Authorship
FOLLOWS 0..1 Authorship

> Authors and other contributors are credited on a book in a specific order. This order is generally preserved in all promotional material, including the bookstore's website.

R2

formalizes association between Author and BookProduct

> Books are generally written by Authors. Some books, however, do not have any authorship credits. For that reason, this association is conditional: Book IS WRITTEN BY 0..* Author. However, every Author has written at least one book.

BookProduct

A Book is a product that can be ordered through the online bookstore.

New books can be made available by Marketing at any time. Likewise, the descriptions and prices of these books can be changed as well. If a price change is made, it does not cause current orders to be re-priced. For that reason, when a ProductSelection is created (a customer selects product for an order), the price of the product at the time the selection was made is recorded as part of the ProductSelection (attribute unitPriceForOrder). See the description of ProductSelection for more detail on this matter.

Books are generally never deleted, since we always need the reference to the book for historical tracking. Instead, a book may be discontinued and as such no longer available for ordering. The attribute "currentlyAvailable" tracks whether the book can be added to the order. The only time a book is actually deleted is if the book was created incorrectly and has not yet been made available for sale.

Attributes

bookNumber: ISBNBookNumber

> The International Standard Book Number, a globally unique identifier assigned to every book in print. For a complete description of the role of the ISBN, go to www.isbn.org.

titleCode: ISBNTitleCode

> The unique code assigned by the publisher that becomes part of the ISBN for the book.

title: string

> The title of the book. Note that many books have both a title ("Executable UML") and a subtitle ("A Foundation for Model Driven Architecture").

subtitle: string

> The subordinate title of the book. Not all book have subtitles, but when a book does have a subtitle, it is generally listed along with the main title of the book.

Associations & Relationships

R11

IS A SUBCLASS OF Product

> The bookstore offers three basic types of publications for sale: books, recordings, and computer software. Products are divided into these three different subclasses because each subclass has distinct attributes and associations that are not meaningful for all products. For example, Books have Authors, but computer software is generally not credited to an Author. However, software is offered to run on a particular Platform (e.g., Macintosh), but books do not require a particular configuration of hardware and software.

> (Note: eBooks are somewhere in between—they run on computers like software but have Authors like Books. At present, the bookstore is classifying all eBooks as Books. This is made reasonable by the fact that all eBooks that we offer follow a single standard format that is platform-independent.)

R2

IS WRITTEN BY 1..* Author

> Books are generally written by Authors. Some books, however, do not have any authorship credits. For that reason, this association is conditional: Book IS WRITTEN BY 0..* Author. However, every Author has written at least one book.

RecordingProduct

A Recording Product is a commercially available recording of a performance. This class encompasses videotapes, audio tapes, CDs, phonograph records, and similar products.

Attributes

runningTime: integer

> The total playing time of the recording. If a recording consists of multiple tracks (e.g., an audio tape or a CD), this is the sum of the running times of the individual tracks.

Associations & Relationships

R11

IS A SUBCLASS OF Product

> The bookstore offers three basic types of publications for sale: books, recordings, and computer software. Products are divided into these three different subclasses because each subclass has distinct attributes and associations that are not meaningful for all products. For example, Books have Authors, but computer software is generally not credited to an Author. However, software is offered to run on a particular Platform (e.g., Macintosh), but books do not require a particular configuration of hardware and software.

> (Note: eBooks are somewhere in between—they run on computers like software but have Authors like Books. At present, the bookstore is classifying all eBooks as Books. This is made reasonable by the fact that all eBooks that we offer follow a single standard format that is platform-independent.)

R16

formalizes association between Recording Format and Recording

Each recording is available in one or more formats. Each of these combinations of title and format is a separate product.

SoftwareProduct

A Software Product is a commercially available computer program available for sale in the store. Each title sold by the store may be available on multiple platforms and multiple versions; these may have different prices and are generally represented by different product codes.

Attributes

productVersion: VersionString

A string identifying the product version. Since there is no industry standard for representing this information, the version string as we use it is merely the commonly used text that the product publisher uses to identify the version.

Note that in some cases different "versions" of the same software title may be cataloged as different titles, e.g. "Windows 95" vs. "Windows ME."

Associations & Relationships

R11

IS A SUBCLASS OF Product

The bookstore offers three basic types of publications for sale: books, recordings, and computer software. Products are divided into these three different subclasses because each subclass has distinct attributes and associations that are not meaningful for all products. For example, Books have Authors, but computer software is generally not credited to an Author. However, software is offered to run on a particular Platform (e.g., Macintosh), but books do not require a particular configuration of hardware and software.

(Note: eBooks are somewhere in between—they run on computers like software but have Authors like Books. At present, the bookstore is classifying all eBooks as Books. This is made reasonable by the fact that all eBooks that we offer follow a single standard format that is platform-independent.)

R19

IS AVAILABLE ON 1 Platform

Each software product is capable of running on a particular configuration of computer hardware and software—a Platform. This association captures the product's compatibility.

Some products are compatible with several platforms. In the future, we may make this association many-to-many and/or add a concept of one platform presuming compatibility with other platforms (e.g., if it runs on Windows NT, it is presumed compatible with Windows 2000).

R20

IS AN INSTANCE OF 1 ComputerSoftware

The same software title may be available for several platforms. For example, BridgePoint is published for Microsoft Windows, HP/UX, and Solaris. Since the product contains different executables and may be priced differently, each platform availability is treated as a distinct product.

SpecialOrderProduct

Special order products are products offered for sale by the store that are not stocked but are ordered from the publisher when the customer requests them. These products are directly shipped to the customer.

Attributes

specialOrderInstructions: string

Additional instructions for placing the special order with the publisher. At the moment, all special orders are sent to a separate back-office system that actually places the order with the publisher.

daysToDeliver: Count

The number of days that the publisher requires in order to prepare and ship the order once the publisher receives the order.

Associations & Relationships

R12

IS A SUBCLASS OF Product

> To provide a broad appeal, the bookstore often offers products for sale that are not actually kept in stock. Generally, rare, expensive, or low-volume items are listed as special order items.

> A stocked product may become a special order product if it is discontinued by the publisher. Discontinued products are generally not widely available. Likewise, a popular special order product may be converted into a stocked product. The decision to migrate a product between stocked and special order is made by the marketing department.

StockedProduct

A stocked product is a product that is ordinarily kept in stock by the store and shipped from the store to a customer who orders the product. Each stocked product has a certain quantity on hand and a certain level (the reorderThreshold) at which additional stock is ordered from the publisher.

Attributes

quantityOnHand: Count

> The number of units of the product currently on hand (currently in stock).

reorderThreshold: Count

> The point at which product is reordered from the publisher. When the quantityOnHand reaches or falls below the reorderThreshold, an order is placed with the publisher for stock. The number of units ordered is equal to the reorderIncrement.

reorderIncrement: Count

> The number of units to reorder when the bookstore needs to restock the product.

reorderInstructions: string

> Special instructions for ordering the product from the publisher. Reorders are done by submitting a request to reorder through a different back office system.

Associations & Relationships

R12

IS A SUBCLASS OF Product

> To provide a broad appeal, the bookstore often offers products for sale that are not actually kept in stock. Generally, rare, expensive, or low-volume items are listed as special order items.

> A stocked product may become a special order product if it is discontinued by the publisher. Discontinued products are generally not widely available. Likewise, a popular special order product may be converted into a stocked product. The decision to migrate a product between stocked and special order is made by the marketing department.

ProductCategory

Products are classified into a hierarchy of categories. Each product is classified into a single category, which may be a subcategory of other categories.

Attributes

categoryID: arbitrary_id

> A unique number that is assigned to each category and category in the hierarchy. This ID is necessary because several categories may all have the same name (at different places in the hierarchy, of course).

categoryName: string

> A name for the category. Although no two categories with the same parent category may have the same name, two categories with different parents may certainly have the same name.

Associations & Relationships
R15
CLASSIFIES 0..* Product

> Each product offered for sale is assigned to a particular category that most reasonably characterizes the content or subject matter of the product. Categories provide a way to find similar products or to find products more specialized or more general in nature.

> Product categorizations are sometimes provided by the product's publisher, but the final decision as to a product's category rests with the bookstore's marketing department.

R14
IS PART OF 0..1 ProductCategory
IS DIVIDED INTO 0..* ProductCategory

> Product categories are organized into a hierarchy starting with very general categories (e.g., movies, computer books) and working down to very detailed subcategories. This association captures category hierarchies. The topmost categories are not "part of" any other category. Categories at the bottom of the hierarchy are not "divided into" any other category.

Recording

A Recording Title is a particular work (sound recording, performance, movie) that is available for sale by the store. Often the same recording title is available in multiple formats (e.g., a single film, "Jaws," may be available in DVD, VHS video, and VHS video/letterboxed).

Attributes
title: string

> The actual title of the recording.

Associations & Relationships
R16
IS AVAILABLE IN 1..* Recording Format

> Each recording is available in one or more formats. Each of these combinations of title and format is a separate product.

R17

CREDITS 1..* Artist

> A Performance Credit is a particular mention ("credit") of a performer or contributor to a recording. Generally, several different people are listed on each recording; not just the principal performer(s), but also the director, performer, etc. The Performance Credit is not intended to be a complete listing of all of the credits on a Recording, just enough to provide a way to look up the most popular performers on a recording.

Artist

An artist is an individual who is credited for a performance on a recording. This may be the "star" or a supporting individual (producer, director).

Attributes

artistID: unique_id

> A unique identifier of the artist. Since several different artists and authors may have the same name (e.g., "Michael Jackson" the performer vs. "Michael Jackson" the software methodologist), we use a scheme whereby the name is not the unique identifier of an artist.

artistName: PersonalName

> The name of the artist.

Associations & Relationships

R17

IS CREDITED ON 1..* Recording

> A Performance Credit is a particular mention ("credit") of a performer or contributor to a recording. Generally several different people are listed on each recording; not just the principal performer(s), but also the director, performer, etc. The Performance Credit is not intended to be a complete listing of all of the credits on a Recording, just enough to provide a way to look up the most popular performers on a recording.

Performance Credit

A performance credit is a particular mention ("credit") of a performer or contributor to a recording. Generally, several different people are listed on each recording; not just the principal performer(s), but also the director, performer, etc. The performance credit is not intended to be a complete listing of all of the credits on a recording, just enough to provide a way to look up the most popular performers on a recording.

Attributes

role: string

> The role of the performer as credited on the recording (e.g., directed by, produced by) Not all Performance Credits will have a value for Role. In particular, the "stars" of the recording will simply be listed by name with no particular value for "Role."

Associations & Relationships

R17

formalizes association between Artist and Recording

> A Performance Credit is a particular mention ("credit") of a performer or contributor to a recording. Generally, several different people are listed on each recording; not just the principal performer(s), but also the director, performer, etc. The Performance Credit is not intended to be a complete listing of all of the credits on a Recording, just enough to provide a way to look up the most popular performers on a recording.

R18

IS CREDITED BEFORE 0..1 Performance Credit
IS CREDITED AFTER 0..1 Performance Credit

> Performance credits are typically specified in a particular order on a recording. This association captures that ordering.

R18

IS CREDITED BEFORE 0..1 Performance Credit
IS CREDITED AFTER 0..1 Performance Credit

> Performance credits are typically specified in a particular order on a recording. This association captures that ordering.

Recording Format

A recording format is a format in which a recording product is available for sale. At present, most recordings are sold as VHS videotapes, compact discs (CDs), digital video discs (DVDs), and cassette tapes. Some recordings are available in other formats, such as long-playing records.

We've chosen to abstract the recording format as a specification class rather than as an enumerated type since it's quite likely that new recording formats may be introduced and we don't want to have to change the models to accommodate the new formats.

Attributes

formatID: arbitrary_id

> A short code that identifies the format.

formatName: string

> A more extensive name that describes the format.

Associations & Relationships

R16

IS AN AVAILABLE FORMAT FOR 1..* Recording

> Each recording is available in one or more formats. Each of these combinations of title and format is a separate product.

Platform

A platform is a particular configuration of computer hardware and system software on which a particular software product can be run.

Platform names are not intended to be exhaustive enumerations of the hardware and system software requirements for a particular software product, merely enough information necessary to distinguish different variations of the same title.

Attributes

platformID: arbitrary_id

> A unique ID for a Platform. This ID is only used by the store—there is no general industry standard identifier for software platforms.

platformName: string

> The general name of a software platform, e.g., Linux, Macintosh, Windows NT.

Associations & Relationships
R19
SUPPORTS 1..* SoftwareProduct

> Each software product is capable of running on a particular configuration of computer hardware and software—a Platform. This association captures the product's compatibility.

> Some products are compatible with several platforms. In the future, we may make this association many-to-many and/or add a concept of one platform presuming compatibility with other platforms (e.g., if it runs on Windows NT, it is presumed compatible with Windows 2000).

ComputerSoftware

Instances of Computer Software are programs and their supporting files and documentation. A particular program title may be available on more than one program and is often available in several different versions.

Attributes
title: string

> The title of the program.

Associations & Relationships
R20
IS AVAILABLE FOR SALE AS 1..* SoftwareProduct

> The same software title may be available for several platforms. For example, BridgePoint is published for Microsoft Windows, HP/UX, and Solaris. Since the product contains different executables and may be priced differently, each platform availability is treated as a distinct product.

B.2   Subsystem Ordering

The Ordering subsystem contains those classes and relationships that deal with the process of ordering merchandise from the bookstore.

The class diagram for this subsystem is shown in Figure B.2.

Customer

A customer is an individual or organization that has placed orders for books and other products offered by the store.

A customer must have purchased books; a user who simply browses to the site is not considered a customer until he or she places an order.

Customers remain active for six months after their last order. An active customer receives periodic e-mail reminders of sales and can be eligible for discounts based on how much he or she has previously purchased.

Attributes

email: InternetEmailAddress

> The customer's e-mail address, also used as the customer's login and unique identifier.

name: PersonalName

> The customer's name.

shippingAddress: MailingAddress

> The address to which the customer's orders are normally sent.

phone: TelephoneNumber

> The customer's telephone number.

purchasesMade: Count

> How many purchases the customer has made since becoming a customer.

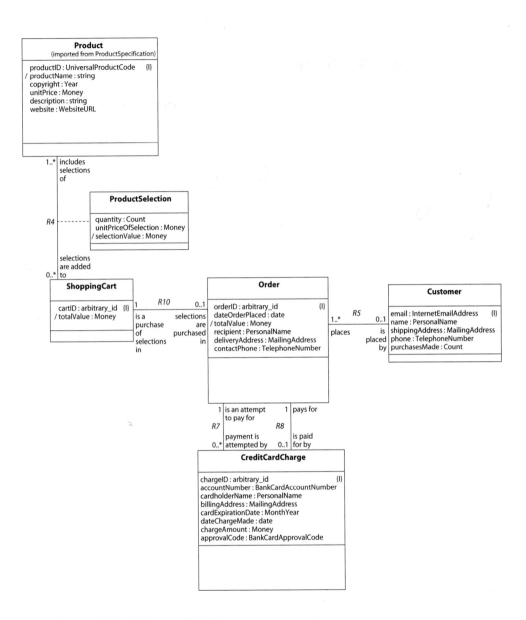

Figure B.2   *Ordering Subsystem Class Diagram*

Associations & Relationships

R5

PLACES 1..* Order

> Customers place orders for products. An order that is not yet checked out does not have to be associated with a customer, but every customer must have placed at least one order.

Order

An order is a request to purchase one or more books. An order is started when a customer checks out a shopping cart by specifying a credit card number and shipping address. If the credit card charge is approved, the contents of the order are shipped to the customer.

State Machine

> See Figure B.3.

Attributes

orderID: arbitrary_id

> A unique number assigned by the bookstore to the order.

dateOrderPlaced: date

> The date the order was started—when a shopping cart is checked out. In some instances, this may be different from the date that the order is shipped.

totalValue: Money

> The total value of the order: the sum of all of the product selections on the order.

> The bookstore does not collect tax or shipping charges on orders.

recipient: PersonalName

> The name of the person to whom the order is to be shipped. This is generally the same as the customer, but a customer may place an order to be shipped to someone else (as a gift, for example).

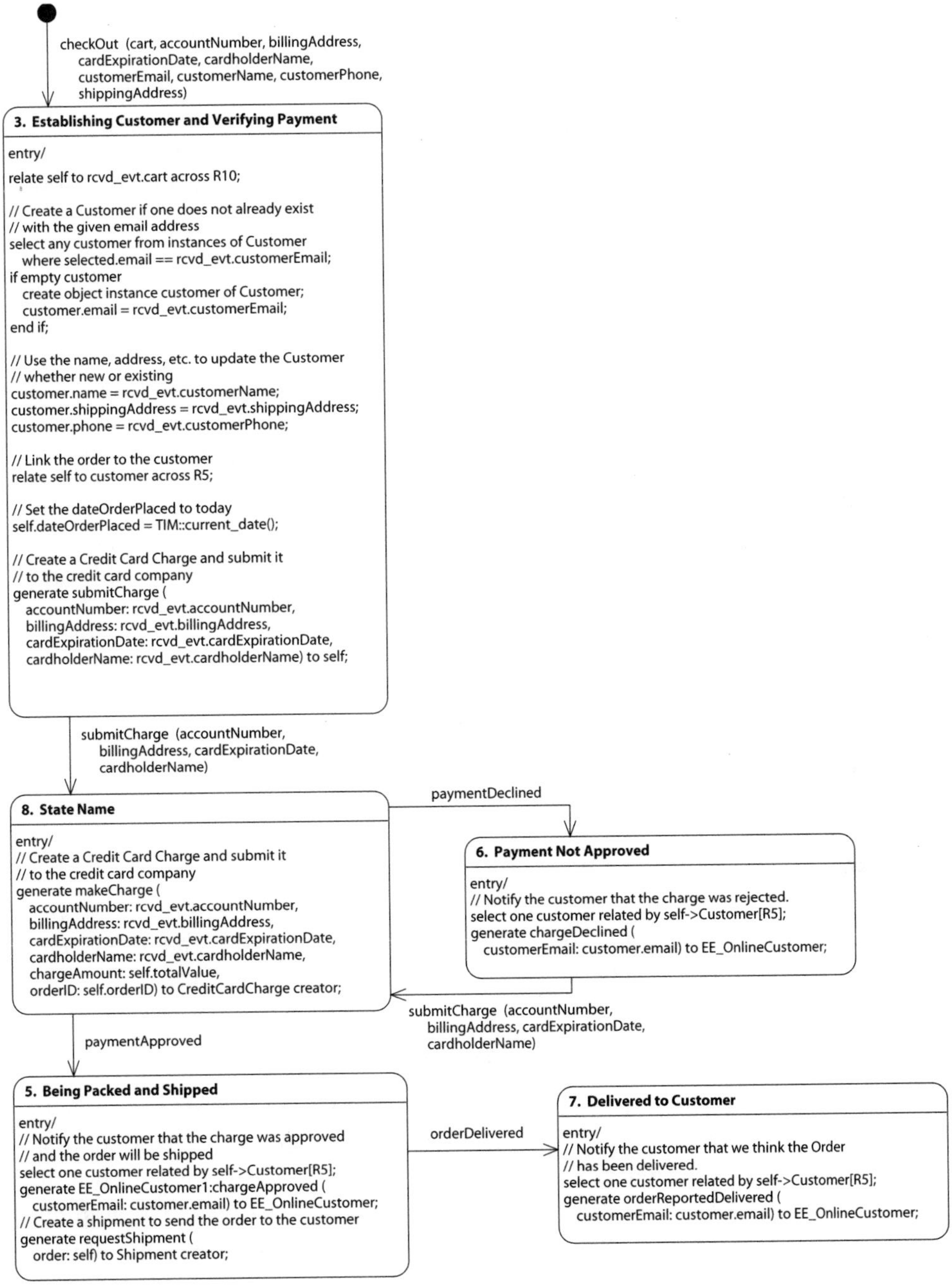

checkOut (cart, accountNumber, billingAddress,
cardExpirationDate, cardholderName,
customerEmail, customerName, customerPhone,
shippingAddress)

3. Establishing Customer and Verifying Payment

entry/

relate self to rcvd_evt.cart across R10;

// Create a Customer if one does not already exist
// with the given email address
select any customer from instances of Customer
  where selected.email == rcvd_evt.customerEmail;
if empty customer
  create object instance customer of Customer;
  customer.email = rcvd_evt.customerEmail;
end if;

// Use the name, address, etc. to update the Customer
// whether new or existing
customer.name = rcvd_evt.customerName;
customer.shippingAddress = rcvd_evt.shippingAddress;
customer.phone = rcvd_evt.customerPhone;

// Link the order to the customer
relate self to customer across R5;

// Set the dateOrderPlaced to today
self.dateOrderPlaced = TIM::current_date();

// Create a Credit Card Charge and submit it
// to the credit card company
generate submitCharge (
  accountNumber: rcvd_evt.accountNumber,
  billingAddress: rcvd_evt.billingAddress,
  cardExpirationDate: rcvd_evt.cardExpirationDate,
  cardholderName: rcvd_evt.cardholderName) to self;

submitCharge (accountNumber,
billingAddress, cardExpirationDate,
cardholderName)

8. State Name

entry/
// Create a Credit Card Charge and submit it
// to the credit card company
generate makeCharge (
  accountNumber: rcvd_evt.accountNumber,
  billingAddress: rcvd_evt.billingAddress,
  cardExpirationDate: rcvd_evt.cardExpirationDate,
  cardholderName: rcvd_evt.cardholderName,
  chargeAmount: self.totalValue,
  orderID: self.orderID) to CreditCardCharge creator;

paymentDeclined

6. Payment Not Approved

entry/
// Notify the customer that the charge was rejected.
select one customer related by self->Customer[R5];
generate chargeDeclined (
  customerEmail: customer.email) to EE_OnlineCustomer;

submitCharge (accountNumber,
billingAddress, cardExpirationDate,
cardholderName)

paymentApproved

5. Being Packed and Shipped

entry/
// Notify the customer that the charge was approved
// and the order will be shipped
select one customer related by self->Customer[R5];
generate EE_OnlineCustomer1:chargeApproved (
  customerEmail: customer.email) to EE_OnlineCustomer;
// Create a shipment to send the order to the customer
generate requestShipment (
  order: self) to Shipment creator;

orderDelivered

7. Delivered to Customer

entry/
// Notify the customer that we think the Order
// has been delivered.
select one customer related by self->Customer[R5];
generate orderReportedDelivered (
  customerEmail: customer.email) to EE_OnlineCustomer;

Figure B.3   *Order Statechart*

deliveryAddress: MailingAddress

> The location where the order is to be shipped.

contactPhone: TelephoneNumber

> A telephone number to contact someone (generally, the customer) in case of problems or questions about the order, the charge, or the shipments.

Associations & Relationships

R8

IS PAID FOR BY 0..1 CreditCardCharge

> Each order must be paid for using a credit card. When the order is checked out, a credit card charge is created and submitted for approval (association R7). Only if the charge is approved (and therefore actually pays for the order) is this association created.
>
> Consequently, there may be many attempts (R7) but only one actual payment (R8).

R6

IS SENT TO CUSTOMER AS 0..1 Shipment

> When an order's payment is approved, a Shipment is created and associated to the Order.

R5

IS PLACED BY 0..1 Customer

> Customers place orders for products. An order that is not yet checked out does not have to be associated with a customer, but every customer must have placed at least one order.

R7

PAYMENT IS ATTEMPTED BY 0..* CreditCardCharge

> When a customer checks out an order, he provides a credit card number, expiration date, and such. This information is submitted to the credit card company, who may approve or decline the charge. This association represents the attempted charge: An instance of this association is created each time a charge is submitted to pay for an order, regardless of whether

or not the charge is actually approved. Contrast this with association R8, the actual payment.

R10
IS A PURCHASE OF SELECTIONS IN 1 ShoppingCart

The Shopping Cart is distinct from the Order. The Shopping Cart has Product Selections added to and removed from it. The Order, on the other hand, is not placed until the Shopping Cart is checked out.

ProductSelection

Each ProductSelection represents a single selection by a customer of products in a shopping cart. A ProductSelection is created each time a customer adds a product to a cart.

State Machine
See Figure B.4.

Attributes
quantity: Count

The quantity of the related product that the customer has selected.

unitPriceOfSelection: Money

Represents the unit price of a product added to a shopping cart at the time the product is selected and added to the cart. This attribute is initialized with Product.unitPrice but is kept separately so as to capture the price the customer actually pays even if the actual product price changes.

selectionValue: Money

The total price of the selection.

Associations & Relationships
R9
IS INCLUDED IN 0..* Shipment

When an order is paid for, the selections in the order are shipped to the customer. This association identifies which selections are shipped in which shipment.

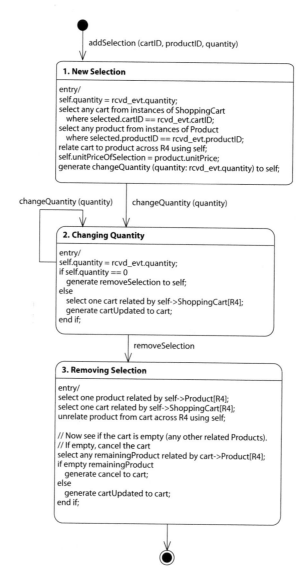

Figure B.4 *ProductSelection Statechart*

Some selections are not shipped from the bookstore because they are selections of special-order products shipped directly from the publisher. It is even possible for a paid order to have no shipment. However, a shipment must contain at least one selection.

Future versions of this system will also support partial shipments in which items are shipped only when there is sufficient stock on hand. In that situation, we will need to identify which shipments contain which selections. This association will capture this information.

R4

formalizes association between Product and ShoppingCart

Each time a customer makes a selection, the customer's cart is linked to the corresponding selection, creating an instance of a ProductSelection.

ShoppingCart

A shopping cart contains a customer's product selections. A cart is started when a customer selects a first product. Additional products may be added to the cart. The customer then checks out the cart to place an order.

State Machine

See Figure B.5.

Attributes

cartID: arbitrary_id

An arbitrary ID to refer to a specific cart.

totalValue: Money

The total value of all of the items in the cart.

Associations & Relationships

R4

INCLUDES SELECTIONS OF 1..* Product

Each time a customer makes a selection, the customer's cart is linked to the corresponding selection, creating an instance of a ProductSelection.

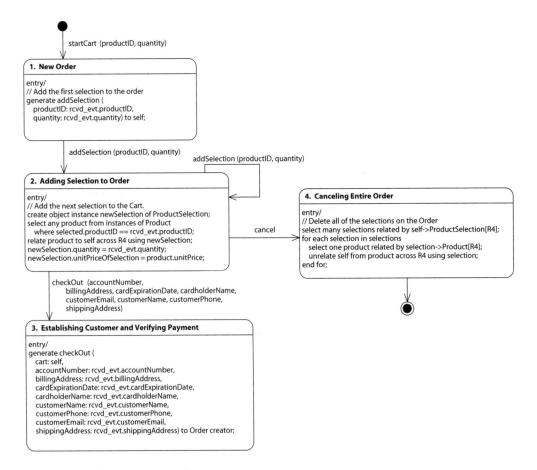

Figure B.5 *ShoppingCart Statechart*

R10

SELECTIONS ARE PURCHASED IN 0..1 Order

The Shopping Cart is distinct from the Order. The Shopping Cart has Product Selections added to and removed from it. The Order, on the other hand, is not placed until the Shopping Cart is checked out.

CreditCardCharge

All purchases are paid by credit card. A credit card charge is created when an order is placed. The charge is submitted to the bookstore's credit card processing company. This company either approves or declines the charge. When the charge is approved, the order can be packed and shipped to the customer.

State Machine

See Figure B.6.

Attributes

chargeID: arbitrary_id

A unique identifier assigned by the bookstore to the charge submission.

accountNumber: BankCardAccountNumber

The credit card account to be charged.

cardholderName: PersonalName

The name of the accountholder as it appears on the credit card.

billingAddress: MailingAddress

The billing address on the credit card account. The credit card processing company compares this to the account's billing address to ensure that the charge submission is correct.

cardExpirationDate: MonthYear

The expiration date as shown on the credit card. The credit card processing company compares this to the account's expiration date to ensure that the charge submission is correct. The processing company will not accept a charge for an expired card, even if a future (but incorrect) expiration date is submitted.

dateChargeMade: date

The date that the charge is sent for processing.

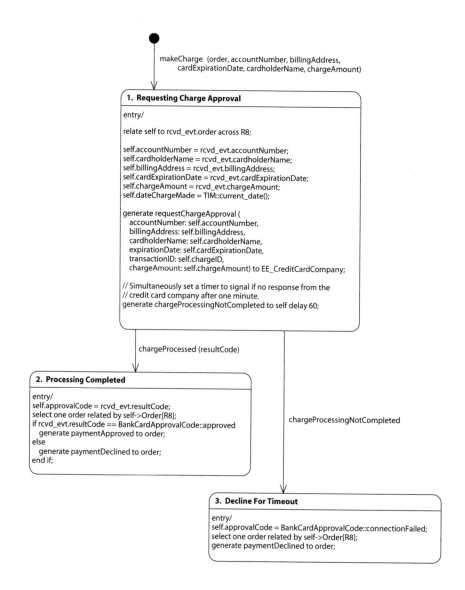

Figure B.6   *CreditCardCharge Statechart*

chargeAmount: Money

The amount of the charge submitted for processing. Normally this is the same as the totalValue of the related order.

approvalCode: BankCardApprovalCode

The result code returned from the credit card processing. See the definition of the datatype BankCardApprovalCode for the possible values of this attribute.

Associations & Relationships

R8

PAYS FOR 1 Order

Each order must be paid for using a credit card. When the order is checked out, a credit card charge is created and submitted for approval (association R7). Only if the charge is approved (and therefore actually pays for the order) is this association created.

Consequently, there may be many attempts (R7) but only one actual payment (R8).

R7

IS AN ATTEMPT TO PAY FOR 1 Order

When a customer checks out an order, he provides a credit card number, expiration date, and such. This information is submitted to the credit card company, who may approve or decline the charge. This association represents the attempted charge: An instance of this association is created each time a charge is submitted to pay for an order, regardless of whether or not the charge is actually approved. Contrast this with association R8, the actual payment.

B.3   Subsystem Shipping

The Shipping subsystem contains those classes that deal with the work of packing and shipping orders to customers.

The class diagram for this subsystem is shown in Figure B.7.

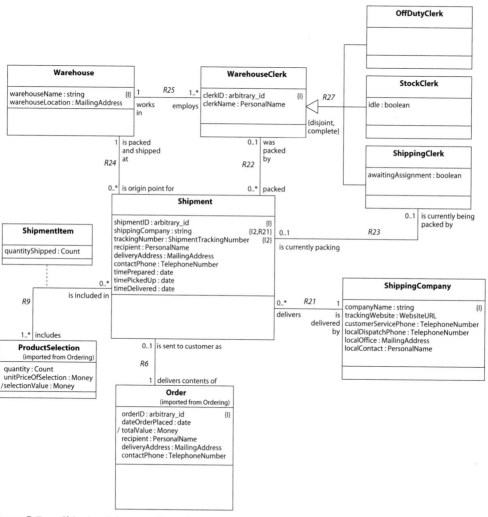

Figure B.7   *Shipping Subsystem Class Diagram*

Shipment

A Shipment is prepared to send a customer's product selections to the customer.

State Machine

See Figure B.8.

Attributes

shipmentID: arbitrary_id

A unique ID assigned by the bookstore to the shipment.

shippingCompany: same_as

The shipping company who delivers the shipment. This attribute, together with the trackingNumber, also uniquely identifies a shipment.

trackingNumber: ShipmentTrackingNumber

The package tracking number (sometimes called the "Airbill Number") assigned to the shipment by the package delivery company.

recipient: PersonalName

The customer to whom the shipment will be delivered.

deliveryAddress: MailingAddress

Where to deliver the order (the address on the shipment).

contactPhone: TelephoneNumber

A telephone number used to contact the customer about the shipment.

timePrepared: date

When the shipment was prepared (the box was packed and made ready for shipment).

timePickedUp: date

When the package delivery company picks up the shipment from the bookstore shipping department.

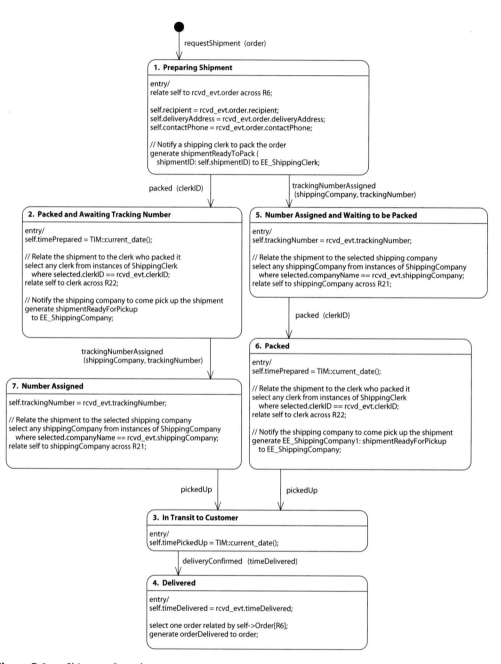

Figure B.8 *Shipment Statechart*

timeDelivered: date

The time that the package delivery company delivers the shipment to the customer, as reported by the package delivery company.

Associations & Relationships

R6

DELIVERS CONTENTS OF 1 Order

When an order's payment is approved, a Shipment is created and associated to the Order.

R9

INCLUDES 1..* ProductSelection

When an order is paid for, the selections in the order are shipped to the customer. This association identifies which selections are shipped in which shipment.

Some selections are not shipped from the bookstore because they are selections of special-order products shipped directly from the publisher. It is even possible for a paid order to have no shipment. However, a shipment must contain at least one selection.

Future versions of this system will also support partial shipments in which items are shipped only when there is sufficient stock on hand. In that situation, we will need to identify which shipments contain which selections. This association will capture this information.

R21

IS DELIVERED BY 1 ShippingCompany

Each shipment is sent to the customer via a delivery company. Ordinarily all shipments are sent using the same delivery company; however, under special circumstances another company may deliver the shipment.

R22

WAS PACKED BY 0..1 WarehouseClerk

This association captures the history of which clerk packed which shipment. The bookstore needs to be able to track the work actually done by each clerk and to identify which clerk packed which shipment. Although clerks are generally very careful, they do make mistakes.

R23
IS CURRENTLY BEING PACKED BY 0..1 ShippingClerk

This association captures a shipping clerk's current assignment. When a shipping clerk is assigned to pack and ship a shipment, the clerk is linked to the shipment. When the clerk completes the job, this link goes away. However, the history of all jobs packed by the clerk is captured in association R22.

R24
IS PACKED AND SHIPPED AT 1 Warehouse

Each shipment is assigned to be packed at a warehouse based on two criteria: (1) whether the warehouse has the product selections in stock and (2) which warehouse is closest to the customer in terms of shipping costs and delivery time. An outside logistics system is responsible for computing the shipping time and costs.

ShippingCompany

A shipping company is an organization that contracts with the bookstore to deliver merchandise ordered to customers. Generally, all shipments are sent via a single company, although in special circumstances other shipping companies can be used.

Attributes
companyName: string

The name of the company.

trackingWebsite: WebsiteURL

The webpage provided by the shipping company that provides package tracking information.

customerServicePhone: TelephoneNumber

The telephone number customers can call for tracking, billing, or pickup information. This is generally not the same as the phone number of the corporate account manager.

localDispatchPhone: TelephoneNumber

The telephone number of the local dispatch office.

localOffice: MailingAddress

The address of the shipping company office that serves the bookstore warehouse.

localContact: PersonalName

The name of the account manager at the shipping company's local office.

Associations & Relationships
R21
DELIVERS 0..* Shipment

Each shipment is sent to the customer via a delivery company. Ordinarily all shipments are sent using the same delivery company; however, under special circumstances another company may deliver the shipment.

WarehouseClerk

A warehouse clerk is any employee of the bookstore who can be assigned to either pack and ship orders or to restock merchandise in the warehouse.

Attributes
clerkID: arbitrary_id

The clerk's company ID number.

clerkName: PersonalName

The clerk's name.

Associations & Relationships
R22
PACKED 0..* Shipment

This association captures the history of which clerk packed which shipment. The bookstore needs to be able to track the work actually done by each clerk and to identify which clerk packed which shipment. Although clerks are generally very careful, they do make mistakes.

R27

IS A SUPERCLASS OF StockClerk

IS A SUPERCLASS OF OffDutyClerk

IS A SUPERCLASS OF ShippingClerk

> In the bookstore, the warehouse makes a policy of hiring clerks who can take on several roles, so that the shipping clerk is really just one kind of a more general warehouse clerk. Sometimes a warehouse clerk may be processing shipments, at other times the same clerk may be assigned to restock product, and at still other times the clerk may be off duty.

R25

WORKS IN 1 Warehouse

> Each clerk works in one warehouse.

Warehouse

A facility where merchandise is stored for shipment to customers. Warehouses are located in specific locations throughout the country (and soon, the world).

Note that the instance-based statechart for the Warehouse serves as an assigner for Shipping Clerks.

State Machine

> See Figure B.9

Attributes

warehouseName: string

> The name of the warehouse, generally the name of the city or town in which the warehouse is located.

warehouseLocation: MailingAddress

> The actual physical location of the warehouse.

Associations & Relationships

R24

IS ORIGIN POINT FOR 0..* Shipment

> Each shipment is assigned to be packed at a warehouse based on two criteria: (1) whether the warehouse has the product

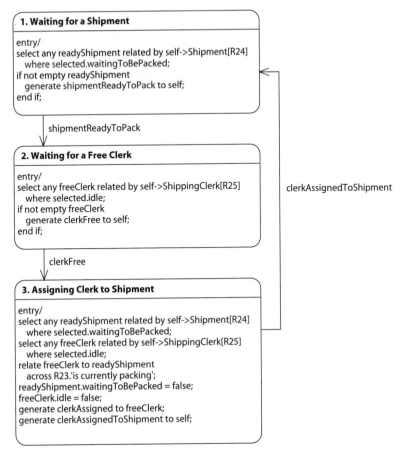

Figure B.9   *Warehouse Statechart (Serving as a Shipping Clerk Assigner)*

selections in stock and (2) which warehouse is closest to the customer in terms of shipping costs and delivery time. An outside logistics system is responsible for computing the shipping time and costs.

R25
EMPLOYS 1..* WarehouseClerk

Each clerk works in one warehouse.

ShippingClerk

A Shipping Clerk is a Warehouse Clerk who is assigned to pack and ship customer orders.

The Shipping Clerk, once assigned to pack a shipment, gets the stock for the shipment, packs the box, affixes the shipping label (with a tracking number assigned by the delivery company), and puts the shipment in a bin for pickup by the delivery company.

The actual assignment of clerks to shipments is handled by the state machine for the Warehouse class. Only shipping clerks on duty at a given warehouse may be assigned to shipments that originate from that warehouse.

State Machine

See Figure B.10

Attributes

awaitingAssignment: boolean

> True if the shipping clerk is idle and able to be assigned to another shipping job.

Associations & Relationships

R27

IS A SUBCLASS OF WarehouseClerk

> In the bookstore, the warehouse makes a policy of hiring clerks who can take on several roles, so that the shipping clerk is really just one kind of a more general warehouse clerk. Sometimes a warehouse clerk may be processing shipments, at other times the same clerk may be assigned to restock product, and at still other times the clerk may be off duty.

R23

IS CURRENTLY PACKING 0..1 Shipment

> This association captures a shipping clerk's current assignment. When a shipping clerk is assigned to pack and ship a shipment, the clerk is linked to the shipment. When the clerk completes the job, this link goes away. However, the history of all jobs packed by the clerk is captured in association R22.

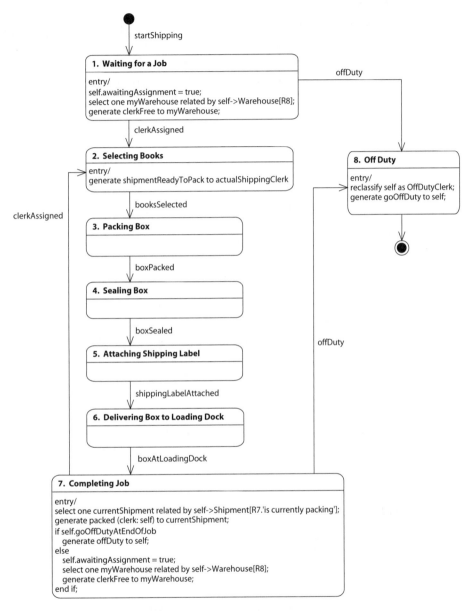

Figure B.10   *ShippingClerk Statechart*

StockClerk

A Stock Clerk is a Warehouse Clerk who is assigned to restock product in the warehouse. The bookstore system only needs to track stock insomuch as it can determine which clerks on-duty at the warehouses are currently available to pack and ship customer orders. (Clerks assigned to stock jobs are not available to pack and ship customer orders.)

Attributes

idle: boolean

> Whether the clerk is assigned to any warehouse restocking task or not.

Associations & Relationships

R27

IS A SUBCLASS OF WarehouseClerk

> In the bookstore, the warehouse makes a policy of hiring clerks who can take on several roles, so that the shipping clerk is really just one kind of a more general warehouse clerk. Sometimes a warehouse clerk may be processing shipments, at other times the same clerk may be assigned to restock product, and at still other times the clerk may be off duty.

OffDutyClerk

An OffDutyClerk is a clerk who is currently not on duty at the warehouse (sick, vacation, not on shift) and is therefore not available to restock the warehouse or to pack and ship orders.

Attributes

Associations & Relationships

R27

IS A SUBCLASS OF WarehouseClerk

> In the bookstore, the warehouse makes a policy of hiring clerks who can take on several roles, so that the shipping clerk is really just one kind of a more general warehouse clerk. Sometimes a warehouse clerk may be processing shipments, at other times the same clerk may be assigned to restock product, and at still other times the clerk may be off duty.

ShipmentItem

Each ShipmentItem represents an individual component of a shipment. If sufficient merchandise is in stock when an order is shipped, then a ShipmentItem is created with a quantity equal to the quantity requested. If there is not sufficient merchandise in stock, then the ShipmentItem is created to ship only what is in stock. Later, when additional product is received from the publisher, subsequent ShipmentItems are created.

Attributes

quantityShipped: Count

> The number of units shipped to the customer in the shipment. Generally, this is the same as the number ordered, but if merchandise is back-ordered then an order is sent in multiple shipments.

Associations & Relationships

R9

formalizes association between Shipment and ProductSelection

> When an order is paid for, the selections in the order are shipped to the customer. This association identifies which selections are shipped in which shipment.

> Some selections are not shipped from the bookstore because they are selections of special-order products shipped directly from the publisher. It is even possible for a paid order to have no shipment. However, a shipment must contain at least one selection.

> Future versions of this system will also support partial shipments in which items are shipped only when there is sufficient stock on hand. In that situation, we will need to identify which shipments contain which selections. This association will capture this information.

B.4   Domain Data Types

arbitrary_id

An attribute whose value is unique for all instances of the class, but whose content is unimportant.

Count

A nonnegative number used to indicate a count of items, e.g., the number of items in an order.

Money

An amount of money. All bookstore orders are handled in U.S. Dollars.

Note: In a multicurrency system, this type would also identify the currency (U.S. Dollar, Euro, British Pound, etc.) and quite possibly conversion rate information.

date

A calendar date and time.

ElapsedTime

The time that elapses between two points in time, expressed in terms of days, hours, minutes, and seconds.

MonthYear

A date specified only to the precision of a month and year.

Year

A calendar year, used primarily for specifying copyright dates. Since the bookstore does not handle books copyrighted prior to the 20th century (copyrights, after all, ultimately expire within a century or so), this does not need to deal with dates prior to 1900.

ISBNBookNumber

The ISBN (International Standard Book Number) is a unique identification number for any book in publication.

The ISBN is defined in ISO Standard 2108. It consists of ten digits organized into four parts: group identifier, publisher identifier, title identifier, and check digit. Each part is separated by hyphens or spaces, e.g. "ISBN 0 571 08989 5" or "ISBN 90-70002-34-5."

The number of digits in the first three parts of the ISBN (group identifier, publisher prefix, title identifier) varies. The number of digits in the group number and in the publisher prefix is determined by the quantity of titles planned to be produced by the publisher or publisher group. Publishers or publisher groups with large title outputs are represented by fewer digits.

For more information on the ISBN, see www.isbn.org.

ISBNGroupIdentifier

A unique code that identifies a country, area, or language area participating in the ISBN system. Some members form language areas (e.g., German language group = group number 3) or regional units (e.g., South Pacific = group number 982).

Each agency is responsible for assigning codes to publishers who, in turn, complete the ISBN by assigning codes to the books they publish.

ISBNPublisherPrefix

A code that uniquely identifies a publisher and that becomes the publisher component of the book's ISBN (International Standard Book Number).

The U.S. ISBN Agency is responsible for the assignment of the ISBN Publisher Prefix to those publishers with a residence or office in the U.S. that are publishing their titles within the U.S. Similar agencies exist for other countries.

ISBNTitleCode

The part of the ISBN assigned by the publisher to identify the books published by that publisher. Contrast this with ISBNBookNumber and ISBN-PublisherPrefix.

PersonalName

A name of a person, consisting of an optional title (Mr., Ms., Dr., etc.), a required first and last name, a suffix (Jr., Sr.), and an optional middle name or initial.

WebsiteURL

A Uniform Resource Locator (URL), commonly known as a "web address," used to identify a site on the World Wide Web.

InternetEmailAddress

An ordinary e-mail address, generally of the form user@domain. The bookstore performs no validation on the e-mail address other than to check that there is an @ somewhere in it (without an @, the address would be considered local to the bookstore's domain).

MailingAddress

An address sufficient for the delivery of mail or packages. This may be a street address or a post office box.

ShipmentTrackingNumber

A number assigned by a package delivery company (sometimes called an "airbill" or "waybill" number) to identify a shipment uniquely in the system.

TelephoneNumber

A telephone number, specified in a way that it can be dialed from the bookstore's offices in the United States. Numbers without country codes are assumed to be in the North American Numbering Plan (United States,

Canada, and Caribbean); all other telephone numbers will include a country code.

BankCardAccountNumber

An account number for a standard credit or debit card (commonly known as a "bank card") that can be used for payment.

BankCardApprovalCode

One of several response codes that the credit card company can return to indicate whether a charge has been approved or declined and the reason for approving or declining the charge.

Enumeration:

approved

> Charge is approved for the amount requested.

overLimit

> The charge would put the credit card over its limit, or the credit card is already over its limit. This error may also be returned if a charge is declined because account is overdue.

noAccount

> No account has been found with this account number. The account number may have been entered incorrectly.

connectionFailed

> No decision could be made, as the connection to the credit card company failed. Retry the charge.

accountDataMismatch

> The supporting data (name, address) provided with the charge do not match the account.

expired

> The card is expired. This does not mean that the expiration date entered is incorrect (the expiration date input parameter is checked only against the bank's records), but rather that the account is expired regardless of the date entered on the charge

request. This usually happens when a new card is mailed to the customer but the card has not yet been activated.

UniversalProductCode

A unique code assigned to all commercial products. This is the famous "bar code" found on everything from groceries to books, recordings, and software. UPC Codes are assigned by the Uniform Code Council (UCC: website http://www.uc-council.org/).

For a detailed explanation of UPC codes, see http://www.howstuffworks.com/upc.htm.

VersionString

A string used to identify the version of a software product. Every product seems to have its own scheme for version numbering, so we treat this as merely an arbitrary string.

B.5   Object Collaboration Diagram

Figure B.11 shows the collaboration diagram for the bookstore domain.

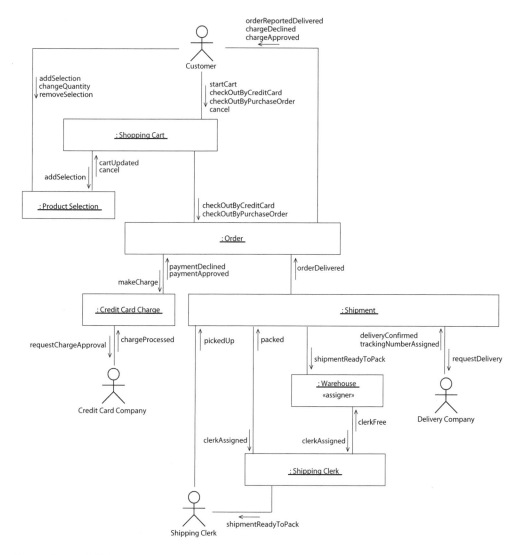

Figure B.11   *Collaboration Diagram*

Index

Also from Addison-Wesley

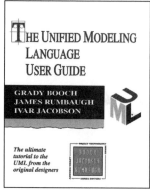

0-201-57168-4

0-201-57169-2

0-201-30998-X

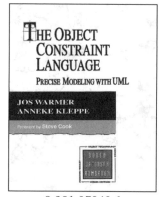

0-201-37940-6

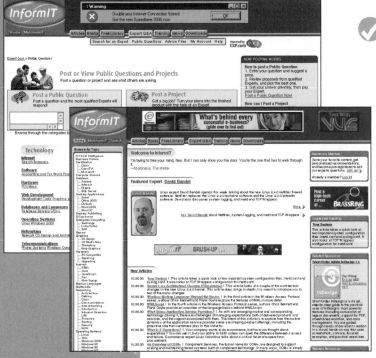